Coalitions of the Weak

For the first time since Mao, a Chinese leader may serve a lifetime tenure. Xi Jinping may well replicate Mao's successful strategy to maintain power. If so, what are the institutional and policy implications for China? Victor C. Shih investigates how leaders of one-party autocracies seek to dominate the elite and achieve true dictatorship, governing without fear of internal challenge or resistance to major policy changes. Through an in-depth look at late-Mao politics informed by thousands of historical documents and data analysis, *Coalitions of the Weak* uncovers Mao's strategy of replacing seasoned, densely networked senior officials with either politically tainted or inexperienced ones. The book further documents how a decentralized version of this strategy led to two generations of weak leadership in the Chinese Communist Party, creating the conditions for Xi's rapid consolidation of power after 2012.

VICTOR C. SHIH is Ho Miu Lam Chair Associate Professor in China and Pacific Relations at the School of Global Policy and Strategy at the University of California, San Diego. He is the author of *Factions and Finance in China: Elite Conflict and Inflation* (2007) and the editor of *Economic Shocks and Authoritarian Stability: Duration, Institutions and Financial Conditions* (2020).

Cambridge Studies in Comparative Politics

General Editor

Kathleen Thelen *Massachusetts Institute of Technology*

Associate Editors

Catherine Boone *London School of Economics*
Thad Dunning *University of California, Berkeley*
Anna Grzymala-Busse *Stanford University*
Torben Iversen *Harvard University*
Stathis Kalyvas *University of Oxford*
Margaret Levi *Stanford University*
Melanie Manion *Duke University*
Helen Milner *Princeton University*
Frances Rosenbluth *Yale University*
Susan Stokes *Yale University*
Tariq Thachil *University of Pennsylvania*
Erik Wibbels *Duke University*

Series Founder

Peter Lange *Duke University*

Other Books in the Series

Christopher Adolph, *Bankers, Bureaucrats, and Central Bank Politics: The Myth of Neutrality*

Michael Albertus, *Autocracy and Redistribution: The Politics of Land Reform*

Michael Albertus, *Property Without Rights: Origins and Consequences of the Property Rights Gap*

Santiago Anria, *When Movements Become Parties: The Bolivian MAS in Comparative Perspective*

Ben W. Ansell, *From the Ballot to the Blackboard: The Redistributive Political Economy of Education*

Ben W. Ansell and Johannes Lindvall, *Inward Conquest: The Political Origins of Modern Public Services*

Ben W. Ansell and David J. Samuels, *Inequality and Democratization: An Elite-Competition Approach*

Ana Arjona, *Rebelocracy: Social Order in the Colombian Civil War*

Leonardo R. Arriola, *Multi-Ethnic Coalitions in Africa: Business Financing of Opposition Election Campaigns*

Adam Michael Auerbach, *Demanding Development: The Politics of Public Goods Provision in India's Urban Slums*

David Austen-Smith, Jeffry A. Frieden, Miriam A. Golden, Karl Ove Moene, and Adam Przeworski, eds., *Selected Works of Michael Wallerstein: The Political Economy of Inequality, Unions, and Social Democracy*

S. Erdem Aytaç and Susan C. Stokes, *Why Bother? Rethinking Participation in Elections and Protests*

Andy Baker, *The Market and the Masses in Latin America: Policy Reform and Consumption in Liberalizing Economies*

Coalitions of the Weak

*Elite Politics in China from Mao's Stratagem
to the Rise of Xi*

VICTOR SHIH
University of California, San Diego

CAMBRIDGE
UNIVERSITY PRESS

CAMBRIDGE
UNIVERSITY PRESS

University Printing House, Cambridge CB2 8BS, United Kingdom

One Liberty Plaza, 20th Floor, New York, NY 10006, USA

477 Williamstown Road, Port Melbourne, VIC 3207, Australia

314–321, 3rd Floor, Plot 3, Splendor Forum, Jasola District Centre,
New Delhi – 110025, India

103 Penang Road, #05-06/07, Visioncrest Commercial, Singapore 238467

Cambridge University Press is part of the University of Cambridge.

It furthers the University's mission by disseminating knowledge in the pursuit of
education, learning, and research at the highest international levels of excellence.

www.cambridge.org
Information on this title: www.cambridge.org/9781316516959
DOI: 10.1017/9781009022859

First published 2022

A catalogue record for this publication is available from the British Library.

Library of Congress Cataloging-in-Publication Data
NAMES: Shih, Victor C., author.
TITLE: Coalitions of the weak: elite politics in China from Mao's stratagem to the rise of Xi /
Victor Shih, University of California, San Diego.
DESCRIPTION: First Edition. | New York : Cambridge University Press, [2022] |
Series: Cambridge Studies in Comparative Politics | Includes bibliographical
references and index.
IDENTIFIERS: LCCN 2021046581 (print) | LCCN 2021046582 (ebook) |
ISBN 9781316516959 (Hardback) | ISBN 9781009016513 (Paperback) |
ISBN 9781009022859 (ePub)
SUBJECTS: LCSH: Political leadership–China. | Coalition governments–China. |
Comparative government. | China–Politics and government. | Mao, Zedong, 1893–1976. | Xi,
Jinping. | BISAC: POLITICAL SCIENCE / General
CLASSIFICATION: LCC JC330.3 .S544 2022 (print) | LCC JC330.3 (ebook) |
DDC 324.2/20951–dc23/eng/20211210
LC record available at https://lccn.loc.gov/2021046581
LC ebook record available at https://lccn.loc.gov/2021046582

ISBN 978-1-316-51695-9 Hardback
ISBN 978-1-009-01651-3 Paperback

For my teacher, mentor, and friend, Roderick MacFarquhar

Contents

Figures

Tables

Acknowledgments

This book is the culmination of over two decades of puzzling, research, and writing, all triggered by an oft-repeated observation of Professor Roderick MacFarquhar. In class discussions, which I had the privilege of being a part of, he observed that after the beginning of the Cultural Revolution, Mao did not have to worry about the bulk of the People's Liberation Army (PLA), Lin Biao being the exception of course. Although at first I did not think much of this truism, the more I studied the comparative politics of authoritarian regimes, the more I found this puzzling. In other authoritarian countries, control over the military was rarely as unproblematic as the case in the late-Mao years, especially after the Lin Biao incident. The light finally turned on for me when I coded the data on the CCP elite in 2008 and found that Fourth Front Army (FFA) veterans were systematically placed in powerful positions in the PLA during the Cultural Revolution. After writing up the initial results in 2011, I presented the paper on the FFA to Professor MacFarquhar, who assured me that this finding was novel and strongly encouraged me to continue down this line of inquiry. This gave me the courage and perseverance to continue with this project, even through my sojourn into the private sector and transition to University of California, San Diego (UCSD). On top of his encouragement, so many aspects of this project were built on his magisterial works on the origin and history of the Cultural Revolution. Although he read through key chapters of this book, one of my greatest regrets is that he passed away before I could give him the full manuscript for review. This book owes its existence to the intellectual foundation he had built and to his encouragement.

The book also owes a great deal to my other Harvard teacher, Professor Elizabeth Perry, who encouraged me and gave me extensive guidance in the latter stages of this project. At a certain point, I realized that a theory of weak officials needed an in-depth treatment of the ideologues who had helped Mao launch the Cultural Revolution and the Red Guard movement, two topics in which Professor Perry is an expert. At various conferences and meetings, she provided me with valuable suggestions on sources – and their quality and reliability – as well as on the minutiae of the argument of this book. She also provided me with comprehensive suggestions on an earlier draft of the completed manuscript.

A crucial aspect of this book is the quantitative metrics on factional affiliation and the elite networks of high-level officials from the 1956 8th Party Congress onward. Zhang Dong supplied crucial research assistance in coding the first version of the CCP elite data. It has been a great pleasure to work with him over the years, first as a mentor and now as a research collaborator as his career prospered. At UCSD, Jonghyuk Lee managed an army of research assistants as we engaged in a large-scale updating of the biographical data set. Jonghyuk Lee and Geoff Hoffman also perfected the network affiliation identifying software, which was crucial to deriving metrics on elite network size. My long-time collaborator Liu Mingxing at PKU (Peking University) helped with historical sources for this research and spent untold hours discussing with me the logics of early CCP politics on my many trips to Beijing. My understanding of Chinese politics, both past and present, has benefited enormously from these conversations. Nancy Hearst at the Fairbank Center Library tolerated me popping in from time to time to find missing sources and to verify data points. Sebastian Heilmann and Max Zenglein provided a hospitable environment and encouragement at the Mercator Institute for China Studies (MERICS) in 2017, where I made substantial progress on the manuscript. Since 2008, Northwestern University, the US Department of Defense, and UCSD have provided crucial funding for the updating of the elite biographical data set. The Chiang Ching Kuo Foundation deserves a special mention for funding my sabbatical leave in 2011 to work on this project.

Over the years, colleagues and students at both Northwestern and UCSD have provided much-needed encouragement and feedback on this project. At Northwestern, Kathy Thelen and Ben Ross Schneider strongly encouraged me to embark on this historical project, as did Will Reno, Andrew Roberts, Mike Hanchard, and Hendrik Spruyt. My PhD students, Zhu Jiangnan, Zhang Dong, Zhang Qi, Sun Xin, David Steinberg, Chris Swarat, and Olivier Henripin, provided friendship, research assistance, and feedback on the various aspects of the project. At UCSD, Susan Shirk supplied a very hospitable research environment as well as intellectual stimulation and steadfast friendship as I completed the manuscript. Other UCSD China faculty, Guang Lei, Karl Gerth, Richard Madsen, Tai-ming Cheung, Molly Roberts, Jia Ruixue, Shi Weiyi, Jude Blanchette, and Michael Davidson, generously shared their friendship, encouragement, and support. Steph Haggard, ever the master in political economy, helped me think through some core logics of the book. Barry Naughton deserves special gratitude for spending hours discussing the minutiae of late-Mao elite politics with me and for giving me nearly ten pages of detailed suggestions. These recommendations significantly improved the quality of the manuscript.

PhD students at UCSD, including Debbi Seligsohn, Jack Zhang, Jason Wu, Brian Tsui, Jonghyuk Lee, Yuan Yin, and Duy Trinh, provided research assistance, friendship, and intellectual stimulation that kept me going. Over the years, colleagues and mentors in the field, including Ezra Vogel, Bruce Dickson, Melanie Manion, Tony Saich, Harry Harding, Joseph Wong, Dwight Perkins, Minxin Pei, Yasheng Huang, Tom Pepinsky, Dan Slater, Mary Gallagher, Bill Hurst, Joe Fewsmith, Susan Whiting, Doug Fuller, Martin Dimitrov, Matt Ferchen, Ed Cunningham, Peter Lorentzen, Pierre Landry, Chris Adolph, Kevin O'Brien, Tony Saich, Avery Goldstein, Rana Mitter, Meng Tianguang, Tia Thornton, Meg Rithmire, Hans Tung, and Zhang Pengfei, provided helpful suggestions, encouragement, and friendship. The long journey to write this book has been much enriched by conversations and exchanges with them.

Finally, this long journey would have been impossible without my family. My parents, James and Sophia, and my sister Clara continue to be sources of inspiration and examples of hard work and perseverance. It has been wonderful to be based near them in recent years, allowing several visits a year. My nieces and nephew provided much-needed distractions in the form of singing the "Baby Shark" song across two different continents. My partner, Maria, stood by me through the ups and downs of this journey. Even through the horrors of Covid, I found the courage to complete this manuscript because of our deep and unwavering bond.

I

Introduction

In mid-1975, a sickly Mao had one of the last meetings with the Politburo. During the meeting, Mao shook hands with the entire Politburo, probably for the last time in his life. When he greeted alternate Politburo member and Vice Premier Wu Guixian, Mao confessed, "I don't know who you are." An embarrassed Wu said, "Chairman, we met in 1964 during the national day parade." Mao compounded her embarrassment by responding, "I didn't know that" (Mao 1975).

It was both surprising and expected that Mao had failed to recognize Wu. On the one hand, Wu's elevation into the Politburo and into the vice premier position had been recommended by Mao himself at the 10th Party Congress less than two years before Mao shook her hand (Teiwes and Sun 2007: 101). It was therefore astonishing that Mao failed to remember the name of his handpicked political rising star. On the other hand, Wu was far from a revolutionary veteran with whom Mao had worked for decades like Deng Xiaoping or Ye Jianying. Mao greeted those two warmly at the meeting by calling them by their nicknames, "Xiaoping" for Deng and "Old Marshal" for Ye (Mao 1975). In contrast, Wu had only joined the party in 1958 and had been nothing more than a model worker until the beginning of the Cultural Revolution (Huang 2007). With the formation of the revolutionary committees at every level of government starting in 1967, Wu found her career enjoying a rocket-like rise toward the center of power. Still, among the millions of model workers who had benefited from a class-based promotion system instituted during the Cultural Revolution, Wu's elevation to the Politburo was striking.

Overall, rather than a lineup of battle-tested guardians of the regime, the majority of the Politburo elected at the 1973 10th Party Congress had great weaknesses on their CVs. In the cases of Wu Guixian, Jiang Qing, Wang Hongwen, and Chen Yonggui, they had been workers, farmers, or someone with only junior official positions prior to the beginning of the Cultural Revolution in 1966. In Chen Yonggui's case, he had been a semiliterate leader of a collective farm until his farm had become a national model for socialist zeal. By 1973, Mao had given him a seat in the Politburo and the vice premier position in charge of China's agricultural policy (Chen 2008: 10). Politburo members such as Yao Wenyuan, Hua Guofeng, Ji Dengkui, Wu De, and Zhang Chunqiao had been subprovincial level cadres who only had a long shot of rising to national-level positions under ordinary circumstances. Li Desheng, Xu Shiyou, Chen Xilian, and Li Xiannian – all Politburo members in the twilight of Mao's life – belonged to a group that had been branded as "counterrevolutionary splittists" by the Party's Central Committee in the 1930s. Despite having damning historical guilt, they commanded the bulk of the People's Liberation Army (PLA) in the late Cultural Revolution period until Mao's death. This was extraordinary considering that a main objective of the Cultural Revolution had been to struggle against "a group of anticommunist, anti-people counterrevolutionaries," according to the May 16th circular, which had launched the Cultural Revolution (Central Committee 1966).

If the dictator – in this case Mao – had wanted lieutenants with the gravitas and influence to defend his and the regime's interests, he would have promoted cadres with rich military or administrative experience to be part of the elite ruling coalition of China. Instead, Mao came to favor either very junior or historically tainted officials, whom I call *coalitions of the weak*. Cadres with whom he had shared decades of experience in revolutionary struggle or seasoned cadres from younger generations, in contrast, were either purged or forced into early retirement, to the extent that Mao could have orchestrated it. This was extraordinary in the 1960s and 1970s, when so many revolutionary veterans were still in their fifties and sixties and in relatively good health. Instead of relying on these seasoned revolutionaries, Mao reshuffled almost the entire top leadership into a coalition of the weak, who did not have the capacity to challenge his rule even as his health failed him.

In contrast to our expectation of an accomplished Spartan guardianship (Bell 2016; Nathan 2003; Yao 2016), why did Mao favor leaders with such thin or questionable qualifications? This was especially puzzling in institutionalized one-party dictatorships that came to power after decades of revolutionary struggle, because presumably the pool of experienced, dedicated cadres would be large relative to the number of senior positions (Bueno de Mesquita et al. 2003; Levitsky and Way 2012). With such a large pool of potential leaders, dictators presumably would have chosen battle-tested and well-networked lieutenants who could mobilize lower-level officials in the service of the regime's quest to dominate and transform society in accordance to the totalistic ideology of communism (Brzezinski and Friedrich 1956; Linz 2000; Wintrobe 1990).

However, in the information-poor environment of authoritarian politics, dictators often made trade-offs between having experienced lieutenants, which favored institutional development and crisis management, and having security from internal challenges to their power. Experienced lieutenants had accumulated political capital and reputation, which provided them with the capacity to mobilize resources across the regime in times of emergency (Levitsky and Way 2012). However, their extensive elite networks also increased their capacity to usurp the incumbent's power. By appointing novices with few ties to the elite, dictators delegated to lieutenants with less political capital, thus obtaining higher certainty of reduced threats to their power. A similar tactic involved appointing veteran cadres who had been tainted by historical guilt, ethnicity, or religious affiliations (Gregory 2009: 54). Although they had networks among high-level officials in the regime and had greater capacities to mobilize resources than novice officials, they had limited means to challenge the dictator's power. Such groups were used in the Soviet Union to run the secret police (Gregory 2009: 54). In China, both Mao and Deng appointed a large group of officers tainted by historical guilt to maintain control over the military.

At critical junctures, triggered by significant redistribution of power among the top elite or by strong expectation of such redistribution, dictators decided on the extent to which they would pursue the coalition of the weak strategy of replacing experienced, well-networked officials with junior or tainted officials. Dictators and their rivals were incentivized to reassess and refashion their strategies when power redistributed because such redistribution potentially gave rise to new equilibria and new winners (Acemoglu et al. 2008). Similar to critical junctures that led to the establishment of welfare and workers' training institutions in advanced democracies (Pierson 2000; Thelen 1999; Williamson 2000), successful pursuit of the coalition of the weak strategy ultimately minimized destabilizing redistribution of power both today and in the future, which provided increasing returns to the dictators in the form of elevating their relative power vis-à-vis their colleagues. This allowed dictators who had unleashed terror on both the population and on the ruling party to live out the last part of their lives in relative tranquility, even as their health and cognition failed them. Those who could not or would not form coalitions of the weak might not fall from power immediately but must guard against potential challenges from colleagues constantly.

Coalition of the weak politics was not a costless exercise for authoritarian regimes, but the trade-off also was not a simple "loyalty-competence" one suggested by the literature (Egorov and Sonin 2011; Zakharov 2016). First, densely networked, experienced officials were not necessarily more loyal to the dictator, and politically weak officials were not necessarily incompetent on narrow technical issues. Empirically, there is little prima facie evidence from the case of China for a strict loyalty-competence trade-off. Mao fully deployed the coalition of the weak strategy in 1972, but the Chinese economy in the 1970s was characterized by steady growth averaging 4 percent in real terms, among the highest in developing countries (Brandt et al. 2014). China also scored a major diplomatic success in this period by having closer ties with the US. Into the 1980s, which saw high growth averaging over 8 percent in real terms (Bosworth and Collin 2008), a group of politically inexperienced technocrats managed the minutiae of economic policies at the ministerial level, guided by a few veteran economic planners (Shih 2008a). Appointing these novices to ministerial or even national-level positions by the late 1980s apparently did not slow China's growth visibly.

However, coalitions of the weak resulted in indirect policy trade-offs in other dimensions. First, the full adoption of this strategy by the dictator ultimately led to policy making that heavily depended on the preferences and cognitive horizon of the dictator. If the dictator had heavily biased policy preferences relative to society or even relative to regime insiders, policies followed suit in that direction, at times resulting in heavy costs to the economy. Also, the quality of such policy making likely declined as the cognitive ability of the dictator diminished. Second, the coalition of the weak completely depended on the patronage and protection of the dictator and could not rule on their own. Thus, after the dictator's passing, a period of political instability likely ensued as relatively weak successors jockeyed for power.

Wholesale investment in the coalition of the weak, moreover, is inimical to institutional building in authoritarian regimes. In order to purge veteran revolutionaries from their bureaucratic powerbases thoroughly at the beginning of the Cultural Revolution, Mao hollowed out the bulk of the state and party bureaucracies. Although this might have helped

China's growth trajectory by decentralizing economic decisions, it destroyed the central bureaucracy of both the state and the party (Liu et al. 2018; Oksenberg and Tong 1991). Full adoption of the coalition of the weak strategy led to the abolition or neglect of institutionalized channels for policy discussion and making, replaced by personal audience with the dictator. Institutions and norms surrounding the cultivation of potential successors also were abolished, in favor of idiosyncratic promotion of weak officials. This could result in a series of potential successors who were chosen but then purged or sidelined after the dictator had changed his mind. In other words, the dictator's success in installing coalitions of the weak in a regime paved the way to patrimonialism and institutional devolution, two concepts well known in the literature (Rudolph and Rudolph 1979; Snyder 1992).

In China, Mao decided to pursue a coalition of the weak strategy in earnest after his power was challenged vigorously in the aftermath of the disastrous Great Leap Forward. This ultimately endowed Mao with true dictatorial power in the twilight of his life, even as party and state institutions remained in stasis. Deng, in contrast, did not pursue a similar strategy at the top level both because he had to contend with a much more stable coalition of veteran revolutionaries in the 1980s and because of the dearth of major policy failure for much of the 1980s. For much of the decade, some degree of institution building occurred in the party partly because the elite at the top knew that dictatorial power was beyond their reach or the reach of their colleagues. Instead, they invested in the institutions over which they had power, expanding them, defining their authorities, and placing trusted followers in these institutions. At the same time, the veteran elites each sought to extend their postretirement influence by appointing weakly networked and inexperienced followers to senior positions in their respective jurisdictions. The shock of the Tiananmen Square protests and the failing health of the revolutionary generation then saw the elevation of a slate of weak, "always nice" officials to the highest positions in the regime after 1989. Rule by two generations of weakly networked officials in the CCP laid the groundwork for Xi Jinping, endowed with a revolutionary pedigree and an extensive elite network, to claim ultimate power in the party.

Examining late-Mao politics through the lens of coalitions of the weak also provides much more satisfying explanations to the evolution of Chinese elite politics up to the present, including Xi Jinping's surprising domination of the CCP after decades of power sharing. This framework provides an analytical explanation backed up by historical evidence of why Mao's appointed successors fell from power so soon after his death. In brief, Mao's main concern late in his life was the maintenance of absolute power in the face of declining health rather than prolonging his ideological legacy. Thus, the weak figures Mao had installed in top-level positions fell in quick succession, when experienced and networked veterans came back to power. The ideologues that had helped Mao launch and sustain the first phase of the Cultural Revolution were immediately arrested after Mao's death in a military coup. Even Mao's final designated successor, Hua Guofeng, soon faced serious challenges from much more experienced and networked cadres, ultimately forcing him to relinquish power.

Furthermore, Mao's reliance on the historically tainted Fourth Front Army (FFA) made Deng, who had "adopted" the tainted faction in the 1940s, a natural successor after Mao's passing because he had the allegiance of the majority of senior PLA officers at the time. More so than other traits suggested by the literature, this made Deng uniquely qualified to be China's leader in the 1980s. At the same time, other leaders entwined with the tortuous history of the FFA – Li Xiannian, Ye Jianying, and Chen Yun – also became top leaders in the emerging ruling coalition in the 1980s because of the continual importance of FFA veterans in the People's Liberation Army.

Finally, the coalition of the weak logic also provided one of the preconditions for Xi Jinping's dominance of the party after he came to power in 2012. In the 1980s, the coalition of rehabilitated and tainted veterans each sought to maximize their own postretirement influence by promoting young, inexperienced technocrats to senior positions on the periphery of the Politburo. When Deng and his elderly colleagues decided to reshuffle China's top leadership in the aftermath of the 1989 shock, a generation of technocrats with relatively narrow power bases rose to the top of the regime. At the same time, ambitious children of revolutionary veterans, who had greater networks than their technocrat colleagues, were systematically excluded from the race for top-level positions by those in power in the 1980s. This left room for the few children of revolutionary veterans who had survived in the elite political game to use their large networks in the military, the party, and in the commercial world to trump their technocratic colleagues after the mid-2000s. The biggest beneficiary of the weak collective leadership fashioned by veteran revolutionaries in the 1980s was Xi Jinping, who came to dominate the Chinese Communist Party.

THE BENEFITS AND PITFALLS OF ONE-PARTY DICTATORSHIPS

Although observers of global politics often labeled authoritarian politics as a "black box," decades of research on dictatorships have yielded some consistent insights. For one, the literature agrees that having to delegate power to lieutenants, dictators on average did better to reward lieutenants through institutionalized channels such as a ruling party than through uninstitutionalized channels. This book adds to the extant literature by highlighting the persistent information asymmetry problem faced by dictators even in institutionalized regimes through the case of late-Mao China. Moreover, if dictators had greater influence over the composition of their ruling coalitions than their colleagues, they could reduce the odds of potential challenges down the road by refashioning the composition of these coalitions. Thus, a fundamental trade-off for dictators, even those in *ex ante* institutionalized regimes, is a choice between having experienced and well-networked lieutenants overseeing and potentially strengthening institutions in the regime and having clear information about the ruling coalitions' ability to usurp their power accompanied by institutional devolution.

In contemporary research on authoritarian regimes, scholars have converged on the insight that dictators and juntas, like their counterparts in democracies, must maintain the support of a group of selectorates in order to stay in power (Bueno de Mesquita et al. 2003; Gandhi 2008: 845; Shirk 1993; Svolik and Boix 2013). Because in every political system, a subset of individuals controlled "the essential features that constitute political power in the system," leaders had to maintain the support of these individuals (Bueno de Mesquita et al. 2003: 8). The support of a sizable ruling coalition was even more essential in regimes that sought to completely transform and control society because a greater number of state apparatus were needed (Wintrobe 1998: 67).

Dictators maintained the support of this coalition by distributing material benefits or by making policy concessions (Gandhi and Przeworski 2006; Gandhi 2008). Dictators further formed legislative bodies to obtain information about the preferences of the selectorates and to assure supporters and potential opposition alike that the flow of benefits to them would continue into the future (Gandhi 2008; Svolik and Boix 2013; Way and Levitsky 2002). Scholars further recognize that the ruling party supplied a uniquely robust set of institutions to deliver spoils to regime supporters because the party structure created expectation of future payoffs for supporters (Brownlee 2007; Geddes 1999; Svolik 2012). Recent research suggests that even among one-party regimes, "identities, norms, and organizational structures forged during periods of sustained, violent, and ideologically-driven conflict" further helped dictators maintain power in the face of external challenges (Levitsky and Way 2012).

The decades of research about one-party regimes have uncovered a deep robustness in many such regimes born of insiders' unwillingness to defect to rival camps in the face of hardship or of sizable opposition (Brownlee 2007; Levitsky and Way 2012; Magaloni 2006). When regimes held the line, the opposition, unless aided by an external power, remained weak and often divided (Brownlee 2007: 3). The robustness of one-party regimes was further helped by strong policing institutions and loyalty bonds developed during the struggle for power (Gregory 2009; Levitsky and Way 2012; Slater 2003). Within the China literature, works by Huang (1996) and Landry (2008) show that even at a time of vast changes in the economic structure and with the rise of new economic classes, the Chinese Communist Party relied on its personnel control of officials to stay in power and to maintain some degree of control over policy implementation at the local level.

In addition to these advantages, one-party systems organized along Leninist principles further narrowed the field of potential challengers to the incumbent tremendously. Because power and control over state resources were only allocated to senior officials in these regimes, junior officials in one-party regimes found it much more difficult to challenge incumbents directly without coordination with senior officials. Also, in established Leninist regimes, information about public discontent and the vulnerability of the senior elite only flowed to the top few leaders of the country, making them indispensable to coalitions that challenged incumbents (Lieberthal et al. 1978; Nathan and Gilley 2002; Wu 1995). This institutional feature allowed incumbents to focus on the scheming of senior officials, which drastically reduced the costs of coup prevention.

Yet, despite all the positive incentives provided by the party structure and the bonds of loyalty between revolutionary veterans, crippling internal strife often plagued one-party regimes. Both Stalin and Mao faced serious challenges to their authority – the 1934 17th Congress in Stalin's case and the 7000 Cadre Conference in Mao's case (MacFarquhar 1997a; Montefiore 2003). Both ended up purging the vast majority of revolutionary veterans from the upper echelon of the ruling party (MacFarquhar and Schoenhals 2006; Montefiore 2003). Throughout the 1970s and the 1980s, China was beset by large-scale urban unrests caused by leadership splits, culminating in the 1989 protests, which precipitated another round of elite purges (Zhao 2009).

The root of political instability in one-party regimes was twofold. First, although the pyramidal political structure provided incentive for officials to fulfill objectives for the regime and prevented coups from the bottom, officials in the upper echelons of the regime also had much stronger incentive to engage in mutual backstabbing in their quest for ultimate power. At the apex of power, competitors for the top office in the regime did not hesitate to mobilize government bureaucracies, the secret police, or even the armed forces in aid of their struggle in the absence of constitutional constraints against these actions. The mobilization of these instruments of state power gave rise to political instability. Without credible constitutional constraints on the actions of elite political actors, models of nondemocratic politics predict that subtle changes in power balance can produce destabilizing political equilibria that lead to elite infighting and mutual elimination (Acemoglu et al. 2008; Slantchev and McMahon 2015).

Second, the one-party structure still failed to deliver at least two vital pieces of information typically available to politicians in democracies, giving rise to political instability. First, dictators often did not know the identity of their enemies, and many dictators were assassinated or removed by their close lieutenants (Iqbal and Zorn 2006; Svolik 2009; Tullock 1987). Even in one-party regimes, top leaders, including Khrushchev and Hu Yaobang, suddenly found themselves removed from power due to scheming by their senior colleagues in the ruling party (Deng 2005; Taubman 2003). Second, the relative strength of the members of the ruling coalition was at best vaguely observable. Power struggles, which provided credible information about the relative distribution of power, only happened occasionally even if power redistributed frequently between members of the party elite in one-party regimes. Potential opponents of the incumbent could not be certain that the power redistribution had provided sufficient advantage to them such that they could confidently defeat the incumbent dictator or junta. Furthermore, challengers could not be certain that the resulting winning coalition could be stable due to uncertainty about the relative distribution of power (Acemoglu et al. 2008). Likewise, dictators also faced this information gap about their own power and the power of their potential challengers, which increased their incentive to purge potential challengers preemptively. This information asymmetry inherent to authoritarian regimes likely led to more intense political conflicts than in democracies as aspirants to high offices gauged relative power by instigating political conflicts.

In response to the intense competition for power and information asymmetry, dictators resorted to frequent rotation of officials, taking hostages from families of senior officials, and erecting extensive spy networks within regimes (Debs 2007; Gregory 2009; Wintrobe 1998). In addition to solving the information asymmetry problem with institutional features, political leaders in autocracies also addressed the problem by refashioning ruling coalitions. Due to the malleability of constitutions in typical authoritarian regimes, the size and the composition of the selectorate were not entirely exogenous to the dictator's survival strategy (Pepinsky 2014). Unlike in most democracies, no credible constitution imposed a strict size to the selectorate. Also, unlike most consolidated democracies, dictators had some degree of discretion over the composition of the selectorate, the very people who were vital to the dictators' power (Shirk 1993).[1] This provides potential leeway for dictators to manipulate the composition or even the size of the selectorate in order to minimize serious challenges to their power.

First, to prevent coups, dictators often deployed highly repressive means of removing members of the selectorate from power, sometimes based on mere suspicion (Debs 2007; Svolik 2009; Tullock 1987). Furthermore, as Slater (2003) observes, dictators could "pack" elite governing bodies with loyal supporters so as to enhance their power. However, historically loyal followers of dictators may well usurp their power if they gained the capacity to do so. Thus, a rational response by dictators was simply to increase the share of selectorate members whom they knew to lack the means to usurp their power.

COALITIONS OF THE WEAK

Throughout this book, I assume that the ultimate goal of leaders in one-party regimes is to stay in power. As such, some manipulation of the selectorate both served to increase the dictator's chance of survival and provided the dictator with vital information about the relative distribution of power among the party elite. In particular, by placing known weak figures in the selectorate, dictators swung the distribution of power to

---

[1] This, of course, does not hold true for competitive authoritarian regimes. These countries hold democratic elections, but the executive can still manipulate outcomes effectively, making them de facto dictatorships. See (Way and Levitsky 2002).

their favor and became more certain about the relative distribution of power both presently and into the future. It would be even more ideal if the dictator appointed individuals whose power could not grow over time, at least not until they could be replaced by someone else equally weak, if not weaker.

The coalition of the weak strategy was the most effective in institutionalized regimes with well-defined selectorate bodies and hierarchies. As discussed, a crucial aspect of Leninist institutions was the concentration of power in the hands of the upper-echelon elite in the party, including greater discretion over the appointment of senior officials than leaders in other forms of authoritarian regimes. Within the broad confines of Leninist hierarchies, which their leaders were incentivized to maintain, the dictators' agency made a difference. By populating elite decision-making bodies with weak figures, dictators reduced the chance of rival coalitions emerging because while a small number of well-connected veteran officials could successfully conspire against the dictator, even a large number of weak officials likely lacked the power to usurp the dictator. By introducing known weak figures, the dictators also obtained more information about the relative distribution of power among those in elite decision-making bodies, given the relatively fixed sizes of these elite bodies in Leninist regimes.

By "weak" officials, I mean two types of officials. First, I mean tainted individuals, defined as actors whose rehabilitation within a given set of institutions required the payment of audience costs (Lohmann 2003). They were valuable to the dictator precisely because they needed to pay costs in addition to the usual costs of rebellion if they decided to rise up against the incumbent.[2] The audience costs arose from the fact that within the social construction embedded in a set of institutions, these individuals were considered to be highly undesirable due to the dominant discourse in that set of institutions (Berger and Luckmann 1990). This typically pertained to ethnic or religious affiliations, which through generations of folk or officially sanctioned discourses, had made certain groups undesirable to the rest of the members in these institutions (Berger and Luckmann 1990). Thus, to remove that stigma, actors had to either invest in new

---

[2] According to Lohmann (Lohmann 2003), "an institutional commitment has bite only if it is made vis-a-vis an audience that can and will punish institutional defections." Thus, when an individual is tainted due to violation of rules set forth by an existing set of institutions, the removal of that taint within that set of institutions will lead to costs imposed by an audience.

discourses or make use of some element of the existing social construction to relegitimize the tainted figures. Neither action was costless.

Because audience costs were high and relatively fixed over time, dictators could make use of tainted individuals over the entire duration of their rule. For one, stigmatized member of the selectorate were much less acceptable as coalition partners in rival coalitions, making it more difficult for rival coalitions to emerge if the top echelon of the party was filled with such individuals. Alternatively, even if they were accepted into potential rival coalitions, their tainted status placed a ceiling on the potential payoffs to them of a successful rebellion, which disincentivized them from participating in plots to remove the incumbents in the first place. For example, if ethnic minority or historically tarnished officials could at most serve as vice-ministers regardless of who was in charge, their preferred choice in most cases was to support the incumbents, which entailed less risk compared with a conspiracy to overthrow the incumbent. For the dictators, such tarnished figures also provided vital information even through future shocks that redistributed power because they knew that at least these individuals had a lower chance of being a part of any potential rival coalitions, leaving the untainted elite as the chief suspects of any suspected plot. As the chapters on the FFA reveal, being on the wrong side of history placed one in an extremely vulnerable position, which ironically helped one survive a suspicious dictator.

The other type of weak officials included individuals who were inexperienced in politics at the national level and who lacked national-level political networks. By appointing such individuals to top-level decision-making bodies, dictators minimized the chance that senior officials could launch coups. Dictators also reduced, although they did not eliminate, the principal–agent problem by appointing inexperienced officials because these officials, not familiar with the exact extent of the dictator's monitoring capacity, at first followed the dictator's instructions to the letter. Finally, this strategy also reduced the costs of purging officials who deviated from the wishes of the dictator. Inexperienced officials without vast support networks across the regime could be dispensed overnight with little repercussion to the dictator.

Unlike some existing works on incompetent officials in dictatorships (Egorov and Sonin 2011; Zakharov 2016), this framework does not see a strict trade-off between loyalty and competence. For one, the concept of loyalty provided limited analytical purchase in authoritarian politics because of the information asymmetry about the distribution of power, especially after major shocks that redistributed power. If an exogenous shock distributed a great deal of power to a previously loyal official, could the dictator still trust that individual? Furthermore, a subordinate's technical competence in itself did not threaten the dictator's power, although political skills can be threatening (Egorov and Sonin 2011). Instead, the density of an official's elite network, which was more correlated with loyalty than competence per se, constituted the threatening variable for the dictator. For example, if an official had a past history of loyalty but also a sizable power base as a result of being a party veteran, he was a greater threat to the dictator than an official without a past history of loyalty and a weak network.

Instead of a loyalty-competence trade-off, the coalition of the weak framework suggests a trade-off between ensuring short- and medium-term dominance for the dictator and long-term institutionalization of the ruling party, a personal power-institutionalization trade-off. As the extant literature suggests, institutionalization took place when stakeholders negotiated with one another over a set of rules to distribute resources and power (Moe 2005; Thelen 2004). In postrevolutionary regimes, this process was helped by the dense social networks that revolutionary veterans had forged with one another during the revolutionary struggle (Easter 1996; Levitsky and Way 2012). Coalitions of the weak undermined the process of institutional consolidation in several ways. First and foremost, by claiming dictatorial power after the coalition of the weak was installed, the dictator abandoned the use of existing institutions for decision-making in favor of personal audiences, thus leading to institutional stasis. This took place to a large extent in the late-Mao years. Even if existing institutions continued to meet and make decisions, weak members of the elite nominally in charge of them knew they could be removed from their positions at any time by the dictator and thus had no incentive to negotiate with other actors to define the rules and resources of those institutions. In any event, all decisions needed the personal approval of the dictator. Other elite actors, knowing that they were negotiating with dispensable officials without authorities, also had few incentives to cede power and resources to these institutions, leading to persistent ambiguity about the authorities of and rules governing the operation of these institutions. Subordinates of weak officials in charge of institutions also were more likely to take advantage of their weak bosses to circumvent previously defined procedures for their own benefits, thus undermining these institutions. Although the literature has long identified "patrimonial" states where personal authority dictated policy-making (Rudolph and Rudolph 1979; Snyder 1992), the coalition of the weak framework provides a mechanism for institutionalized regimes to devolve toward patrimonialism.

To clarify the advantages of appointing a coalition of the weak for the dictator, I provide the following algebraic expression. This illustration only considers the benefits of pursuing the coalitions of the weak strategy, not the potential costs outlined previously. Suppose there are N number of individuals in the selectorate, and in each turn, each member of the selectorate will win with a probability of P_i, thus becoming the dictator of the group. In the simplest setup, nature uniformly assigns probability to the ith selectorate member to win in a given turn. Thus, $P_i = 1/N$, where N is the total number of members in the selectorate. In the highly uncertain environment of authoritarian politics, the objective probability of winning a power struggle may not be uniform, but senior leaders in one-party regimes certainly behave as if there are persistent threats to their power. For example, Mao often talked of the need for him to "go back to Bandit Hill" if forced out of power by rivals (Mao 1987f). Also, unlike the Acemoglu et al. paper (2008), which takes power level of selectorate members as a given, the model expressed in Equation 1.1 examines how dictators can maximize their chance of victory if allowed to manipulate the composition of the selectorate.

In essence, dictators can make two important choices about the members of the selectorate to enhance their chance of victory at each turn. First, dictators can choose selectorate members who are weak in various degrees. Second, dictators can decide on the share of the selectorate composed of weak members. In the first case, a dictator can replace an ordinary (and strong) member of the selectorate with another strong member, who has $P_i = 1/N$. Alternatively, she can choose a replacement who is weak and tainted and only has, for example, half the probability of winning as the other members. In this case, the replacement's probability of winning would be $P_{i*} = 1/2N$. More generally, a weakened member of the selectorate would win with a probability of $P_{i*} = 1/QN$, where Q is some existing constraint on the power of a particular or a group of selectorate members $i*$. The dictator and perhaps her colleagues have discretion over how large Q is in the replacement because they can choose the replacement from a large pool of potential elites (Bueno de Mesquita et al. 2003). As mentioned in the previous discussion on weak officials, this constraint can be inexperience, which prevents an official from fully exercising the power of her office. It can also be membership in an ostracized ethnic or religious community, which imposes costs on this official and potential coalition partners when joining rival coalitions.

The tainted status also can stem from historical guilt. The historical material in the rest of the book will flesh out how various vulnerabilities prevented "weak" coalition members from seriously challenging the power of the dictator.

Second, through manipulating the size and through reshuffling the top leadership, dictators or an oligarchy can also influence the share of the selectorate composed of weak figures, that is, figures with $Q > 1$. The share of weak figures in the selectorate is represented by λ. The manipulation of λ can come about in two ways. First, dictators or a small group of oligarchs can enlarge institutionalized bodies of senior officials, such as the Politburo, and pack them with weaklings, thus increasing the share of senior officials over whom they have a great deal of control. Mao famously called this tactic "mixing in sand" (Mao 1987b). Second, the dictator can replace veteran officials with weak figures in a selectorate body of fixed size. So as not to alarm one's opponent of an impending purge, "mixing in sand" may be an advantageous first step in forming a coalition of the weak.

From the perspective of members of the selectorate who do not face such a constraint on power, especially the dictator, having a weak member in the selectorate is obviously a superior choice. If a member of the selectorate is weak in some sense, then the other members of the selectorate win with higher probability (Tullock 1987: 145). Similarly, when the share of weak members in the selectorate goes up (λ increases), unconstrained members of the selectorate, presumably including the dictator, should also benefit from a higher probability of obtaining victory at every turn.

Since the sum of the probabilities of all the members winning in a given turn is 1, the probability of the unconstrained members winning in a given turn, given that some share of the selectorate has been filled with weak members of a certain level, is given in equation below where N is the number of actors in the selectorate, Q is the extent to which weak members' power has been discounted, and λ is the share of the selectorate made up of weak members:

$$P_i = \frac{1}{N} + \lambda N \left(\left(\frac{1}{N} - \frac{1}{QN} \right) * \frac{1}{N - \lambda N} \right)$$

Or

$$P_i = \frac{1}{N} + \frac{1}{N} \left(\frac{\lambda}{(1-\lambda)} - \frac{\lambda}{Q - \lambda Q} \right)$$

For example, in a selectorate of five individuals, a uniform distribution of power provides each individual with one-fifth chance of winning in each turn. However, if one member of the selectorate could only win with a probability of one-tenth (i.e. Q = 2, λ = 0.2), the other members of the selectorate would have this probability of winning:

$$P_i = \frac{1}{5} + \frac{1}{5}\left(\frac{0.2}{(1-0.2)} - \frac{0.2}{2-0.2(2)}\right)$$

In other words, unconstrained members of the selectorate only obtained a 2.5 percent increase in the probability of victory from the uniformly distributed power case after the replacement of one ordinary selectorate member with one member with half the power as the others. Obviously, the more one can constrain a member's power, that is, the higher Q is, the more winning probability redistributes to the other members of the selectorate. Likewise, the larger share of the selectorate is subjected to power restrictions, the more winning probability redistributes to members of the selectorate whose power is not constrained. But which of the two tactics is more advantageous for the incumbent?

In Figure 1.1, I plot out the additional probability of winning bestowed on an ordinary member of the selectorate as Q rises for the one weak member appointed to a three-player selectorate, a five-player selectorate, and a ten-player selectorate. One should note that although in all three

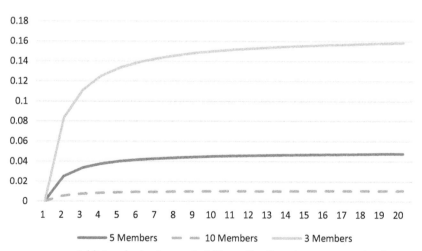

FIGURE 1.1 Additional winning probability redistributed to unconstrained players as Q increases: selectorates with three members, five members, and ten members

cases only one weak member is appointed, λ differs in each case due to variation in selectorate size. Thus, λ are 0.33, 0.2, and 0.1, respectively. Figure 1.1 shows the marginal effect of rising Q, or power constraints, on the unconstrained members' chance of winning in a given turn. Two clear patterns emerge in this exercise. First, there is a diminishing return for the unconstrained players as Q rises, regardless of λ. At a certain point (such as when Q > 5), it doesn't matter if a person with a blemished record or an illiterate farmer is made a Politburo member; appointing the farmer without any experience would redistribute only very marginal gains to the other members of the selectorate. Second, increasing λ, the share of weak members, obtains significant gains for unconstrained members of the selectorate. In Figure 1.1, the placement of a single weak member, if he is at least one-fifth as strong as the others, has a drastic effect on a three-person selectorate, a mild effect on a five-person selectorate, and a minute effect on a ten-person selectorate.

We further explore this logic in Figure 1.2, which plots Pi as λ, the share of weak selectorate members, rises in a ten-person selectorate. Q, the power constrained on the weak members, is set at two and at five, giving weak members half and one-fifth the probability of winning as the other members. As we can see, without any weak member in a ten-member selectorate, each member can win with one-tenth probability. As the share of weak members rises, unconstrained members' winning probability rises also. However, unconstrained members do not become

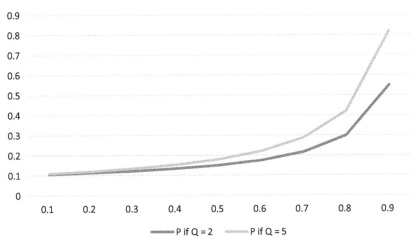

FIGURE 1.2 The probability of unconstrained players winning (P_i) as λ rises in a ten-member selectorate

dominant until λ is at 0.9, when the dictator remains the only unconstrained member of the selectorate and obtains a higher than 0.5 probability of staying in power. This is the case even if Q is high, that is, if very weak members are introduced into the selectorate.

This result is intuitive. As weak members are introduced to the selectorate, other unconstrained members in the selectorate besides the dictator also benefit from the presence of weak members, which limits the gains of the dictator. It is only when everyone but the dictator is weak in the selectorate that the dictator can truly enjoy the fruits of, well, being a dictator. To prevent other unconstrained members of the selectorate from benefiting from weak members, dictators must engineer wholesale removal of their colleagues to maximize the benefits of the coalition of the weak strategy. True dominance does not occur until weak members make up the vast majority of the selectorate. After the coalition of the weak is fully in place, the difference between having moderately weak and very weak members in the selectorate is the level of security for the dictator. As Figure 1.2 shows, when the dictator corules with moderately weak figures with half the ordinary strength, his probability of victory is only at 55 percent, whereas very weak figures with one-fifth of ordinary strength would provide the dictator with a 82 percent chance of winning.

Figure 1.2 also suggests the possibility of oligarchic rule. If a self-enforcing coalition of unconstrained elite decided to increase their power bases without a dictator emerging, they can introduced a wave of weak officials to boost λ to a range between 0.5 and 0.8 (Figure 1.2). This arguably was the politics in the 1980s in a nutshell, as discussed in Chapter 7.

Because of this logic, weak members of the selectorate may survive a suspicious dictator better than strong members who have proven themselves loyal for years. In fact, the findings about military officers during the Cultural Revolution suggest that tainted officials who had a history of splitting the party were preferred over those with years of loyal service.

Departing from the aforementioned abstract setup, dictators or members of a junta often secured these appointments because they, at a given point in time, had some superiority in power. Thus, in every turn, the dictators' probability of winning was likely over 50 percent in any event. By appointing weak figures in the selectorate, dictators further bolstered their chance of success in the future because the weak members were much less likely to challenge the incumbent in the future. Furthermore, placing known weak figures in the selectorate also elevated the dictators' certainty of the relative distribution of power, compared to placing experienced and unblemished officials who could be quite powerful.

Moreover, similar to new institutions, constructing a coalition of the weak likely provided increasing returns to the dictator (Pierson 2000). Concretely, as the share of weak figures in the selectorate rose, the possibility of a sufficiently powerful rival coalition diminished, thus allowing the dictator to remove remaining strong members with fewer risks. This further incentivized the dictator to remove additional strong members from the selectorate, potentially until achieving true dictatorship. Because politically inexperienced replacements feared the dictator's wrath much more so than their predecessors, they were much more likely to follow the dictator's instructions to the letter and report deviations of others to the dictator, thus alleviating the agency and information asymmetry problems that typically plagued the dictator (Gregory 2009). This tendency thus reduced the risks faced by the dictator temporarily until the political novice began to learn more about the information deficits faced by the dictator. However, this fear-driven concentration of power also militated against institutional development, which required leaders of institutions to exercise authorities delegated to these institutions.

The theory of coalition of the weak thus has the following empirical predictions, many of which manifested in the late-Mao period starting with the beginning of the Cultural Revolution (1966–1976) and also in the politics of the 1980s. First, when faced with a potentially disadvantageous redistribution of power, which took place after a political shock or during times of succession, dictators might have pursued a coalition of the weak strategy. The manifestation of the coalition of the weak strategy included purging experienced officials with dense political networks and replacing them with either historically blemished officials or inexperienced junior cadres. The dictators might have chosen to enlarge the size of key decision-making institutions such as the Politburo or the Central Committee, inducting only weak new members. Related, we would expect the replacement of veteran cadres by young or tainted counterparts to occur in large waves instead in a gradual fashion over time. That is, when dictators took the risk of eliminating veterans who posed potential threats, they had incentive to get rid of large groups of colleagues with no weaknesses, since the payoffs of replacing them remained limited until a sizable share of the selectorate had been replaced. When such a purge occurred, veterans with major blemishes in the past or stigmas attached to them were expected to survive at a higher rate than veterans without blemishes.

In terms of patterns of promotion, instead of requiring candidates for top leadership positions to undergo an extensive trial period, the theory of coalitions of the weak predicts the systematic "helicoptering" of extremely junior officials into the center of power without any significant trial periods. Such wholesale promotions of junior officials left a large number of mid-ranking officials with much richer experience in their place. Furthermore, dictators asserted close control over the "helicopters" instead of encouraging them to become autonomous leaders in their own right or to exercise autonomous power in the institutions over which they nominally presided. However, besides the dictator, other veteran members of the ruling coalition also might have taken advantage of the ignorance of newly promoted junior officials, thus limiting the gains of the dictators. Instead of protecting the newly promoted novice and grooming them for future leadership positions, the "helicoptered" officials were sacrificed wholesale for political expedience, replaced by other junior officials with little experience.

Full implementation of the coalition of the weak strategy, that is, the replacement of the vast majority of the selectorate with weak cadres, resulted in significantly fewer serious challenges to the dictator's power and greater ease for the dictator to make major policy changes. In essence, once incumbents appointed coalitions of the weak, they could expect to rule as dictators, facing few serious threats to power or entrenched opposition to policy changes. This applied to major policy changes preferred by the dictator, even if they were detrimental to vested interests in the upper echelon of the regime, including personnel changes. In comparison, leaders who had not fashioned coalitions of the weak faced serious challenges to their power and high hurdles in making preferred policy changes. Even if they ultimately got their way, dictators sharing power with veteran colleagues needed to engage in months, sometimes years, of scheming in order to enact preferred policy changes. Full implementation of the coalition of the weak strategy also led to policy-making resembling that seen in neopatrimonial regimes, where the personal authority of the dictator trumped established laws, institutional procedures, or even ideology tenets (Snyder 1992). Policies, including major changes in personnel, depended only on the whims of the dictator instead of on established rules or norms. If an oligarchy pursued a limited weak coalition strategy, unconstrained members of the coalition likely enjoyed a high degree of control over members of the weak coalition but not on other members of the oligarchy.

The coalition of the weak theory also predicts that once the dictator died naturally, members of these weak coalitions became vulnerable to challenges from any surviving senior leader with rich experience and extensive political networks and without any historical baggage.

Members of the previous leader's coalition faced a sharp increase in political risks in the transition period, which was settled with either their purges or their convergence toward a stable power-sharing arrangement.

ALTERNATIVE EXPLANATIONS

The literature on elite Chinese politics have provided a number of explanations for outcomes in the late-Mao period. However, these accounts have left unexplained gaps. For example, the existing accounts of Mao's last years never provided a convincing rationale of why after the Lin Biao incident in 1971, serious challenges to Mao's power suddenly ceased, even as the Great Helmsman's health failed rapidly. Some scholars argued that the relative tranquility of Mao's last years stemmed from him pursuing more moderate policies, which presumably decreased the level of conflict (Teiwes and Sun 2007: 14). In other words, Mao moved his policies closer to those preferred by the "median voter" in the elite selectorate, thereby garnering him greater support in the elite circle. Others argue that the rehabilitation of Deng Xiaoping afforded Mao better control over the military, which had been weakened by the Lin Biao incident in any event (Dikötter 2016; MacFarquhar and Schoenhals 2006: 379). Party historians in China argue that Zhou Enlai's tireless effort to preserve stability prevented all-out clashes from emerging between high-level leaders after the beginning of the Cultural Revolution (Gao 2003).

None of these accounts, however, provides entirely satisfactory explanations for the tranquility of Mao's last years, nor can they explain the strange patterns of elite promotions seen in the last years of Mao's life. First, the radical Red Guard phase of the Cultural Revolution ended in 1968, when the young Maoists were sent off to the countryside en mass. Yet Lin Biao still challenged Mao's power by having his subordinates resist Mao's call for self-criticism after the 1970 Lushan Conference (Wu 2006: 807). After the Lin Biao incident, Mao indeed began the process of rehabilitating some purged veterans, but few returned to high-level offices before Mao's death. Many were merely moved back to Beijing for "medical care" from their work farms (Gao 2003: 387). In their place, inexperienced cadres and military men still held the vast majority of senior positions in Mao's last years. If the moderates were not in any position to challenge Mao, why would Mao pursue "moderate" policies to appease them?

Indeed, the rehabilitation of Deng was related to Mao's wish to control the military, especially the faction in the PLA that had become dominant after the Lin Biao incident. However, Mao very easily removed Deng at the end of 1975, in sharp contrast to the beginning of the Cultural Revolution, when Mao spent months plotting the demise of Liu Shaoqi and Deng (MacFarquhar and Schoenhals 2006). Both before and after Deng's removal, the military showed little sign of disobedience to Mao or indeed any serious engagement in politics, except for carrying out the Anti-Lin Biao, Anti-Confucius Campaign on behalf of Mao, which led to an additional wave of purges. As for Zhou, he was unable to prevent the Lin Biao incident from occurring despite some effort to smooth the relationship between Lin and Mao (Gao 2003). He also failed to prevent clashes between a newly rehabilitated Deng Xiaoping and the Gang of Four. Finally, he withdrew from active engagement with party affairs long before Mao's own death. The key in the late-Mao period was that after Lin Biao's aborted flight and the purge of his close followers, the military became an almost trouble-free organization for Mao and even his successors. But after high-level military figures such as Peng Dehuai and Lin Biao had challenged Mao's absolute authority, why had the military transformed into a politically quiescent organization, even as Mao's health failed? None of the existing accounts can provide a satisfying answer to this puzzle.

In addition, the China field has long interpreted the appointment of inexperienced, young officials to high-level offices as one of succession and preserving the revolutionary zeal. As MacFarquhar (1997b: 249) points out, "[i]n the storm of the Cultural Revolution, new leaders were to emerge, steeled in struggle, 'proletarian' in outlook, in whose hands the Maoist brand of socialism would one day burn fiercely." Similarly, Teiwes and Sun (2007: 10) contend that Mao's objective after the Lin Biao incident was to "create a wider corps of successor generation leaders." Li also argues that the appointment of ideologically enthusiastic activists aimed to ensure "continuous revolution," a principle that was even enshrined in the Party Constitution at the 10th Party Congress (Li 2007).

Indeed, during the 9th Party Congress, Mao enlarged the number of Central Committee members to 170 in order to introduce rebels and mass representatives into the ruling elite (MacFarquhar and Schoenhals 2006: 292). Some of the rebels from the first stage of the CR were inducted into the Central Committee as full or alternate members, including Wang Hongwen, Wang Xiuzhen, and Nie Yuanzi. Mao further imposed a quota system on the new revolutionary leadership at the local level, mandating an "old, middle age, young" age distribution for leaders in the revolutionary committees (Ye 2009: 992).

This explanation of the promotion pattern during the CR contains some inconsistencies, however. For one, very few of the radical activists from the first stage of the CR survived as political elite by the 1973 10th Party Congress. Besides key members of the Central Cultural Revolution Group (CCRG) – Jiang Qing, Zhang Chunqiao, and Yao Wenyuan – many of their assistants, including Wang Li, Guan Feng, Qi Benyu, Nie Yuanzi, had been purged by the 10th PC. Wang Li, a key member of the CCRG until the day of his downfall, was arrested on verbal instructions by Mao and put in solitary confinement without trial for fourteen years (Wang 2001: 152). Nie Yuanzi likewise was sent to the countryside soon after she was inducted into the Central Committee as an alternate member. If these radicals had been groomed to be successors, why did Mao remove so many of them from power without giving them a second chance? At the 10th Party Congress, Mao inducted mass representatives from the grassroots into the elite, including an illiterate vice premier Chen Yonggui and the miracle textile worker Wu Guixian. Unlike Red Guard activists, this wave of elite took no part in instigating the Cultural Revolution and proved to be helpless defenders of Mao's legacy, switching immediately to support the post-Mao leadership and its policies after the fall of the Gang of Four (MacFarquhar and Schoenhals 2006: 447). If Mao's objective was only to preserve the revolutionary legacy of the CR, why were the radical Red Guards, some of whom with a great deal of charisma and organizational skills, treated so badly?

Also, if the promotion of junior radicals during the Cultural Revolution had been aimed at cultivating a new generation of leaders, Mao would have put them through longer trial periods to work alongside more experienced veterans to accumulate experience. Instead, officials like Wang Hongwen, Wang Li, and Qi Benyu were thrown into the labyrinth of elite politics without any training or preparation. As MacFarquhar observes about Wang Hongwen's sudden elevation to be nominally the third most powerful official in China at the 10th Party Congress "with only six years' experience of revolutionary struggle and politics, he was expected to keep up with and contend against men like the premier, who had survived six decades of revolutions, civil wars, foreign invasion, and party infighting. It was a grossly unequal contest, another Maoist gamble that would fail" (MacFarquhar 1997b: 281). Instead of a failed gamble, this book argues that placing clueless junior officials in positions of great authority was a deliberate strategy by Mao to enhance his personal power while he still lived. Postmortem legacy or even the long-term rule of the party likely was not a high priority for Mao.

Another frequently used framework to explain late-Mao politics is one of factionalism, which saw Mao coalescing officials who historically had served him against officials from other "mountaintops" in the revolution (Dittmer 1998; Huang 2000). In a factional framework, a patron was expected to protect one's loyal followers rather than the followers of former enemies (Pye 1995; Shih 2008b). To be sure, the first phase of the Cultural Revolution saw this logic unfold with the purge of Liu Shaoqi and the consolidation of power by Lin Biao and others who had followed Mao since the Jinggangshan Base Area in the late 1920s. The latter part of the Cultural Revolution, however, was highly inconsistent with the factional framework. The Cultural Revolution ultimately saw the removal of scores of Mao's most trusted and oldest followers, including Lin Biao himself, as well as Deng Xiaoping, Wu Faxian, and Qiu Huizuo. In the meantime, the followers of Mao's most serious usurper from the 1930s, followers of Zhang Guotao in the Red FFA, were systematically saved and promoted. Mao's protection of Zhang Guotao followers in the midst of the Cultural Revolution made little sense from a factional perspective, which a coalition of the weak perspective could remedy.

To be sure, the replacement of experienced revolutionaries with the coalition of the weak was highly correlated to the level of power enjoyed by the incumbent dictator at the time of the reshuffling. In a sense, coalition of the weak was such a sensible tactic that dictators with sufficient power likely would have done so (Acemoglu et al. 2008). But even conditioning on the level of power dictators enjoyed, dictators did not have perfect information on the power of their colleagues, thus deterring them from purging the selectorate at a whim. Exogenous historical shocks and the personalities of dictators ultimately also drove the timing and extent to which dictators could pursue the coalitions of the weak strategy. For Mao, rising challenges to his authorities after the Great Leap disaster meant Mao either had to accept gradual decline of his power, perhaps culminating to his own purge, or to take the risky gamble of purging his experienced colleagues. As the pre–Great Leap period showed, without his prestige falling so precipitously because of the Great Leap disaster, Mao could have maintained his dominance through a divide and rule strategy for decades longer (MacFarquhar 1997a). His risk-accepting style compelled him to put his coalition of the weak strategy in motion after his senior colleagues had criticized him after the Great Leap, culminating in the wave of purges between 1966 and 1967. Once Mao removed his potential challengers, the benefits of the coalitions of the weak strategy reinforced each other, and elite politics in China went down a path toward total dictatorship in the late-Mao period.

Finally, FFA veterans might have been saved during the Cultural Revolution because their tainted status compelled them to follow Mao's instruction to the letter, which made them less vulnerable targets of Mao's wrath. Their different behavioral profiles, instead of Mao's power strategy, might have saved them from purges. To be sure, they, by and large, carefully followed Mao's wishes. Some, like Xie Fuzhi, went out of their way to help Jiang Qing and Kang Sheng concoct evidence against veteran cadres targeted by Mao (Central Committee 1982c). However, carefully following Mao's instructions did not stop many other cadres from being purged during the Cultural Revolution. Furthermore, Li Xiannian and Xu Xiangqian, both senior members of the FFA group, displayed anger and dissatisfaction against the Cultural Revolution during the February Countercurrent in 1967 (MacFarquhar and Schoenhals 2006). They survived the repercussions relatively unscathed. Xu Shiyou, the leader of an "armed counterrevolutionary plot" in the 1930s, personally ordered the Nanjing Military Region to resist Red Guard activities in military units as late as December 1966 (Zhang 2007). When the Red Guards came to arrest him in 1967, he ran away to the Dabie Mountains, where he had fought guerilla warfare in the 1930s and threatened to shoot anyone who tried to bring him to a struggle session. Instead of arresting and purging him, a fate that had befallen officers who had committed much lesser infractions, Mao invited Xu to live next to him in Zhongnanhai in Beijing (Wen and Li 1998)! Thus, behaving carefully also did not explain the systematic retention and promotion of FFA veterans during the Cultural Revolution.

COALITIONS OF THE WEAK AND THE INNER POLITICS OF THE MAO AND DENG PERIOD

The historical and quantitative research conducted for this book also sheds new light on the elite politics of the Mao and Deng Eras, as well as on the origin of Xi Jinping's total domination over the CCP. First, the story of Zhang Guotao's FFA is a major gap in the political history of the Mao and Deng Eras. The obscure but traumatic political struggle toward the end of the Long March in 1935, often glossed over in official party history and history textbooks, produced hundreds of military officers and civilian cadres who were politically scarred for life. As followers of the "Zhang Guotao counterrevolutionary splittist line," half of them were sent on a death march from which only a handful returned, while the other half underwent intense political struggle and torture for years. When these officers and cadres emerged from years of rectification, however, most of them were never purged again in subsequent decades.

The rise of Zhang Guotao's remnant faction in the entire postliberation period is puzzling because Zhang Guotao split from the Central Committee by setting up a "Provisional" Central Committee at the end of the Long March. Furthermore, Zhang was the most senior member of the CCP to have survived defection.[3] Thus, if the Cultural Revolution aimed at struggling against class enemies and traitors within the party, followers of Zhang Guotao, who actually had been enemies of Chairman Mao in the 1930s, should have been purged immediately. After all, Mao spent months trying to prove that Liu Shaoqi was at the head of a ring of traitors dating back to the 1930s (MacFarquhar and Schoenhals 2006). For Zhang Guotao followers, no investigation into their past sins would have been necessary because numerous party documents issued in the 1930s documented their counterrevolutionary crimes. Instead of purging them, Mao went out of his way to save them from Red Guard rampage. Even as Mao encouraged Lin Biao to systematically wipe out the faction of He Long, another faction from the 1930s, veterans of the renegade FFA largely retained their positions (Wu 2006: 636). Even after the Wuhan incident, which saw conservative Red Guards supported by former Zhang followers kidnapping Mao's personal representatives, Mao actively intervened to prevent an army-wide purge of this faction. Chapters 3 and 5 of this book will discuss the origin of the FFA faction in the Chinese military, as well as their crucial roles in late-Mao power strategies and in the Deng Era.

Despite a torrent of literature about the Deng Era, crucial aspects of the period remain murky (Baum 1994; Deng 1995; Fewsmith 1994; Goodman 1994; Ross 1989; Ruan et al. 1994; Shambaugh 1993). First and foremost, the rise of Deng has never been satisfactorily explained. To be sure, there is a host of explanations. He headed the Second Field Army, but there were a dozen or so other commanders who had his command experience in the 1980s, including Huang Kecheng, Li Jingquan, Tan Zhenlin, Su Yu, and Xiao Ke. What made Deng unique? Second, Deng took a tough stance against "Two Whateverism," but why was he able and willing to do so, but not others (Ruan et al. 1994)? His willingness to

---

[3] The other senior defectors, including Gu Shunzhang, Xiang Zhongfa, and Lin Biao, were killed either before or soon after their defections. Zhang lived out his days in Canada.

take a tough stance stemmed from his support base in the military, but this leads back to the first explanation. Another related explanation was that Mao needed Deng rehabilitated so that he could strengthen command over the military (MacFarquhar and Schoenhals 2006: 358; Vogel 2011: 80). Again, when there were still so many veterans who had joined the party before the end of the Long March, why was Deng uniquely suitable to put the military in order? Why was he rehabilitated so soon after the fall of the Gang of Four?

More generally, the composition of the core leadership group in the 1980s – Deng Xiaoping, Chen Yun, Ye Jianying, and Li Xiannian – in many ways seemed unlikely. Deng Xiaoping had been purged twice during the Cultural Revolution and came from a relatively weak faction that had been wiped out in battles in the early 1930s. Li Xiannian, the veteran of a group that had been accused of "counterrevolutionary splittism" in the 1930s, served mainly in technocratic positions, managing China's budget for much of the 1950s and 1960s. Dozens of other technocrats in Li's position never had nearly the same level of influence in politics in the 1970s and 1980s. Yet Li was regularly consulted on major decisions throughout the entire Deng period until his death. Li's prominence becomes especially puzzling when one considers his high-level position during the Cultural Revolution, which implied cooperation with the Gang of Four, and his role as a supporter of Hua Guofeng. The conventional framework of victims, beneficiaries, and radicals simply cannot explain Li Xiannian's continual power into the 1980s because Li was certainly a major beneficiary of the late Cultural Revolution. Similarly, Ye Jianying was a weak military figure who had not commanded troops directly since the early 1930s. Throughout the Cultural Revolution, he continuously held some of the most powerful positions in the PLA, and yet, when Deng came to power, Ye continued as a high-level military leader whom Deng consulted regularly (Zhang 2008a: 415).

The influence exercised by Chen Yun in the 1980s likewise was puzzling. To be sure, Chen was enormously prestigious as an early revolutionary and as the economic czar of China in the 1950s, but other early revolutionaries, including Cai Chang and Li Weihan, never returned to any position of great authority after 1978. Mao and Zhou Enlai found Chen to be replaceable as an economic planner for much of the late 1960s and the 1970s. Yet, suddenly and effortlessly, Chen Yun found himself back in the pinnacles of power in the late 1970s, where he stayed until his death.

This book is the first to argue that Mao's appointment of Fourth Front Army (FFA) veterans in the 1970s to control the military greatly influenced the composition of the ruling coalition not only in the late Mao period but also through much of the Deng Era in the 1980s. FFA commanders Li Xiannian and, to a lesser extent, Xu Xiangqian and Xu Shiyou, retained a great deal of influence over the military and over the party throughout the latter parts of their lives. Their former underlings continued to serve in senior army positions until well into the 1990s. In Mao's own words, Li Xiannian was "the representative of the Fourth Front Army" faction, which gave him enormous clout as one of the three veto players in elite decision-making in the 1980s (Huang et al. 2010: 812).

Others who had played crucial roles in the FFA's tortuous history likewise became key actors in the 1980s. As a way of ensuring absolute control over this group of tainted officers, Mao elevated Ye Jianying, the man who likely fabricated a story in the 1930s to deepen the guilt of FFA veterans, to be in charge of the military. This made Ye Jianying and his children a formidable force in the party for much of the 1980s and into the 1990s. The dominance of FFA veterans in the military provided Deng Xiaoping, who had taken over command of the FFA after Zhang Guotao's defection, much-needed political resource as he struggled for supreme power in the late 1970s. When he took power, Deng, like Mao, continued to make heavy use of FFA veterans in the 1980s and into the 1990s. The last FFA veteran to hold substantial power, Liu Huaqing, did not retire until 1998. Finally, Chen Yun, in combination with his long history in the party, was also the only surviving elite witness to the legitimacy of the Western Legion, which he used to great effect to maintain influence over FFA veterans. In sum, many of the great figures of the 1980s – Deng, Chen, Li, and Ye – have all derived a substantial portion of their power because of historical brushes with the "splittist" FFA.

Most treatments of the Central Cultural Revolution Group (CCRG) have focused on their role in helping Mao launch and sustain the Red Guard movement within the Cultural Revolution, as well as their role as the guardians of Mao's vision for a "continuous revolution" (MacFarquhar and Schoenhals 2006; Pantsov and Levine 2012; Perry and Li 1997; Walder 2009). To be sure, the junior radicals played those roles during the Cultural Revolution. This book, in contrast, focuses on the political roles they and the other "scribblers" (笔杆子) played in Mao's coalition strategy. From a purely strategic perspective, the scribblers, who included veterans such as Chen Boda as well as younger theorists such as Guan Feng and Wang Li, were nothing more than pawns to Mao and Lin Biao, who readily sacrificed them to serve their immediately political needs. Although Mao might have hoped that one or two of the scribblers and workers' radicals would have emerged as worthy revolutionary successors, he stood ready to sacrifice most of them to political struggles. The purge of the scribblers seen after the Wuhan incident in late 1967 attests to the callousness with which scribblers were treated. As the struggle between Mao and Lin heated up, Lin Biao, who instigated the "genius" and state chairmanship debates at the 1970 Lushan Conference, barely hesitated in putting the entire blame on Chen Boda. For Mao and Lin Biao, ideologues and scribblers were not so much the future of the revolution but rather ready fodder for power struggles among the surviving Long March military commanders. Instead of nurturing and correcting them when they committed errors, Mao loyalists such as Wang Li and Guan Feng spent the better half of their lives in solitary confinement because they were expendable and knew too many secrets.

Finally, as observers of China grapple with the rising dictatorial rule of Xi Jinping in China (Johnson and Kennedy 2015; Li 2016a; Saunders et al.), this book provides a historical account that partly explains Xi's rapid consolidation of power over the party and the military. When revolutionary veterans were rehabilitated in the 1980s, they each pursued their own weak successor strategy by elevating technically competent but obedient and fawning novices to ministerial-level positions just outside of the Politburo. Meanwhile, the most politically savvy and well-connected young officials, namely the children of the revolutionary veterans, faced resistance to their promotion due to their mistakes during the Cultural Revolution and due to status quo power-holders' fear of their meddling. After the political shock of the Tiananmen Square Crisis in 1989, Deng and surviving veterans opted to promote a slate of relatively inexperienced young technocrats to lead China instead of younger revolutionary veterans or densely networked princelings. This inaugurated an era of collective leadership by technocrats with limited factions.

By the mid-2000s, as the succession competition to choose the post-Hu leadership heated up, the few surviving princeling officials in elite politics only had to contend with technocrats with narrow power bases instead of with a large number of their well-connected peers from revolutionary families. This created preconditions for a previously inconspicuous "bloodline" prince, Xi Jinping, to rally support from his princeling network to triumph over other entrenched networks in the Communist Party.

METHODOLOGICAL APPROACH AND SOURCES

The main approach of this book is analytical historical case comparison, augmented by statistical analysis to provide more robustness to the empirical claims. The three cases include two from the Mao period (1960–1966, 1967–1976) and one from Deng's rule (1978–1992). The goal of these cases is to examine whether the empirical predictions generated earlier played out in these cases. To test the hypotheses generated from the theory of the coalition of the weak, this book mainly leverages within regime variation in the extent to which Mao and Deng were able to appoint coalitions of the weak at the top level (King et al. 1994; Mill 1846). In these cases, I first examine the political shocks that led these two leaders to pursue and not pursue the coalition of the weak strategy. I then discern whether significant variation in serious threats to these leaders' power and the ease of major policy changes depended on their pursuit of the coalition of the weak strategy at the top level, that is, the Politburo and its Standing Committee, as well as in the Central Military Commission. Because detailed political history of the late-Mao period and the Deng period already exist, these cases instead focus on the causal mechanisms in question instead of on providing complete political histories of these periods (Dikötter 2016; Fewsmith 1994; MacFarquhar and Schoenhals 2006; Pantsov and Levine 2012; Teiwes and Sun 2007; Walder 2015).

To be sure, variation in the outcome between these leaders may be due to differences in their initial endowment of power. For example, because Hua was a member of Mao's coalition of the weak, his relatively quick downfall was almost inevitable (Shih et al. 2010a). To hone in on the causal impact of the coalition of the weak, I break down the Mao period into two separate cases to exploit within leadership variation. During Mao's rule, there was a clear divide between the post–Great Leap, pre–Cultural Revolution period, when he had to contend with various "mountaintops" with extensive factions, and his rule after the beginning of the Cultural Revolution, when he actively pursued a strategy of appointing weak individuals at the top level. I only focus on the post–Great Leap portion of Mao's rule because Mao was beset by the guilt of having caused the death of tens of millions of people between 1959 and 1961 (Meng et al. 2015). This enormous policy misstep likely enhanced the importance of political machination in Mao's survival strategy after 1960, compared with the first ten years of the People's Republic. Even after the beginning of the Cultural Revolution, there was a difference between the power dynamics faced by Mao prior to Lin Biao's doomed flight to the Soviet Union and afterward. Whereas Lin Biao had emerged as a powerful challenger to Mao between 1967 and 1971 (Chapter 4), his eradication finally realized Mao's coalition of the weak, as detailed in Chapter 5. Careful comparison of these two periods distilled the advantage of the coalition of the weak strategy for Mao, as suggested in Figure 1.2.

In addition, like any in-depth historical studies, this book also ensures robustness of the argument by looking for "smoking guns," that is, empirical observations whose presence lend credence to the theory (Mahoney 2012). For example, one of the strongest "smoking guns" was the statistical finding that in the midst of the Cultural Revolution, when hundreds of senior military officers were purged, officers who had actually been labeled "counterrevolutionaries" in the 1930s were systematically spared by Mao. Other smoking guns include behavioral patterns of the members of the coalition of the weak. The cases in Chapters 4 and 7 reveal that weak members in the upper echelon constantly asked Mao and Deng for instructions and reported all significant conversations to the dictator or to someone representing the dictator, such as Zhou Enlai. They also did nothing to protect one another when one of them faced Mao's wrath. Mao also did not show a pattern of protecting young radicals who eagerly defended his ideological legacy. Instead, they were readily sacrificed in power struggles.

In contrast, members of established, untainted factions coordinated with one another to deflect Mao's policy intentions and to protect one another, even when one of them was on the receiving end of Mao's wrath. Another key "smoking gun" to the theory was Mao's explicit articulation of his power strategy on the eve of Lin Biao's doomed flight to the Soviet Union. Mao explicitly labeled the strategy of diluting Lin Biao's power in the military and in the Party as "mixing in sand" (Mao 1987b). Throughout the book, such "smoking guns" will be flagged as empirical implications of the theory.

In terms of measuring the dependent and independent variables, the independent variable of the theory, the appointment of the coalition of the weak, can easily be traced using biographical data of the political elite (Shih et al. 2008). Chapter 2 displays several graphs that trace the evolution of junior officials (defined as Politburo members with ties to fewer than 10% of the Central Committee) and tainted officials (defined as members of the FFA) in the upper echelons of the party. Because the dependent variable, the probability of staying in power, is difficult to directly measure in one-party dictatorships, I make use of historical material to assess two key outcomes: whether there were serious challenges to the incumbent's de facto position as the head of the Chinese Communist Party and whether the incumbent could change major policies without entrenched opposition. By and large, after Mao successfully deployed the coalition of the weak strategy after Lin Biao's fall in 1971, no other elite could credibly challenge his power, and he made dictatorial decisions over all major aspects of the party, even as his health and cognition declined. Likewise, by appointing weak successors to the upper echelons of the party in the 1980s, revolutionary veterans, even those who had retired from formal offices, still retained a final say over key policies, such as deploying troops in Tiananmen Square in 1989.

The main primary sources used in this book are threefold. First, the independent variables are derived from a quantitative data base of the Chinese elite (Shih et al. 2015). Second, I make use of dozens of elite biographies and autobiographies, written by participants of elite politics or their close confidants. Such accounts have multiplied in recent years and provide valuable, if biased, insights into the machination at the elite level. Highly informative volumes include those written by Deng Liqun, Wang Li, Xu Jingxian, Wu Faxian, Xu Xiangqian, Zhao Ziyang, Yan Huai, and Zhang Guotao. The secretaries of senior leaders, such as Jiang Qing's secretary Yang Yinlu and Lin Biao's secretary Shu Yun, also wrote several highly informative volumes revealing the dynamics between Mao and weak and compromised members of the ruling coalition. Finally, this volume benefited greatly from the original documents collected by Song Yongyi and published in the *China Contemporary Political Movement Archive*, which contains thousands of original documents recording the conversations and instructions of central leaders and high-level party organs such as the Central Committee Administrative Office. Without these documents, this book would be incomplete and much more speculative.

A BRIEF OUTLINE

The rest of the book will proceed as follows. Chapter 2 describes the ruling coalition in China in the early 1960s, in the aftermath of the disastrous Great Leap Forward. Although Mao preferred to preserve the legacy of the Great Leap Forward, other members of his ruling coalition, each a "mountain top" with extensive factions in the military and in the Party, successfully overruled Mao and even began to sideline him from power. Fortunately, his loyal follower Lin Biao rose to defend him, thus planting the seeds for Mao's plan to overthrow his veteran colleagues. Chapters 3 and 4 provide historical background on the origins of two key components of Mao's emerging coalition of the weak strategy: FFA veterans and young scribblers. Both groups had major flaws in their biographies, which challenged their roles as future senior officials in the Maoist one-party state. Yet, as Mao launched the political campaign to remove his veteran colleagues, each group began to serve their roles in the emerging coalition. For the tainted members of the former FFA, they increasingly became a valuable counterweight against Lin Biao's rising influence. For the scribblers, they took great risks for Mao and also for Lin Biao as they tested the power and determination of Mao's rivals.

Chapter 5 first examines the circumstances under which the coalition of the weak finally came to power, replacing the last veteran faction that challenged Mao, Lin Biao's faction. It then compares the policy-making process in the late-Mao period with that of the early 1960s, when revolutionary veterans still occupied senior offices. Mao was finally able to exercise power as a dictator in China, but party and state institutions also entered stasis. Also, as Chapter 6 outlines, not having to contend with serious challengers did not mean the end of the agency problem for Mao. As his health declined, even the scribblers began to position themselves for post-Mao politics, often ignoring Mao's call for them to rule in harmony with the other members of the ruling coalition. Likewise, rehabilitated veterans, especially Deng Xiaoping, also actively positioned and signaled for post-Mao politics, which ultimately led to Deng's downfall in the last year of Mao's life. After Mao's death, Deng almost immediately returned and ruled in a coalition with FFA veterans and rehabilitated veterans, demonstrating the fragility of the coalition of the weak after the dictator's passing. The late-Mao coalitional arrangements had a profound impact on the composition of Deng's own ruling coalition, ensuring important roles for both FFA veterans and their historical detractors.

Chapter 7 examines the consequences of the 1980s oligarchy on politics in the 2010s. The ruling coalition in the 1980s genuinely worried about the fate of the party with the passing of the revolutionary generation. Instead of promoting seasoned and well-networked successors, however, the veteran selectorates of the 1980s promoted young technocrats with a talent for fawning over veteran officials. Even children of veteran revolutionaries faced discrimination in the 1980s, which eliminated the vast majority of them from the race for the top positions in the party in the 2000s. This opened the way for the few surviving children of revolutionary veterans to dominate politics in the 2010s. Chapter 8 recaps the argument and discusses the implications of the coalition of the weak for the Xi Jinping Era.

2

Coalition of the Strong

Mao's Predicament after the Great Leap Forward

As reports of mass famine turned from a trickle to a flood in 1960, the leadership slowly realized that the party had made a mistake of historical proportion. According to Ministry of Public Security data, 675 counties and cities had death rates exceeding 2 percent of population in the early 1960s, compared to the normal 1 percent or so. In forty counties, mainly in Anhui, Sichuan, Henan, Guizhou, and Qinghai, the death rates exceeded 10 percent of the population (Yang et al. 2012: 395). Economists and demographers estimate that the Great Leap Forward caused sixteen to thirty million unnatural deaths in the early 1960s (Kung and Lin 2003). The policy of using confiscated grain to finance a rapid buildup of industrial capacity championed by Mao and his colleagues had led to one of the greatest man-made disasters in the twentieth century.

In the first decade of the People's Republic, Mao and his colleagues were largely content with a system of power sharing with Mao being the ultimate arbiter among competing factions of revolutionary veterans (Teiwes 1993). However, in the six-year period between the 1959 Lushan Conference and the commencement of the Cultural Revolution in 1966, Mao found that his prestige had taken a heavy toll as several powerful factions in the regime took advantage of the policy disaster to diminish his role in the party and to advance their own influence. His firm grip on power was slowly slipping, while uncertainties about his future role in the party increased. Although Mao had shared power with the same revolutionary comrades who had helped him survive a harsh Japanese occupation, triumph over the well-armed KMT, and fought the US Army to a standstill on the Korean Peninsula (Mitter 2004), they each also had entrenched influence over various parts of the party-state through factional followers.

In the aftermath of the Great Leap disaster, the presence of so many revolutionary veterans in the upper echelon of the party prevented Mao from exercising dictatorial power over major policies and subjected him to harsh criticism and even implicit threats of usurpation. Even his designated successor in the early 1960s, Liu Shaoqi, explicitly criticized Mao for pursuing radical economic policies and entrusted economic policy making to a group of men who had resisted Mao's mobilization method of economic management. Liu even built up his own cult of personality based on his pre–Long March revolutionary credentials (Perry 2012). Most insidiously, Liu Shaoqi institutionalized policy-making processes that increasingly isolated Mao and also successfully directed a major political movement, the Socialist Education Movement, proving that he, too, was capable of galvanizing the entire party into actions (MacFarquhar 1997a). Although Liu's maneuvers likely strengthened state and party institutions, Mao felt increasingly isolated from the policy process. Even at the beginning of the Cultural Revolution, Peng Zhen, a core member of Liu's Northern Bureau faction, resisted Mao's attempt to purge a relatively junior official. Rather than making decisions and seeing them faithfully executed immediately, Mao had to scheme and plot constantly against his colleagues just to maintain his status as the first among equals in the party's upper echelon between 1960 and 1966. With the coalition of the strong cogoverning with him, Mao's power was constrained.

Fortunately for Mao, he still had a loyal soldier in Lin Biao, who refused to join in the wave of implicit and explicit criticism against Mao after the Great Leap famine. At the same time, Mao also began to cultivate a group of junior propagandists who took great risks to help him overcome the strong coalition. After the purge of the strong coalition of revolutionary veterans, Mao fashioned a coalition composed of junior propaganda officials with sparse political networks and of military veterans found guilty of "counterrevolutionary" crimes from an earlier period. This finally allowed Mao to exercise his power without constraints from his colleagues during the latter phase of the Cultural Revolution.

COALITION OF THE STRONG

Although Mao became the most revered figure in the party after the Communists achieved victory in 1949, the party was an amalgamation of several communist movements that had carried out prolonged struggles in relative isolation from one another. Because these movements mainly carried out guerilla activities in remote mountainous areas close to the boundaries of two or more provinces, the party had coined the factional loyalty that derived from the hardship of guerilla warfare "mountaintopism" (*shantouzhuyi*) (Huang 2000). As the new regime put in place the enormous party-state bureaucracy after 1949, senior leaders in these various factions filled senior positions in the party, the state, and the military. In other words, Mao now ruled with the help of hundreds of senior functionaries with different histories and loyalties, each with a great deal of formal power. Most problematically for Mao, because each of the major "mountaintop" had followers throughout various apparatus in the party, the state, and the military, they were constantly jostling for greater power for themselves. Until the Great Leap Forward, this did not trouble Mao because of his high prestige as the party's savior and of the absence of major policy disagreements between Mao and the vast majority of the political elite.[1] When factional conflicts flared up, Mao inevitably became the ultimate arbiter of power struggles, further cementing his power in the party. In both the Gao–Rao affair and in the attempted purge of Su Yu, Mao played a pivotal role in determining the outcome, deciding on the purge of Gao Gang in the former case and the protection of Su Yu in the latter case (Jiangsu Party History Work Office 2012: 408; Teiwes 1993: 130).

At the 1956 8th Party Congress, representatives of the various "mountaintops" took seats in the Central Committee and the Politburo, thus formally cementing a collective leadership of experienced, densely networked revolutionary veterans (Yang and Chen 2006). The representation of these various factions reflected the tortuous course of the Chinese Revolution, but the tension and competition for senior positions between these factions also served to consolidate Mao's role as first among equals in the party. The major factions included the group of military and civilian leaders who had built up the Jiangxi Soviet along with Mao, as well as several other factions that had fought guerilla warfare in relative isolation for years. Even within the First Front Army led by Mao, there were different tendencies with divided loyalty. Lin Biao, Chen Yi, Zhu De, and Song Renqiong, among others, were with Mao when he established

---

[1] There were, of course, minor policy differences such as the pace of collectivization and the pace of grain production in 1957–1958, but Mao won these debates with the support of the vast majority of the Politburo. See (Teiwes 1993: 130).

his first base area on Jinggangshan in late 1927 (Editorial Staff of One Spark Lighting the Plains 2006). In 1929, Peng Dehuai, who had operated his own "mountaintop" in the Hunan-Hubei-Jiangxi border area for months, joined with Mao's forces on Jinggangshan. Although this union had created the core of the First Front Army, Peng's relationship with Mao was a tumultuous one for the rest of their lives, beginning with their dispute in the early 1930s on the extent of the anti–AB League purge (Gao 2003: 101). Although many native Jiangxi communists joined Mao's First Front Army when it shifted from Jinggangshan to Ruijin, some bore grudges against Mao for launching the bloody AB League purge targeting Jiangxi natives upon entering the province (Gao 2000: 17). In other words, although some in the dominant First Front Army faction had very deep history with Mao and were very loyal to him, others had earlier allegiance or bore historical grudges against him. Because the survivors of these political struggles had endured the Long March with Mao, most of them occupied senior positions in the party-state by the 1950s and enjoyed sizable networks of close comrades from the revolutionary period, who also occupied important positions.

Three other major factions also had sizable representation in the upper echelons of the party in the late 1950s. First, followers of He Long, who had commanded the Second Front Army in the 1930s, had had their own base area and had embarked on a different Long March than the one of Mao's forces. Thus, He Long's followers had a sizable presence in the CCP upper echelon and in the military by the late 1950s (Gao 2003: 99). Another "mountaintop" was the Northwest Base Area faction based in northern Shaanxi Province and led by Liu Zhidan, Gao Gang, and Xi Zhongxun. This faction "saved" Mao's First Front Army by providing it with food and shelter when Mao's beleaguered forces stumbled into northern Shaanxi after an exhausting Long March in 1935 (Gao 2000: 247). After Liu Zhidan had died in battle in 1936, Gao Gang became the de facto head of this faction and came to be the communist overlord over the industrial heartland in northeastern China after Japan's surrender in 1945. More important, because Gao's jurisdiction was on the Soviet border, he met regularly with Soviet officials, even Stalin himself, and became one of Stalin's confidential informants in the CCP (Pantsov and Levine 2012: 395). Knowing that, Mao managed to purge Gao Gang in 1954 after Stalin's death (Pantsov and Levine 2012: 395). Despite Gao's purge, the northwestern base area faction continued to have a significant presence in the senior leadership in the form of Vice Premier Xi Zhongxun, the father of Xi Jinping.

The most troublesome faction for Mao in the 1950s was the so-called white area group, whose members had spent much of the 1930s and 1940s in urban centers occupied by the KMT or by the Japanese carrying out underground activities on behalf of the party (MacFarquhar 1997a). Many of them were Soviet educated and spoke fluent Russian, often to one another as a secret language (Yang 1980). Others had spent stints in KMT prisons but were miraculously released without harm (Central Committee 1982d). Because white area cadres had been some of the most educated party members, they also held senior positions in the new party-state bureaucracy, which earned them Central Committee membership at the 8th Party Congress. Their high representation in the upper echelon was helped by the fact that a core member of the group, An Ziwen, served a twenty-plus-year stint in powerful positions in the Central Organization Department that selected cadres for promotions. According to Red Guard accusations, also corroborated by a memoir published years later, An Ziwen systematically protected other members of the white area cadre group from charges of wrongdoings during the Socialist Education Movement in the early 1960s, which increased the representation of cadres from that faction in the senior ranks (Li 2005b: 104; Revolutionary Masses of the Central Organization Department 1967).

As Figure 2.1 shows, the 8th Party Congress elected nearly a majority of cadres associated with Mao's First Front Army faction into the 97-member Central Committee (CC). This affiliation was coded based on whether these officials fought with Mao on Jinggangshan in the late 1920s and whether they had been a part of the Jiangxi Soviet in the early 1930s (Shih et al. 2008). This was not a surprising result considering that the majority of Central Committee members in 1934 went on the Long March with Mao's First Front Army instead of the other two long marches.[2] Members of that faction dominated the selection process prior to the 8th Party Congress, which facilitated the dominance of the First Front Army group at the congress (Yang and Chen 2006: 249).

Still, with Liu Shaoqi as the second in command in the party and the patron of the white area cadres, their representation in the Central Committee was nearly one-third. More important, members of the white area faction occupied some of the most powerful positions in the regime

---

[2] After the Central Committee moved from Shanghai to the Jiangxi Soviet in the early 1930s, previously "internationalist" cadres such as Zhou Enlai, Zhang Wentian, and Wang Jiaxiang were folded into Mao's camp in subsequent struggles within the party. See (Gao 2000).

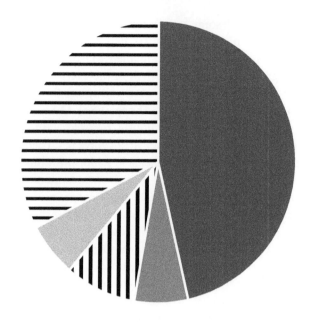

■ First Front Army   ▨ Second Front Army   ❙❙ Fourth Front Army

▨ Northwest Base Area   ☰ White Area Cadres

FIGURE 2.1 Factional affiliations of Central Committee members at the 1956 8th Party Congress

at the time. Besides Liu's own position as vice chairman of the party after the 8th Party Congress, An Ziwen headed the Organization Department, which determined promotions throughout the party (MacFarquhar 1997a). Peng Zhen, another stalwart in the white area faction, was the party leader of Beijing. Finally, Bo Yibo, who had led the revolutionary effort in Shanxi, became the vice premier of China in charge of industries (Bachman 1991). In addition to occupying powerful positions, the head of the faction, Liu Shaoqi, also cultivated a personality cult of himself based on his role in the first large-scale strike of industrial workers the CCP had organized (Perry 2012). This cult of personality paved the way for his eventual replacement of Mao, a plan that Mao had nominally endorsed at the 8th Party Congress.

Second Front Army veterans and Northwest Base Area cadres each took up around 6 percent of CC seats (Figure 2.1). Although numerically few, veterans of these two factions nevertheless occupied some of the most powerful positions in the regime. Xi Zhongxun, the leader of the

Northwest faction after Gao Gang's purge, for example, was a vice premier of China, while fellow northwest base area compatriot Jia Tuofu was the minister of light industry (Li 2005b). Meanwhile, Second Front Army veterans such as He Long, Xiao Ke, and Xu Guangda occupied some of the highest positions in the military, including vice chairmanship of the Central Military Commission for He Long. The remaining 8 percent of seats were taken by Fourth Front Army (FFA) veterans, who will be discussed extensively in Chapter 3.

With officials with differing loyalty occupying such powerful positions in the new regime, it was no surprise that several low-intensity conflicts emerged between the various factions in this period. Mao, however, took advantage of his role as the great balancer to use these conflicts to maintain his dominance over the party and the military. In early 1958, for example, Mao first approved Peng Dehuai's plot to remove his rival in the PLA, Su Yu, from the powerful position of the chief of the general staff (Jiangsu Party History Work Office 2012: 401). Before an enlarged Central Military Commission meeting unleashed harsh punishment on Su for charges of "anti-party, anti-leadership extreme individualism," Mao intervened to prevent his purge without fully exonerating him, thus maintaining his hold over Su (Jiangsu Party History Work Office 2012: 402).

POST–GREAT LEAP REBUKE

As scholars have pointed out, the Great Leap Forward was an enormous shock to the equilibrium of collective leadership achieved after the 8th Party Congress (MacFarquhar 1997a; Yang et al. 2012). The Great Helmsmen, whom the various factions had enthroned as their leader because of his brilliant political and military insights during the long struggle for victory, suddenly made an error of historical proportion. Mao's position as first among equal in the leadership began to wobble. Both his long-time partner Peng Dehuai and his designated successor Liu Shaoqi questioned Mao's leadership. Given their networks of followers, their challenge of Mao's authority posed a potential threat to Mao's power. This especially pertained to Liu Shaoqi, whose followers and allies occupied significant positions in the party-state. Sensing this vulnerability, Mao began to rely on one of his most loyal lieutenants from the earliest days, Lin Biao, for support. Lin Biao's forceful intercession on Mao's behalf quickly consolidated support around Mao, turning the table against Peng Dehuai. Lin Biao's unwavering support for Mao continued to be important even as Liu Shaoqi joined a wave of criticism against

Mao's Great Leap policies. Although Mao stayed in power, Mao's prestige, if not de facto power, diminished in the party between 1959 and 1962.

After Communist forces had conquered much of mainland China by the mid-1950s, Mao became increasingly impatient with China's economic backwardness and continual dependence on Soviet aid. In 1956, Mao pressured the central economic planners to accelerate the pace of investment, but after a period of imbalance, Premier Zhou Enlai and Chen Yun, a party veteran steeped in Soviet method of the planned economy, persuaded Mao that such a breakneck pace of growth would stretch the productive capacity of the country (Teiwes and Sun 1997: 152). Still frustrated by the conservative economic approach of the central bureaucrats, Mao convened a series of ad hoc conferences starting in early 1958 with local party secretaries to once again build policy momentum for high-speed growth. These conferences were held outside of Beijing to discourage participation by central bureaucrats. Since these were not formal Central Committee or Politburo meetings, Mao could set the agenda and create the political momentum for his radical economic policies and, more importantly, for the decentralization of power to the provinces, away from the hands of the central planners. Starting in the first Hangzhou meeting in January 1958, the chairman directed his harsh criticism at Zhou Enlai and Vice Premier Bo Yibo, who was in charge of light industries, and accused them, not inaccurately, of shutting him out of the economic policy process (Teiwes and Sun 1999: 73). The Hangzhou Conference also called for the decentralization of economic planning to regions, which presumably would spur competitive fervor between local leaders to increase grain and steel production (Teiwes and Sun 1999: 73). If the central government procured a much higher level of grain production for export and a heightened level of steel output for industrial equipment and infrastructure, China's economy would soon catch up to those of England and even the United States.

The Nanning Conference, convened later in January, saw another round of criticism against central technocrats, as well as the passage of the "60 Articles on Work Methods," which called for the disastrous "double accounting system," deep ploughing, close cropping, as well as concrete plans to decentralize economic planning power to the regional level (Bo 1993: 682). The radical decentralization measures and Mao's economic agenda were formalized in the Second Session of the 8th Party Congress in May. The Congress promoted a production speed of "one day is equivalent to twenty years" (Fang et al. 1984: 211). Meanwhile, the

Finance and Economic Small Group, a high-level economic policy decision-making body headed by Chen Yun, now had only policy proposal power, rendering it an advisory group (Sun and Teiwes 1999: 99, 107). Local leaders, such as Ke Qingshi of Shanghai, began to set unrealistically high grain and steel production targets and pressured their subordinates to do the same (Bo 1993: 700). While unrealistically high steel production targets diverted resources away from agricultural production, unrealistically high grain procurement targets led to draconian grain confiscation from farmers that directly led to mass starvation and lower agricultural output (Li and Yang 2005a).

By the spring of 1959, words of mass starvation in certain regions of China began to trickle into Beijing. What had been euphoria about sky-high grain and steel production in the previous fall increasingly transformed into a sense of foreboding among the elite. In April 1959, an internal report read by Mao stated that twenty-five million people across six provinces were short on food, but instead of rushing aid, Mao ordered party secretaries of these provinces to deal with the shortage (Yang et al. 2012: 447). In mid-June, Mao conducted self-criticism at a Politburo meeting but still portrayed the food shortage as a relatively minor problem caused by excessive optimism, over-decentralization, and false reporting by local cadres (Yang et al. 2012: 351).

Thus, when Mao convened senior cadres again for a discussion on the emerging famine in July 1959 at the summer resort of Lushan, he likely had not anticipated a serious criticism of the movement overall (Deng 2016: 90). Yet others at the meeting had been much more somber because they had witnessed mass starvation during inspection trips. This included Marshal Peng Dehuai, the Minister of Defense and the second in command of the military at the time. In open discussion at Lushan, Peng put the blame on Mao, saying that Mao knew about false reports of grain production, set unrealistic steel targets, and insisted on communes (Yang et al. 2012: 357). The marshal even went as far as criticizing the lack of collective decision-making in the top leadership, another barely veiled criticism of Mao's work style (Yang et al. 2012: 357). Peng then wrote a letter summarizing his criticism against the Great Leap to Mao (MacFarquhar 1983: 215). Instead of hiding the letter from his colleagues and resolving Peng's concerns privately, Mao distributed the letter to the entire elite in attendance on July 18. Perhaps as Mao had expected, several attendees of the Lushan Conference, including Zhou Xiaozhou, Huang Kecheng, and Li Rui, strongly endorsed the letter (Pantsov and Levine 2012: 464). Zhang Wentian, whom Mao had replaced as secretary general of the party, made a long speech affirming Peng's labeling of the Great Leap as a manifestation of "petty bourgeois fanaticism" (Yang et al. 2012: 363). Veteran revolutionaries who had born grudges against Mao took this opportunity to openly criticize him.

Mao became very alarmed by the emerging wave of criticism against Great Leap policies. He summoned Zhou Enlai and Liu Shaoqi to vent about Peng and Zhang's labeling of the Great Leap as a manifestation of "bourgeois fanaticism" (Yang et al. 2012: 365). The two leaders immediately sided with Mao against Peng. To generate greater momentum against Peng, Mao ordered a break in the meeting and flew several high-level officials, including Zhang Dingcheng, Hu Yaobang, Xu Shiyou, and Xu Guangda, to Lushan to bolster the anti-Peng camp (Man 2005). With Mao making clear his displeasure, the tide soon turned against Peng, and Peng, along with those who had spoken in favor of his letter, were labeled as members of an "anti-party clique" and purged (Goldstein 1991; Pantsov and Levine 2012: 464). Although the criticism against Mao at the Lushan Conference did not stand, opposition to Mao was brazen and likely beyond his expectation. Only the forceful purge of Peng and his supporters overturned the tide of criticism against the Great Leap Policy (MacFarquhar 1983).

At the 7000 Cadre Conference in 1962, criticism against the Great Leap and Mao was much more pervasive and penetrating. Unlike the 1959 Lushan Conference, Mao was unable to overturn the consensus of the conference against the Great Leap Forward. To be sure, by 1961, it was widely known that Great Leap policy had been a great tragedy. Even by the party's own accounting, the policy of forced grain confiscation from peasants led to some thirty-two million unnatural deaths, roughly 5 percent of China's population at the time (Yang et al. 2012: 396). Stories of mass execution to enforce the grain confiscation and of cannibalism were told by survivors in famine-stricken areas who had made their way to Beijing to lodge formal complaints against local officials. In response, the central government also sent inspection teams to stricken areas of Sichuan, Henan, and Anhui to confirm these stories (Deng 2016: 121). Senior leaders such as Liu Shaoqi also had visited rural areas for prolonged investigation trips, which revealed to them the true extent of the famine in rural China (Liu and Chen 1996). China also began to import grain from the rest of the world in 1961, including the US, reversing earlier policies of net grain export (Pantsov and Levine 2012: 474).

Perhaps more important for the leadership and for Mao, the economy was falling apart due to excessive investment and production from previous years and due to the famine. By 1961, China ran an enormous budget deficit of five billion RMB, which threatened high levels of inflation (Deng 2016: 116). After the initial two years of the Leap, grain production also collapsed to levels similar to that during the Chinese Civil War (Li and Yang 2005). If this deterioration had continued, the regime would have lost all the economic gains it had achieved up to 1959. Thus, when Deng Xiaoping suggested holding a meeting that included all provincial, prefecture, and even county party secretaries, to convince them to stop leftist excesses that had led to the famine, Mao immediately agreed to it.

Again, Mao likely was surprised and frustrated by the level of criticism against Great Leap policies and his personal leadership style. In Mao's own speech at the conference, he hardly discussed the famine and spent most of the time expounding on the proper implementation of democratic centrist leadership style and how to treat class enemies (Mao 1986: 1–12). To the extent that he discussed the famine, he tried to reduce his own error to ignorance and lack of experience: "As for me, I still don't understand many issues in economic construction. I really don't understand industry and commerce. I have some understanding of agriculture, but only relatively speaking..." (Mao 1986: 7). In contrast to Mao, Liu Shaoqi, Mao's second in command, leveled harsh criticism against Great Leap policies. During his speech to the participants, he said that 70 percent of the disaster was caused by human errors (Gao 2003: 91). Liu further stated that "the three red banners have undergone a test of history, so why don't we not mention these slogans for now...we made major mistakes and brought losses to the people. This is my first re-examination, but that is not enough; we must re-examine our problems every year from now on" (Deng 2015: 356). The three red banners of socialist construction, agricultural great leap forward, and people's communes had been a hallmark slogan of the Great Leap Forward enthusiastically endorsed by Mao. By calling for the end of this slogan, Liu essentially urged the party to turn away from the Great Leap Forward completely. Peng Zhen, a long-time follower of Liu, directly called Mao into account by stating that no matter what error Mao himself had committed, "it would be odious to us if he did not self-criticize" (MacFarquhar 1997a: 158). Such a direct confrontation against him must have been disturbing to Mao.

Although Liu himself enthusiastically endorsed Great Leap policies in 1958, his repudiation of it in 1961 elevated his stature in the eyes of many mid-level officials. According to Deng Liqun, a supporter of Liu Shaoqi, many attendees of the 7000 Cadre Conference wanted Liu to republish his famous essay *How to be a Good Communist* (Deng 2015: 341). The essay was indeed republished in the leading party publications *Hongqi* and *Renmin Ribao* in 1962. The republication of this essay further added to the growing prominence of Liu in the cultural sphere where novels, plays, and movies about Liu's role in the famous Anyuan Strike in the 1920s had made frequent appearances (Perry 2012: 192).

Lin Biao, who had fought alongside Mao since the Jinggangshan period in the late 1920s, staunchly defended the achievement of the Great Leap Forward at the conference, arguing that although grain production in the past two years had not been great, relative to historical trajectory, the Great Leap made significant achievement. Also, Lin warned that the chance of war was ever present due to the aggressiveness of the imperialist countries as well as Soviet revisionism. Lin thus made the argument that no matter what Mao may or may not have done, the party still needed him (Li and Shu 2009: 832). Mao liked the speech so much that he reprinted and distributed the speech to all the attendees of the conference (Li and Shu 2009: 833). Despite Lin's spirited defense of Mao, however, Liu and Peng's repudiation of the Three Red Banners became the official line. This led to real shifts of power away from Mao.

After the 7000 Cadre Conference, economic policy making began to shift away from the hands of Mao loyalists into the hands of technocrats who had opposed the Great Leap in the first place. This likely was another move orchestrated by Liu Shaoqi and his supporters. After the 7000 Cadre Conference, the leadership immediately convened the Xilou Conference, which featured key speeches by economic planners who had resisted Mao's drive to decentralize the economy at the beginning of the Great Leap Forward. Chen Yun's speech, which called for a high degree of economic centralization and mass import of soy beans to meet the population's protein needs, received enthusiastic applause from the attendees (Deng 2015: 361). Sensing the popularity of Chen's plan, Liu Shaoqi distributed Chen's speech to party officials with a preamble saying that the situation in China was still "very serious," in contrast to Mao's assessment that the worst was over (Deng 2015: 363).

As a part of economic recentralization, the entire leadership, including Mao, agreed that the Central Finance and Economic Small Group (CFESG) had to be given back its decision-making power. Instead of having Mao loyalist Li Fuchun as the head the CFESG, Liu Shaoqi, with the urging of Deng Liqun, proposed Chen Yun as the head (Deng 2015: 366). The CFESG ultimately became a powerful institution for economic policy decision, the descendent organization of which is still the locus of economic policy making today (Shih 2017). Although Mao nominally approved this new arrangement, his control over economic issues was diminished under Chen, who applied the rigid Soviet framework of the "three balances" to economic management. In the meantime, Liu continued to make veiled criticism against Mao. At a May 1962 central work conference on the famine, for example, Liu Shaoqi said, "If someone in the face of obvious difficulties claims that there is no difficulty, he is not a courageous person" (Research Center for Party Material in the Central Archive 1986: 64).

With economic management slipping from Mao's grasp, the technocrats even infringed on some core issues with great ideological significance. During Mao's absence from Beijing in mid-1962, for example, Deng Xiaoping and Chen Yun supported a report drafted by veteran agriculture specialist Deng Zihui on household and individual responsibility farming and private plots, which resembled private household farming prior to collectivization (Research Center for Party Material in the Central Archive 1986: 112). Although he had earlier signaled support for the policy, Mao was incensed by an actual policy push by his colleagues (MacFarquhar 1997a: 262). He immediately convened party secretaries from a few provinces and drafted a decree that called for bolstering collective agriculture and for forbidding individual contracting (Deng 2015: 433). Sensing Mao's disapproval, both Deng and Chen withdrew support for household responsibility farming and praised Mao's decision. Deng Zihui, the author of the report on household responsibility system, faced a week of harsh criticism from the top leadership at a late-August Politburo standing committee meeting (Deng 2015: 433).

Although the termination of the household responsibility experiment was often cited as an example of Mao's continual dominance over his colleagues, it showed that Mao's colleagues in fact were willing to push agendas that went against the Maoist line. The people's commune was a core tenet of the "three red banners" championed by Mao and Mao loyalists such as Lin Biao at the 7000 Cadre Conference (MacFarquhar 1997a: 163). Yet senior officials such as Deng Xiaoping and Chen Yun were ready to abandon it completely in favor of more pragmatic policies in agriculture. Against this subversive tide, Mao felt compelled to warn his colleagues at the August 1962 Beidaihe Conference against a "capitalist resurgence" in China (MacFarquhar 1997a: 275). Just one month after Mao's criticism of household responsibility farming, however, Liu Shaoqi challenged Mao at the 10th plenum to instruct cadres to focus more on economic construction and less on class struggle, to which Mao reluctantly agreed (Deng 2015: 434). Clearly, even suppressing household responsibility farming found Mao no relief from potential challenges from his powerful colleagues.

In addition, by the mid-1960s, Liu Shaoqi controlled one of the most powerful bureaucracies in the Chinese Communist Party, the organization bureaucracy in charge of promotion. Through An Ziwen, a long-time follower from the Northern Bureau days in the 1930s who had become the head of the Organization Department, Liu was able to influence numerous promotions in the upper echelon of the party. For example, at a mid-1964 meeting, senior members of the Liu coterie, including Yang Shangkun, Bo Yibo, and Peng Zhen, got together with An Ziwen to "discuss personnel arrangement in several departments" (Yang 2001b: 363). The result of this coordination was that even relatively junior members of Liu's faction had become ministers by the mid-1960s, ahead of others in their peer groups. Officials who had joined the party in the 1930s, such as Yao Yilin, Zhang Linzhi, and Yang Xiufeng, for example, all became ministers by the mid-1960s, likely due to Liu's patronage (Liu et al. 2018). Subministerial-level cadres also felt the growing influence of Liu in the organization realm. After an early 1960s speech in which Liu said "central cadres must have some experience at the local level before promotion," many bureau-level cadres applied to serve stints at local governments in response, believing that Liu's words were tantamount to official policy on promotion (Gao 2003: 93). This likely alarmed Mao.

Finally, Mao's politically experienced colleagues also showed their ability to mobilize the entire party independently of Mao. In 1963, Mao was intrigued by a local campaign in Baoding, which led to the cleaning up of numerous corruption and power-abuse problems that had built up in the local governments during the Great Leap Forward. Sensing that such problems were common in many localities, Mao convened a group of local leaders to draft a decree on how to carry out similar campaigns in localities across the country (Deng 2015: 457). A high-level coalition including Liu Shaoqi, Deng Xiaoping, and Tan Zhenlin soon took over the campaign and structured it into a top-down mobilization effort that saw the assignment of over one million cadres into work teams, each with over 100 cadres. These work teams took over local governments for months at a time and carried out the Socialist Education Movement, which saw the dismissal and purging of millions of local cadres (Deng 2015: 458). Furthermore, as the head of one of the first work teams assigned to Taoyuan, Liu Shaoqi's wife, Wang Guangmei, wrote a widely circulated report on her experience in the work team. She then traveled around the country to spread the "Taoyuan Experience," thus magnifying her national fame as a first lady in the wings (Thornton 2007: 191).

Although launching a rectification campaign had been Mao's idea, Mao was apparently frustrated by how little control he had over the campaign by late 1964. At a November 1964 meeting, a frustrated Mao told Liu Shaoqi, "[Y]ou be chairman, You be the *Qin* Emperor. I have my weak points. When I tell people, it has no effect...You should take control of Xiaoping and the premier" (MacFarquhar 1997a: 417). Sensing that perhaps Mao had laid a trap for him, Liu suggested an alternative that also took power from Mao – a collective leadership over the campaign composed of Liu Shaoqi, Deng Xiaoping, Xie Fuzhi, and Zhou Enlai (MacFarquhar 1997a: 417). In another example, Mao repeatedly instructed Liu and Deng that he wanted the focus of the Socialist Education Movement to be on the local cadres instead of on the farmers. Yet a key decree for the movement drafted by Liu, Deng, and Tan was not changed in any significant way to reflect Mao's wishes. A frustrated Mao went as far as slamming down copies of the party and state constitutions on the table during a Politburo meeting and accused Deng of ignoring the opinion of a party member, that is, Mao himself (MacFarquhar 1997a: 425). Episodes like this show that although Mao's veteran colleagues still appeared deferential to Mao's wishes on the surface, they were not afraid to spar with him in order to obtain outcomes close to their true preference. In order to put an end to such resistance to his decisions, Mao needed to remove his former comrades-in-arms from power once and for all.

THE PURGE OF THE STRONG COALITION

The purge of scores of revolutionary veterans at the beginning of the Cultural Revolution is a familiar account (Harding 1997; Huang 2000; MacFarquhar 1997a; MacFarquhar and Schoenhals 2006; Teiwes 1993). The theoretical model in the introduction, however, suggests a slightly more nuanced interpretation of the events surrounding the beginning of the Cultural Revolution. An important implication of the theoretical model is that purging strong members of the selectorate and replacing them with other strong members did not obtain any additional gains for the dictator. In fact, the dictator only obtained true dominance in the selectorate if an overwhelming majority in the selectorate had significant constraints on their power. Thus, even in the first year of the Cultural Revolution, one can delineate the period prior to the February

Countercurrent in February 1967 and afterward, when the vast majority of the unsullied revolutionary veterans were purged or sidelined.

The extant literature makes it clear that even in 1965, Mao had begun a campaign to purge a large number of the existing elite, a topic that will be visited in Chapter 3. The targets of the first wave included potential challengers in the military, such as Luo Ruiqing and Yang Shangkun, as well as the entire Northern Bureau cadre faction, which included Liu Shaoqi, Peng Zhen, Lu Dingyi, and Bo Yibo (MacFarquhar 1997a). This faction in particular had sought to undermine Mao's authority since the Great Leap Forward. Besides criticizing Maoist policies at the 7000 Cadre Conference and supporting the household responsibility system, members of the Northern Bureau faction such as Lu Dingyi and Peng Zhen also defied Mao's effort to criticize the author of the historical play "Hairui Dismissed from Office," which portrayed a Ming official dismissed for telling the truth, much like the fate of Peng Dehuai during the Lushan Conference. In late 1965, even after Mao made it clear to Peng Zhen that he was behind the criticism of the play, Peng Zhen still defended author Wu Han, who was another member of the Northern Bureau faction (Zheng 2017: 173).

By the August 1966 11th Plenum, many of those who had been part of the perceived campaign to sideline Mao had been purged or criticized. In their place, a new crop of Long March veterans, such as Tao Zhu, Li Fuchun, and Kang Sheng, were promoted to the Politburo (Gao 2003: 131). Of the twenty-two Politburo members in September 1966, all were Long March veterans from either the First Front Army or the Fourth Front Army (Central Organization Department et al. 1997a: 24). There were no radical upstarts in the Politburo at that time. The result was that many veteran cadres still attended top-level meetings and leveled criticism against the unfolding movement.

The new crop of veteran cadres in the early Cultural Revolution months had their networks of followers, which they protected from Red Guard attacks. Although Mao wanted to protect local leaders in some cases, in many cases, Mao wished for the Red Guards to overthrow existing power-holders. The process of overthrowing veteran power-holders from local authorities was still stymied by the same coalition of the strong that had frustrated Mao after the Great Leap Forward. In Shanghai, for example, when Red Guards sought to overthrow mayor Cao Diqiu and secretary Chen Pixian, Cao called Tao Zhu, a veteran cadre who briefly served as the vice-chairman of the Central Cultural Revolution Group, for help (Xia 2008). Tao backed Cao, thus sealing his own fate later, but Tao Zhu's action temporarily stifled the Red Guard takeover of the Shanghai government. In order to obtain greater power, Mao needed to remove more veterans such as Tao Zhu, which also reduced the marginal costs of removing additional veterans.

Even as Red Guards ransacked central ministries and took over local governments in February 1967, veteran Politburo members such as Chen Yi, Tan Zhenlin, and Ye Jianying attended a meeting organized by Zhou Enlai to discuss how to carry out the Cultural Revolution in the military. This led to the famous ruckus in the Huairentang (大闹怀仁堂) in which veteran cadres angrily lashed out at the various aspects of the Cultural Revolution. Chen Yi went as far as calling members of the Central Cultural Revolution Group "revisionists," a label for the Soviet Union at that time (MacFarquhar and Schoenhals 2006: 196).

Mao, who had wanted a grand coalition including many veteran cadres in the wake of Liu Shaoqi's purge, was surprised by the depth of the veteran cadres' anger at this revolutionary exercise and, perhaps more importantly, at their willingness to resist Mao's revolutionary movement. Two days after the ruckus, Mao convened top cadres to criticize those who had participated in the February Countercurrents, a label that the radicals had slapped on the shouting match in Huairentang. An angry Mao again threatened the prospects of civil war to his veteran colleagues: "Lin Biao and I will leave Beijing and go back to fighting guerrilla warfare on Jinggangshan" (Li and Shu 2009: 1015). After lambasting veteran cadres, he placed Chen Yi, Tan Zhenlin, and Xu Xiangqian on administrative leave. After that point, veteran cadres who were perceived by Mao as disobedient were purged or sidelined.

By the 1969 9th Party Congress, Mao had begun fashioning a coalition of the weak. Of the twenty-one Politburo members elected in 1969, four were from the renegade FFA, and another four were radical beneficiaries of the Cultural Revolution who had been junior officials below the ministerial level prior to 1966 (Central Organization Department et al. 1997a: 32). Although the remaining Politburo members were Long March veterans, three of them were generals close to Lin Biao who had not been in the Central Committee prior to the Cultural Revolution – Wu Faxian, Qiu Huizuo, and Li Zuopeng. Another general, Huang Yongsheng, had only been an alternate member of the Central Committee prior to 1966 (Central Organization Department et al. 1997a: 34). Even though some veteran cadres such as Lin Boqu, Zhu De, and Liu Bocheng held on to their positions, they had no responsibility, and their followers were systematically purged from the central

TABLE 2.1. *The share of "weak" Politburo members at the 8th, 9th, and 10th Party Congress*

	Ties with Less than 10 percent of CC Members	FFA veterans	Coalition of the Weak Share of Politburo
8th PC	0	8 percent	8 percent
9th PC	16 percent	20 percent	36 percent
10th PC	36 percent	20 percent	56 percent

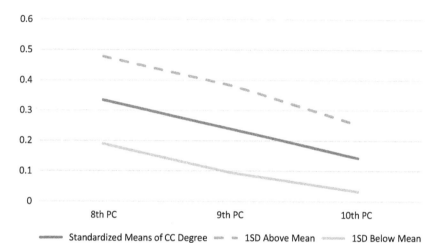

FIGURE 2.2 Mean, one standard deviation above and one standard deviation below the mean of degree centrality of Politburo members: 8th to the 10th Party Congress

ministries. By 1968, between 70 and 90 percent of cadres in the central ministries had been purged and sent down to the countryside (MacFarquhar and Schoenhals 2006: 160). This meant that the factional networks of many of Mao's colleagues had been dismantled. In their place, Mao contended with the growing influence of Lin Biao in the party and in the military, as well as the coalitions of the weak.

Figure 2.2 and Table 2.1 show the evolution of Mao's coalition of the weak strategy from the 1956 8th Party Congress to the 10th Party Congress in 1972. On Figure 2.2, I calculate the mean degree of Politburo members from the 8th Party Congress (PC) through the 10th Party Congress, as well as lines of one standard deviation above and below the means. One should note that degree is slightly different from the notion of faction. Whereas faction implies hierarchical relationships between patrons and clients, degree, or the number of ties, merely denotes previous coworking, cofighting experience between a Politburo member and all Central Committee members at that congress. On Figure 2.2, the vertical axis denotes the share of the full Central Committee (CC) members. The average Politburo member at the 8th Party Congress had ties with 40 percent of full CC members, with Politburo members one standard deviation above the mean having ties with over 57 percent of CC members. Again, the high density of these senior officials' networks with the Central Committee elite may explain why officials such as Liu Shaoqi, Peng Zhen, and Deng Xiaoping had dared to challenge Mao's policies time and again. Each of these officials could have mobilized support from a large share of the Central Committee prior to the Cultural Revolution. By the 1969 9th Party Congress, mean degree of Politburo members had dropped to 30 percent, largely due to the enlargement of the Central Committee and the removal of several major factions from the elite. By the 10th Party Congress, the mean degree of a Politburo member further plunged below 20 percent.

To be sure, Mao maintained some highly networked veterans in the Politburo throughout his life, even if they had no real authority in reality. Also, networks formed during the revolution naturally decayed over time as veterans retired or passed away. However, Mao drastically accelerated the process with the Cultural Revolution, which saw the purge of over 100 veterans from the Central Committee. More important, instead of replacing them with slightly younger but still densely networked revolutionaries, Mao introduced "workers' representatives" with no elite ties and other inexperienced junior officials to replace the purged veterans. At the 8th PC, Politburo members, even someone one standard deviation below the mean in terms of degree centrality, had ties with over 20 percent of the CC, but by the 10th Party Congress, Politburo members one standard deviation below the mean had ties with only 4 percent of the Central Committee. In reality, Politburo members "from the grassroots" – such as Chen Yonggui, Wu Guixian, and Ni Zhifu – had existing ties with only two to five CC members, including themselves (Figure 2.2).

As discussed in detail in later chapters, the 9th Party Congress also saw the elevation of FFA veterans, who bore the guilt of "splitting the party" in the 1930s. Together with thinly networked junior officials, the coalition of the weak made up a rising share of the Politburo from the 8th PC to the 10th PC. Whereas their share had been 8 percent at the 8th PC, it rose to 56 percent by the 10th Party Congress, the last one before Mao's passing. Several of the surviving veterans – Liu Bocheng, Zhu De, and

Zhou Enlai – were by then in worse physical shape than Mao, rendering very few elite who could have challenged Mao's power. As subsequent chapters detail, these two groups, which did not overlap, played a pivotal role in Mao's political strategy in the last years of his life.

CONCLUSION

Even before the disastrous Great Leap Forward, Mao cogoverned China with a coalition of experienced revolutionaries, each with his own faction of loyal followers installed throughout central government agencies, provincial governments, and the military. While Mao was seen as the messianic figure who had delivered ultimate victory to the Chinese communists, few in the ruling coalition thought of sidelining Mao. Mao also maintained supremacy by playing them against each other. However, the disastrous Great Leap Forward, which killed upward of thirty million Chinese, changed the invincible status of Mao. The coterie of followers surrounding these experienced revolutionaries gave them the confidence to criticize Mao's policies, to challenge ideological frameworks on which Mao had invested a great deal of personal prestige, and, ultimately, to sideline Mao from the policy process.

As power slipped out of Mao's hands, he had two courses of action. First, he could have accepted his gradual retirement and allowed a coalition of his colleagues to rule collectively. This likely would have been a fairly stable equilibrium (Acemoglu et al. 2008). Alternatively, he could have destroyed powerful figures in the party, as well as their factions, and replaced them with weaklings who obeyed his every word. Events soon revealed that he chose the latter course of action, thus shaping elite politics in China for decades to come.

3

"Counterrevolutionary Splittists" in Mao's Ruling Coalition

During his ascent to power in the 1930s, 1940s, and 1950s, Mao had "packed" the CCP upper echelon with people who had sided with him in the many internal power struggles in the party, especially those who had served with him in the First Front Army. Yet even this strategy was insufficient to maintain Mao's absolute power in the party. When the unexpected shock of the Great Leap Forward led to a precipitous fall of Mao's prestige within the party, a rival coalition composed of Mao's former allies emerged to sideline him. Even a formerly loyal protégé such as Deng Xiaoping began to display streaks of independence.

Instead of a factional strategy of placing previously loyal followers in senior positions, placing known weak figures in elite decision-making bodies constituted an effective alternative strategy for Mao to pursue. Within this framework, this chapter lays out the historical conditions that allowed Mao to pursue the strategy of replacing strong officials with tainted individuals, especially in the military. The value of historically sullied officials laid in the costliness of their rehabilitation, which deterred their joining of rival coalitions against the incumbent. As long as the institutions that had condemned them continued to dictate the behaviors of political actors, these tainted officials could not participate in politics as ordinary officials of the same rank.

Examining the case of "counterrevolutionary splittists" led by Zhang Guotao, I find that this tainted faction became a central pillar in Mao's manipulation of the elite during the Cultural Revolution (1966–1976). Because of fierce internal power struggle that had ensued in the party in the 1930s, a large group of Long March veterans from the Fourth Front Army (FFA) were branded "counterrevolutionary splittists" and even "armed counterrevolutionary group" by the party authorities, rendering them very vulnerable to Mao's wrath for decades to come. At the height of the Cultural Revolution, when a large share of veteran revolutionaries was removed from power and banished to work farms on trumped-up counterrevolutionary crimes, Mao systematically protected veterans of the FFA from his most trusted lieutenant Lin Biao and from the Red Guards. Many FFA veterans were further entrusted to take over much of the civilian and military apparatus. Mao felt at ease in placing members of this tainted faction in positions of great power because short of overthrowing CCP institutions entirely, the entire party would have rallied around Mao if the tainted faction had plotted against him. Moreover, even if a rival coalition had emerged, it would not have wanted to ally itself with the renegade faction due to the additional audience cost of such an alliance, thus making these sullied individuals more reliable to Mao during times of political struggle. Meanwhile, by continuing to emphasize the second-class status of these individuals, Mao was able to promote them into senior positions without violating the discourse on which their guilt was based. Having created a discourse of "splittism" against Zhang and his lieutenants in the first place, Mao could not have rehabilitated the sullied faction without discrediting himself and paying a large audience cost. Zhang's remnant faction thus knew that they had little chance of rehabilitation while Mao was still alive and that their political survival hinged solely on Mao's good will. Ultimately, the dependence of these tainted individuals on Mao's good graces made them more trustworthy and reliable than even Mao's long-time friends and comrades.

THE INVISIBLE FACTION OF FFA VETERANS

Existing accounts of politics in the Mao period mainly focus on the tension between First Front Army veterans such as Mao, Lin Biao, and Peng Dehuai, as well as the rift between white area cadres such as Liu Shaoqi, Peng Zhen, and Bo Yibo, and Mao (MacFarquhar 1997a; MacFarquhar and Schoenhals 2006; Teiwes 1993; Teiwes and Sun 1996). To be sure, eliminating rivals was a main objective for Mao during the Cultural Revolution, as pointed out by the extant literature (MacFarquhar 1997a; MacFarquhar and Schoenhals 2006). However, so long as Mao preserved the Leninist party structure, he had to promote others to fill the positions left empty by his purged colleagues. As outlined in this and the next chapter, no group benefited from the Cultural Revolution as much as the FFA group. Yet, in the late 1950s, FFA veterans were a largely muted group with little political ambition. Had Mao not launched the Cultural Revolution, Fourth Front Army veterans would have continued to serve in low level or largely ceremonial positions in silence. The reason for this faction's passivity was that they all bore the criminal label of "counterrevolutionary splittists," which left them completely at the mercy of Mao.

Their vulnerability had to do with a largely hidden history in the Chinese Communist Party surrounding Zhang Guotao and the party's split during the Long March. The former leader of the FFA faction, Zhang Guotao, was a giant in the early Chinese Communist Party (CCP), and his stature as well as his command over the largest army in the CCP at the end of the Long March compelled him to make a bid for ultimate power against Mao, thus tainting members of his army with guilt even to this day. In addition to being one of the few founders of the CCP still in the party by the 1930s, he was the only CCP leader to have met Lenin, Stalin, and Bukharin (Zhang 1971: 378). This was especially important in the early days of the party because, until the Long March, the CCP still mainly took orders from the Comintern on important matters.

Although Zhang had been among the top five officials in the CCP throughout the 1920s, he gained real autonomy from the Politburo when he was ordered to take command of a guerilla base in the Hubei-Henan-Anhui (*Eyuwan*) Border Area in the 1930s. The *Eyuwan* area was nearly as big as the Jiangxi Soviet founded by Mao and also produced a major fighting force for the CCP. Within a year of arriving in the isolated base area in 1931, Zhang had consolidated his control through a series of military victories, the promotion of a group of trusted followers, and a purge of political enemies (Xu 1987: 159; Zhang 1998).[1] Zhang Guotao formed long-lasting bonds with Chen Changhao and Shen Zemin, who also had been Central Committee cadres sent to the *Eyuwan* area, as well as with a group of military officers who had been in the base area before Zhang's arrival. Senior figures in the latter group included Xu Xiangqian, Li Xiannian, Xu Shiyou, Wang Shusheng, Han Xianchu, and Xie Fuzhi, all of whom became senior officers in the *Eyuwan*-based FFA (Zhang 1998). The initial success of the base area, however, drew increasingly large-scale attacks from Chiang Kai-shek. In the autumn of 1932, Chiang

---

[1] There are disputes on the scope of Zhang's purge. Zhang himself claimed that although over a thousand were arrested, only thirty were executed. His former subordinate Xu Xiangqian claims that many more were killed. See (Xu 1987: 154; Zhang 1998: 108).

struck with some 500,000 troops attacking from three sides, which was twenty times Zhang's forces (Zhang 1998).

Facing a much stronger enemy, Zhang led the FFA in a westward retreat to northern Sichuan Province. Although the FFA suffered significant losses, Zhang still maintained some 16,000 troops out of the original 25,000 upon arriving in northern Sichuan. This compared much more favorably to Mao's First Front Army, which lost some 90 percent of its original force in the course of the Long March (Braun 1982: 140). To their delight, Zhang's army found a political vacuum in northern Sichuan. Besides opium-growing bandits, the area had few other political authorities, and Chiang's main KMT forces had not penetrated this far west yet. Thus, Zhang's forces quickly consolidated control over a large area and began to recruit new soldiers in earnest (Xu 1987; Zhang 1998).

When Zhang's forces met up with Mao's skeletal column in June 1935 in the snowy highland of Maogong, Zhang had between 50,000 to 60,000 troops (Braun 1982: 123; Xu 1987: 386). Soon after the Maogong reunion, tension flared between the two armies. First and foremost, the FFA was shocked at the small size and the decrepitude of the First Front Army. Zhang's men had expected a well-armed force of tens of thousands. Instead, they greeted a column of around 15,000 starving, sick, and demoralized skeletons dressed in rags (Xu 1987). A serious split soon emerged between Mao and Zhang over the issue of where the combined Red Army should go. In essence, Mao and the majority of the Central Committee wanted to go north in order to link up with the Soviet Union through Outer Mongolia. Zhang, feeling relatively comfortable in Northern Sichuan, opted to remain in place and perhaps explore a Western linkage with the Soviet Union through Xinjiang (Zhang 1998: 235). Meanwhile, the relationship between both men and officers of the two armies deteriorated as each hurled accusations at each other. While Mao's cadres accused Zhang's men of behaving like warlords and cowards, Zhang accused Mao and his men of defeatism and, more seriously, of pursuing an incorrect political line (Xu 1987; Zhang 1998).[2]

The confrontation came to a head after the First Front Army had crossed treacherous grassland in the Sichuan–Gansu border, where thousands more perished. The main contingent of the First Front Army,

---

[2] While Zhang favored a federation loosely based on patriotism, the Central Committee still wanted to form Soviets in China. This ideological disagreement was resolved later when the Comintern ordered the CCP to form an anti-imperialist united front.

composed of the First and Third Army Groups and much of the Central Committee, was traveling north on the east side of the grassland (Xu 1987: 453). This column, however, also included contingents of the FFA led by two of Zhang's core followers, Chen Changhao and Xu Xiangqian (Xu 1987: 454). Meanwhile, the main column of the FFA, which also included elements of the First Front Army and its senior officers such as Zhu De and Liu Bocheng, moved north at a much slower pace on the west side of the grassland (New fourth Army research society et al. 2009). After crossing the grassland in early September 1935, the Central Committee sent numerous telegrams to Zhang urging him to quickly move north through the grassland to join the First Front Army. Zhang, in turn, sent several telegrams to Chen Changhao and Xu Xiangqian asking them to persuade Mao and his colleagues to go south (Wang and Zhu 2004).

According to an account Mao gave in 1937 during a struggle session against Zhang, Zhang sent a secret telegram on September 9, 1935 to Chen Changhao and Xu Xiangqian, asking them to "go south, thoroughly carry out inner party struggle"(Jiang 2004; Wang and Zhu 2004). An even more controversial version of the story contends that the telegram stated to "use force to get rid of the Central Committee." Scholars from the army combed through the Politburo archive in the 1980s and found little evidence to support even the existence of the telegram in the first place (Wang and Zhu 2004).

In Mao's version of the story, Ye Jianying, then Mao's chief of staff, somehow got a hold of this telegram and showed it to Mao (Zhang 2008a: 172). Quickly responding to a possible coup by the FFA contingent, Mao ordered all units of the First Front Army in the column to quickly move north while Zhang's men slept. According to both Chen Changhao and Xu Xiangqian, both FFA officers in Mao's column they never received such a telegram and were shocked to find that Mao's troops had suddenly departed (Liu 2008; Xu 1987: 451). This account was corroborated by Wu Faxian, a First Front Army veteran who was later purged from the party for being too close to Lin Biao. According to Wu, there was a heated argument between the First Front Army and the FFA contingents, but Mao urged calm and told the First Front Army that they would just continue north without the FFA (Wu 2006: 101).

After the departure of Mao's followers, units of the FFA that had been attached to the Central Committee decided to go south and reunite with their brethren. According to Xu Xiangqian, he and Chen indeed ordered the FFA to head south after Mao's departure, "thus committing an error which would shame me for life" (Xu 1987: 454). When the FFA reunited, Zhang Guotao called for the formation of a "Provisional" Central Committee headed by himself, as well as for the expulsion of Mao, Zhou Enlai, Zhang Wentian, and Bo Gu from the CCP (Xu 1987: 460). In a telegram to the Central Committee that was later used as evidence for Zhang's plot, Zhang stated, "[W]e demand that you stop using the false title of the Party Center and change it to the CCP Northern Bureau" (Zhang 1996). In the meantime, Mao engaged in his own war of words against Zhang for committing "the criminal act of splitting the Red Army" (Politburo 1979). For a while, Zhang seemed to have the upper hand because contingents of the First Front Army who had traveled with Zhang became his supporters due to their dissatisfaction with Mao's harsh treatment of them during the Long March (Zhang 1998: 272). Even long-time Mao collaborators Zhu De and Liu Bocheng, who had been traveling with Zhang, did not actively undermine Zhang's leadership (Xu 1987: 458).

The war of words between the two sides continued well into 1936 with no clear resolution. Finally, two important external events redistributed power away from Zhang and to Mao, thus sealing the political fate of Zhang's "splittist" faction. First, Zhang's gambit to expand his power into central Sichuan ended in abject failure because Chiang Kai-shek had shifted substantial forces into Sichuan to augment the local warlords. In a series of failed attacks in the spring of 1936, Zhang's forces lost over 10,000 men and were forced to retreat north (Xu 1987: 472). Meanwhile, although only some 8,000 troops from the First Front Army arrived in northern Shaanxi Province, they were pleasantly surprised by the presence of a sizable Communist force there led by Liu Zhidan (Braun 1982: 140). A few months later, the beleaguered First Front Army managed to persuade the local warlord Zhang Xueliang to join the CCP in an anti-Japan united front. This alliance serendipitously coincided with the Comintern decision to change its line in favor of an antifascist united front in China, which aimed at delaying a Japanese attack of the Soviet Far East (Zhang 1998: 292). Into 1936, Zhang's position collapsed both politically and militarily. Militarily, a large KMT force closed in on Zhang's Sichuan base area from three sides. Politically, Mao's success in uniting with a powerful warlord in accordance to Moscow's wishes dashed Zhang's plan to replace Mao as the new chairman. Both factors compelled Zhang to abandon the "Provisional Central Committee," accept Mao's leadership, and move north with his forces in the spring of 1936 (Xu 1987: 487).

In June 1936, Zhang still did not give up his struggle against Mao. Instead of sending all his troops to northern Shaanxi to join Mao, he ordered Chen Changhao and Xu Xiangqian to take the bulk of the FFA, as well as a few small units of the First Front Army, across the Yellow River into Gansu. Reviving a plan that had been discussed when the two armies first had united, Zhang wanted the FFA to reach Xinjiang, where the Soviet Union could supply and train the Fourth into a powerful fighting force (Zhang 1998: 355). Stalin, wanting to consolidate Communist control over northwestern China, approved Zhang's plan to send the bulk of the FFA west and even ordered weapons to be shipped to Xinjiang (Gao 2000: 102; Zhang 1998: 296).[3] Thus, the 9th, 30th, and 5th Army of the FFA, totaling some 20,000 men and women, crossed the Yellow River in October 1936 (Xu 1987: 310). Zhang's remaining hope was the victorious return of the FFA from Xinjiang.

Instead of a triumphant return, the Western Legion (*Xilujun*), the name of the FFA units that had crossed the Yellow River, was completely annihilated by forces commanded by the Muslim warlord Ma Bufang in the Gansu Corridor. The Gansu Corridor, a narrow strip of flat, barely arable land connecting Shaanxi with Xinjiang, was hemmed in from both the north and the south sides by a desert and a mountain range. Thus, the Western Legion, commanded by Zhang followers Chen Changhao and Xu Xiangqian, had little room to maneuver, and the flat, open topography of the Gansu Corridor was advantageous to Ma's cavalry. Still, writing decades later, Xu was convinced that if the Western Legion had moved quickly, it could have survived relatively unscathed through the Gansu Corridor because the Muslim warlords were in no mood to fight a passing army (Xu 1987: 557). However, in November 1936, the Central Military Commission, then dominated by Mao, ordered the Western Legion to stop at the narrowest point of the Gansu Corridor to start a base area. Not wanting to further offend the Central Committee, Chen Changhao, the political commissar of the Western Legion, ordered his troops to stop and establish a base over the opposition of Xu Xiangqian (Xu 1987: 552).

In subsequent months, the Western Legion was worn down by waves of unrelenting attacks by Muslim warlords until it was completely

---

[3] Zhang Guotao claims that Lin Yuying, who had just returned from Moscow in late 1935, conveyed to him Stalin's wishes for Zhang to head toward Xinjiang. Xu Xiangqian does not mention this, but Xu quotes a Central Committee telegram approving the FFA's move west.

annihilated. Examining historical evidence, Mao and other First Front Army leaders likely ordered the Western Legion to stay put in order to eradicate the main forces of the splittist faction. First, the Western Legion was in radio contact with the Central Committee and reported regularly on its mounting casualties and dwindling supplies (Xu 1987: 546). Zhang Guotao himself also repeatedly implored the other Politburo members to help the Western Legion, but Mao and others were evasive and avoided the subject (Zhang 1998: 329). Instead of giving any help, Mao sent a telegram to Zhang's beleaguered troops stating that "the Central Committee feels that the Western Legion's mistake is the same rightist, retreatist opportunism that the Fourth Front Army committed when a second central committee was set up" (Zhu 2008: 50). As a contrasting case, earlier in 1936, when Lin Biao's forces ran into strong resistance upon crossing into Shanxi Province, Mao and Peng Dehuai immediately ordered him to cross back to the western bank of the Yellow River to avoid losses (Li and Shu 2015a: 132).

On March 11, 1937, the totally depleted remnants of the Western Legion broke out of the fortified hamlet of Nijiayingzi and were quickly cut down by Muslim troops. After two days of massacre in a network of dry riverbeds, only around 1,200 escaped into the mountains (Qin 2007: 73; Xu 1987: 549). In the end, of the over 20,000 troops in the Western Legion, only 400 or so finally made it to Xinjiang, while several dozens of stragglers, including Chen Changhao and Xu Xiangqian, made their way back to Mao's base in Shaanxi (Xu 1987; Zhang and Hu 2010). Waiting for the stragglers in Xinjiang, however, was Mao's chief of secret police Deng Fa, who launched an anti-Trotskyite purge among the survivors of the Western Legion (Liu 1999). Scores of officers, including senior commanders such as Li Te and Huang Chao, were executed.

This fateful march west became another albatross that hung on the necks of FFA veterans. After the failed march, Mao blamed the annihilation of the Western Legion (*Xilujun*) on "the errors of Zhang Guotao opportunism" (Zhang and Hu 2010). Survivors of the Western Legion, including Li Xiannian, insisted all along that the march was authorized by the Central Committee, although they were unable to make their case formally until the 1980s (Zhu 2008). The march westward was pivotal in swinging the power balance between the Fourth Front Army and the First Front Army because the majority of the FFA was annihilated during the march.

After Mao had consolidated his control in northern Shaanxi and after forming an anti-Japan united front with Chiang Kai-shek in 1937,

Mao lost no time launching a fierce political campaign against Zhang Guotao and the survivors of the FFA (Politburo 1996). Considering the thin resources and taxing demands on the party at the time, substantial effort was invested in the tainting of the Zhang Guotao faction. Mao loyalist Kai Feng was tasked with writing a comprehensive denunciation of Zhang Guotao, blaming him for a series of past setbacks going back to the 1920s, as well as for more recent transgressions, including "counter-revolutionary splittism," "banditry," "warlordism," "right opportunist flightism," and neglecting mass work with minorities (Kai 1979). Mao even blamed the annihilation of the Western Legion on the "Zhang Guotao line of retreatism" (Mao 1991). For ten days, officers of the First Front Army hurled these charges at their colleagues in the FFA, thoroughly "exposing" their sins (Wu 2006: 171).

Surviving officers of the FFA then were put in special classes at the newly formed Anti-Japan University and faced daily struggle sessions, carried out by officers from the untainted First and Second Front Armies (Li 2009b; Zhang 1998: 358; Zhu 2008). In some struggle sessions, FFA veterans had to stand on the stage wearing placards stating "I belong to Zhang Guotao" (张国焘的人) while hearing abuses hurled at them by First and Second Front Army veterans (Li 2009b). This struggle caused sharp resentment among the officers of the FFA, and a few of them committed suicide, while others ran away (Li 2009b). As Hong Xuezhi, a FFA officer, recalls, "[W]e did not understand why we were targeted, so we made a ruckus. The ruckus got louder, more fierce" (Li 2009b).

With a rising tide of indignation, a group of thirty FFA officers led by Xu Shiyou attempted to escape from Shaanxi to start a new guerilla base back in Hubei, a region native to many of them. The "armed counter-revolutionary group"(武装反革命集团) was foiled when one of the would-be escapees betrayed Xu Shiyou (Jiang 2004). After the revolutionary court labeled the plotters as an "armed counterrevolutionary group" and death sentences were handed down to its leaders, Mao went to see Xu Shiyou twice to see if he would change his attitude. At the second meeting, Xu broke down and begged Mao for his forgiveness, which led to a stay of execution and eventually the release of Xu Shiyou and his fellow plotters (Mu 2006). Thirty-four years later, Mao entrusted Xu Shiyou, the leader of the "armed counterrevolutionary group," to arrest Lin Biao's followers after Lin had fled to Mongolia.

Just as the campaign against Zhang was reaching a feverish pitch, however, Moscow sent a telegram ordering Mao to refrain from expelling Zhang and his followers from the party (Zhang 1998: 367). Stalin probably wanted to keep Zhang to balance against Mao's rising influence. After Moscow's telegram, Zhang's political fortune recovered slightly, and Mao put him in charge of the relatively powerless Shaanxi-Gansu-Ningxia People's Government (Zhang 1998: 397). Zhang even tried to revive his political fortune by reaching out to staunch Stalinist Wang Ming, who had just returned from Moscow. Given the deep stain on Zhang's record, Wang rejected Zhang's offer of friendship, perhaps missing out on a powerful alliance (Zhang 1998: 425). Around that time, Zhang also found out from Wang that Deng Fa had executed some survivors of the Western Legion in Xinjiang for being Trotskyites. The executions made up his mind to leave the CCP, and Zhang became the most senior CCP leader to defect to the KMT. In Zhang's own words, he "did not want to wait until Mao killed him like Bukharin" (Zhang 1998: 431).[4]

After Zhang's shocking defection to the KMT in April 1938, the position of FFA veterans became even more precarious. They were all "counterrevolutionary splittists" already, and a number of them were part of the "armed counterrevolutionary group" led by Xu Shiyou. The survivors of the Western Legion death march took part in "Zhang Guotao's opportunism." Now, they were also associated with a bona fide traitor. More ominous, Stalin no longer had any incentive to protect Zhang's associates from Mao's wrath, as a traitorous Zhang was politically useless to Stalin. Indeed, Mao launched a large-scale propaganda campaign discrediting Zhang both within the party and to the country (Wang and Zhu 2004). As former Red Fourth Front Army units were then engaged in fierce fighting against Japanese forces, Mao had to make do with a few brief struggle sessions against FFA veterans on the front lines (Xu 1987).

Even without another round of intense struggle, however, the dark stain of Zhang's "splittism" and "opportunism," as well as the defection permanently marked FFA veterans. Numerous Politburo and Central Committee documents exposed Zhang's crimes against the Central Committee (Central Committee 1979; Kai 1979; Politburo 1979, 1996). In a key Central Committee document that summarized CCP history up to 1945, Zhang's actions were labeled "counterrevolutionary" (Central Committee 1990). Although veterans in Zhang's FFA were not expelled

---

[4] Nikolai Bukharin had been a longtime friend of Stalin and his ally during Stalin's struggle against Trotsky. Ultimately, however, Stalin tried and executed him during the Great Terror in 1938. See (Montefiore 2003).

from the party in most cases, they were demoted and sent to raise guerilla forces behind Japanese lines with little funds and weapons. Li Xiannian, who had commanded an army group, was initially assigned to be a battalion commander until Mao intervened to give him a position at the division level, still a major demotion (Huang et al. 2010).

The largest contingent of the FFA was incorporated into the 129th Division of the 8th Route Army, which was led by Liu Bocheng and Deng Xiaoping. Xu Xiangqian, the former commander of the FFA, was given a largely honorary title of vice commander of the 129th division (Xiang 2006). The bulk of the 129th division organized guerilla bands and built base areas behind Japanese lines in northern China (Chen 2007; Xiang 2006; Zhao 1997). During the Chinese Civil War (1946–1949), the 129th Division became the 2nd Field Army, which fought a war of attrition against KMT troops in north central China (Qin 2007; Whitson and Huang 1973). This stands in sharp contrast with Lin Biao's Fourth Field Army, which was given the best equipment and fought fierce battles against KMT crack troops (Zhang 2002). Furthermore, even in the 1940s, Mao did not entirely trust FFA veterans, especially those who had conspired to run away from Yan'an. Until the late 1940s, FFA veterans were not in charge of any army or column-level unit. Even when they had command of a unit, their authority was balanced by a political commissar from either the First Front Army or an intellectual cadre from the Northern Bureau. Xu Shiyou, the ringleader of the "armed counter-revolutionary plot" served as a chief of staff in the Shandong Base Area but was watched over by the person who had betrayed the plot to Mao, Wang Jian'an (Wang 2006). The only exception was Xu Xiangqian, who commanded the 18th Army Group and fought a protracted and bloody battle against Yan Xishan around Taiyuan for much of 1948 (National Defense University Editorial Committee for *Xu Xiangqian Chronicle* 2016: 4). Despite second-class status, fifteen years of constant warfare after the Long March gave FFA veterans steady promotions, even to the army-group level in many cases by 1949.

With the founding of the People's Republic, senior figures from the FFA were integrated into high-level positions in the new regime. Xu Xiangqian, the commander of the doomed Western Legion, became the Chief of Staff of the People's Liberation Army (PLA) for a period after 1949 (Editorial Staff of One Spark Lighting the Plains 2006). Furthermore, Xu was elected into the Central Committee at the 1945 7th Party Congress and remained in that organ until the 1982 12th Party Congress and even served in the Politburo in the 11th and the 12th

Central Committees. Other FFA veterans also prospered under Mao's patronage. Li Xiannian, who had led Western Legion stragglers to Xinjiang and had narrowly missed being labeled a Trotskyite and shot, became the longest serving vice premier of China between 1954 and 1984. At the 1956 8th Party Congress, Li was further elected into the Politburo despite his own objection (Huang et al. 2010). Xie Fuzhi, who had been the political officer overseeing fellow FFA veterans at the Anti-Japan University, perhaps benefited the most from Mao's patronage (Li 2009b). He was promoted to Beijing to serve as the minister of public security in 1959 and became a vice premier of China in 1965 (Xia 2005b).

Despite Mao's patronage of a few of the most senior FFA officers, FFA veterans as a whole still did not fare as well as their counterparts from the First Front Army, who had stood on the right side of the Mao-Zhang struggle in 1936. Despite having more men than the First Front Army even after the Western Legion death march, FFA veterans only took one of the seventeen seats in the Politburo elected in the 1956 8th Party Congress. Only 8 percent of full Central Committee members elected in 1956 came from the FFA (Li 2007: 180). Likewise, of the 886 Long March veterans promoted to the rank of brigadier general or above in 1955, FFA veterans only received 287 of those commissions.[5] Xu Xiangqian became the only FFA veteran to receive the rank of marshal, which was bestowed on nine distinguished commanders in the People's Liberation Army in 1955 (Editorial Staff of One Spark Lighting the Plains 2006). His highest position prior to the Cultural Revolution, vice chairmanship of the Central Military Commission, likely had been a ceremonial post, as Xu had been put in charge of the militia and long-term strategy instead of major departments or branches in the PLA (National Defense University Editorial Committee for *Xu Xiangqian Chronicle* 2016: 82).

FFA veterans, for their part, kept a low profile throughout much of the 1950s and 1960s, making deep self-criticism when necessary. Throughout much of the 1950s and the first half of 1960s, Xu Xiangqian and Li Xiannian seldom met with one another or with former subordinates in the FFA (National Defense University Editorial Committee for *Xu Xiangqian Chronicle* 2016). They likely went out of their way to avoid potential charges of factionalism. They also readily conducted self-criticism even without prompting. At a preparatory meeting of the 8th Party Congress,

---

[5] The other 172 generals joined the Red Army after the Long March.

Li Xiannian forthrightly admitted, "I also committed serious errors in the past by following the Zhang Guotao line. Even if I did it blindly, it still was a mistake" (Jiang and Gao 2006: 37). Although some FFA veterans grumbled about the label of the Western Legion as a product of "Zhang Guotao opportunism," Li Xiannian and other senior FFA veterans never made a fuss about it until the 1980s (Huang et al. 2010). Even FFA veterans at the elite level such as Xu Xiangqian and Li Xiannian only followed the prevailing political wind instead of fighting against it. For example, during the Gao–Rao Affair, Li Xiannian at first took the cue from Gao Gang and criticized Bo Yibo for his proposed new tax system, but when Gao Gang came under criticism, Li was the first one to make a self-criticism to Bo Yibo (Huang et al. 2010). This fear of violating the prevailing political wind made Li and other FFA veterans extremely useful for Mao because to form a coalition on any issue, Mao only needed to signal to FFA veterans that he wished it so. Mao also did not have to fear that they would have joined a rival coalition – given their tainted status, no one would have wanted them as a part of their coalitions.

THE RISING FORTUNE OF FFA VETERANS

Prior to the Cultural Revolution, Mao maintained the tainted status of the FFA by often reminding party elites of their duplicity in the 1930s. For example, at the second plenum of the 8th Central Committee in 1958, Mao reminded his audience that "during the 25,000 li Long March, the party split …. [A]fter Zhang Guotao defected, the party regained unity" (Mao 1967a). In a 1959 speech discussing the fate of Peng Dehuai, who had just been removed from power during the Lushan Conference, Mao distinguished Peng from Zhang Guotao: "[Peng Dehuai and Huang Kecheng] are different from traitors like Chen Duxiu, Luo Zhanglong, Zhang Guotao, and Gao Gang; the first is contradiction within the people, while the second is contradiction between the people and the enemy" (Mao 1967b: 248). In numerous other speeches, Mao casually sprinkled references of Zhang Guotao's rebellion, strongly indicating that Zhang's crime was still common knowledge within the elite circle of the CCP. As such, when the Cultural Revolution was launched, it was surprising that these proven "counterrevolutionaries" did not become the key targets of the movement.

Once the Cultural Revolution commenced, however, FFA veterans experienced a reversal of fortune. Instead of being purged for counterrevolutionary crimes, these bona fide counterrevolutionaries were either protected from purges or promoted into positions left empty by their purged colleagues. In the first stage of the Cultural Revolution, Xie Fuzhi, who had been a senior political officer in the FFA, sided with the radicals and used his authorities as the minister of public security to persecute many veteran cadres (He and Song 2004). He led the special case group gathering evidence of the alleged crimes of the wife of Mao's archrival, Liu Shaoqi, and this case group soon turned its attention on Liu himself (MacFarquhar and Schoenhals 2006: 282). His willingness to side with the radicals, however, was itself insufficient to protect him from the purge, because other top leaders who had cooperated with the Central Cultural Revolution Group (CCRG) soon fell from power, including Wang Renzhong, Liu Zhijian, and Tao Zhu (MacFarquhar and Schoenhals 2006: 183). In contrast to them, Xie was promoted into the Politburo and the Central Military Commission at the 9th Party Congress (He and Song 2004).

Xu Xiangqian meanwhile earned a promotion to the vice-chairmanship of the Central Military Commission at the start of the Cultural Revolution, the core organ controlling the PLA. Mao further put Xu in charge of the Army Cultural Revolution Group in 1966, which coordinated revolutionary activities within the army (Xu 1987: 835). Xu himself was shocked when Yang Chengwu brought him the news: "I have been sick for many years...so please tell Chairman Mao that I cannot do this job!" (Xu 1987: 821) This was indeed a strange appointment considering that Lin Biao had been designated Mao's successor by that time. Clearly, Mao wanted a balance against Lin's power. When Lin Biao tried to stop Xu from becoming a Central Committee member at the 1969 9th Party Congress, Mao personally countermanded Lin Biao and ordered Xu's selection into the Central Committee (MacFarquhar and Schoenhals 2006; Xu 1987: 844). This was despite the fact that Xu was identified by Mao as a "culprit" of the February Countercurrent in 1967. Meanwhile, although Li Xiannian suffered through a few struggle sessions during the Cultural Revolution, Mao directly intervened on Li's behalf so that Red Guards could not remove him from office (Li 2009a).[6] When Zhou Enlai's health began to fail him in the early 1970s, Li Xiannian even

---

[6] When Red Guards in the Ministry of Finance began to put up large character posters against Li, Zhou Enlai reported the situation to Mao. Mao said that Li was "a general who did not step off his horse," implying that Li was only a fighter and did not meddle in politics during the revolution. That comment likely saved Li from the Red Guards. See (Li 2009a).

stood in as acting premier when Zhou took sick leaves (MacFarquhar and Schoenhals 2006: 359).

The political fortune of the members of the "armed counterrevolutionary group" at the Anti-Japan University was even more unfathomable, especially at a time when the Central Case Examination Group scoured the country looking for "counterrevolutionaries" (Schoenhals 1996). Xu Shiyou, who was tried and convicted of counterrevolutionary crimes as the ringleader of the group, had been appointed vice minister of defense and commander of the Nanjing Military Region in 1959. When Red Guards rampaged through the barracks of the Nanjing Military Region in 1967, Xu did not obediently participate in struggle sessions. Instead, he repeated what he had done in the 1930s and ran off to the Dabie Mountains, where he had fought guerilla warfare, with a small contingent of loyal troops (Li 2002). Instead of arresting him and trying him for "counterrevolutionary armed uprising," Mao had Zhou Enlai send a special escort to protect Xu, which included a core member of the CCRG, Zhang Chunqiao (Zheng 2017: 637). When Xu finally left the Dabie Mountains to meet Mao in Shanghai, Mao lightly berated him for moving troops without the Central Military Commission's permission and had a private talk with him without anyone else's presence (Zheng 2017: 636). Afterward, Mao quartered Xu next to him in the Zhongnanhai leadership compound, which was the only place in China beyond Red Guard reach at the time (Wen and Li 1998). At the 9th Party Congress, Xu further was catapulted into the Politburo. Chen Xilian, another plotter in 1937, was handpicked by Mao in early 1976 as the person in charge of the daily affairs of the Central Military Commission (Mao 1987e; Zhao 1997).

Despite Mao's protection of FFA veterans, Mao had no intention of erasing the taint in their past, especially during the Cultural Revolution. In fact, Lin Biao, who had been designated Mao's successor in the first part of the Cultural Revolution, came close to uprooting FFA veterans after the Wuhan incident in 1967, which saw conservative Red Guards close to FFA veterans beat up Mao's personal emissaries right outside of Mao's personal guesthouse in Wuhan (Wang 1995). Despite another political error committed by FFA veterans, Mao's political instinct led him to stop their wholesale purge, even though in the atmosphere of the Cultural Revolution, it would have been easy to justify such a purge. More so than other episodes, the Wuhan incident and the subsequent campaign against "a small handful in the army" showed the vulnerability of FFA veterans in the absence of Mao's protection.

The Wuhan incident began when an element of the Wuhan Military Region sided with conservative Red Guards against radical Red Guards and their allies in Beijing (MacFarquhar and Schoenhals 2006: 200). In other localities, such alliance with conservative Red Guards "against the tide" would have been sufficient ground for a purge of the local military command. Yet Mao clearly wanted to resolve the escalating conflict between conservative and radical Red Guards and sent an emissary to resolve the standoff, which included FFA veteran Xie Fuzhi and radical Wang Li. Meanwhile, Mao himself also secretly arrived in Wuhan, bringing with him an entourage of senior officials (Wang 1995). Instead of calming the factional conflict, the emissary sided with the radicals and enraged the conservative Red Guards backed by two divisions of the Wuhan Military Region: the independent division and the 29th division (Wang 1995). On July 20, 1967, angry conservative Red Guards attacked Wang Li and Xie Fuzhi. Astonishingly, while Xie was unharmed, Wang was beaten up and detained.[7] Only a direct order from Chairman Mao secured Wang's release later in the day.

Missing from the conventional analysis of this event was the fact that the Wuhan Military Region was dominated by FFA veterans because Zhang Guotao's *Eyuwan* guerilla base had centered on Hubei Province, whose provincial capital was Wuhan. Thus, many Hubei natives in the FFA became senior officers in the Wuhan Military Region. Chen Zaidao, the commander of the military region, had been a senior officer of the FFA. Other senior military region officers like Ye Ming and Kong Qingde were also FFA veterans. FFA veterans also served as senior officers of the renegade independent and 29th divisions (Chen 1988).

Mao was shocked by the brazenness of the conservative Red Guards in Wuhan, but Lin Biao, then minister of defense and Mao's designated successor, saw a chance to eradicate the "counterrevolutionary" veterans of the FFA once and for all. With Mao's approval, the main "culprits" of the Wuhan incident, composed mainly of FFA veterans, were brought to Beijing to face criticism. In an expanded Politburo meeting on July 26–27 attended by Politburo members, members of the Central Cultural Revolution Group, and senior officers in the PLA departments and the military regions, historical animosity was added to accusations of a "counterrevolutionary coup" to guarantee severe punishment for senior

---

[7] It remains unclear why Xie Fuzhi was unharmed. The only plausible explanation is that conservative Red Guards recognized Xie as a senior member of the FFA faction, who shared many historical ties with leaders in the independent division and the 29th division.

officers of the Wuhan Military Region. Xie Fuzhi, who had shown a willingness to betray his former comrades in the FFA even back in the 1930s, gave the first remarks and directly accused Chen Zaidao of a "counterrevolutionary rebellion aimed at Chairman Mao, Vice Chairman Lin, and the Central Cultural Revolution Group" (Chen 1988). In the rest of his remarks, however, he did not dwell on past counterrevolutionary crimes that he had shared with Chen and others. Instead, he spent the bulk of his speech accusing Chen of being a poor military leader, a much more innocuous topic than discussion of past counterrevolutionary activities (Wang 2001). Kang Sheng, who had been Mao's rectification specialist since his return from NKVD training in Moscow in the 1930s, laid bare the historical vulnerability of FFA veterans (Chen 1988):

You Chen Zaidao don't act like you have credentials; don't think that just because Chairman Mao calls you a comrade that you are not a counter-revolutionary. 30 years ago Zhang Guotao betrayed the Central Committee in Wuhan. Now you are launching a counterrevolutionary rebellion in Wuhan. This is a repeat of the Zhang Guotao incident.

Likewise, Wu Faxian, a follower of Lin Biao, also accused Chen of being a "modern day Zhang Guotao" (Chen 1988). Xu Xiangqian, former commander of the FFA, was forced to attend the struggle session against Chen and was accused of being the "backstage controller" of this "counterrevolutionary coup d'état" (Chen 2006; Xu 1987: 837). The next day, Lin Biao presided over the meeting and labeled Chen as "the Liu-Deng line with guns" and a "small handful of capitalist roaders in the army" (Zheng 2017: 405).

After the expanded Politburo session, Ye Qun, Lin Biao's wife and the head of his personal office, began to send words to Red Guards that the Wuhan incident was related to FFA veterans' dissatisfaction with Lin Biao's role as the designated successor (Chen 1988). For the following few weeks, the fate of Chen Zaidao and other FFA veterans hung in balance as a national campaign orchestrated by Jiang Qing and Lin Biao to "drag out a small handful in the army" proceeded with great ferocity in the national press (Wang 2001). Within the military, Lin Biao disbanded the renegade independent division of the Wuhan Military Region and sent thousands of officers in Wuhan to labor camps and work farms (Chen 1988: 524). In place of Chen Zaidao and Zhong Hanhua, Lin Biao appointed Liu Feng and Zeng Siyu, both First Front Army veterans, to positions in the Wuhan Military Region leadership (Li and Shu 2009: 1060). Lin Biao also took this opportunity to consolidate control over the military by migrating day-to-day decision-making authority from the Central Military Commission Standing Committee to the newly formed Central Military Commission Administrative Office (CMCAO), composed exclusively of his loyal followers in the military and his wife, Ye Qun (Li and Shu 2009: 1069). Later on, Mao insisted on the addition of Li Desheng, a FFA veteran, to the CMCAO (Gao 2003: 274).

Yet Mao never meant for a thorough purge of FFA veterans to occur. Just two days before the Wuhan incident, Mao personally met Chen Zaidao in Wuhan, and he assured Chen that "they want to overthrow you, but I will make them not overthrow you!" (Chen 1988: 513) The anger of the conservative Red Guards against Mao's emissary exceeded Mao's expectation, thus forcing him to censure Chen Zaidao and the other "culprits" of the Wuhan incident (Wang 1995). After the July 20 incident, Chen Zaidao was removed from his command and forced aside until the Lin Biao incident in 1971. However, Mao made sure that the purge did not extend to other senior members of the FFA. When Red Guards sought to arrest Xu Shiyou in the Nanjing Military Region, Xu ran off to the Dabie Mountains, and Mao offered to fly him to Beijing to live in his compound (Wen and Li 1998). At the same time, Mao also warned Zhang Chunqiao, a core member of the CCRG, off FFA veterans: "I want to protect Xu Shiyou. If you want to overthrow Xu Shiyou, and Han Xianchu, and Chen Xilian, who will command the troops to battle?" (Zheng 2017: 410) Upon hearing about the ransacking of Xu Xiangqian's house, Zhou Enlai, acting under Mao's instruction, ordered Red Guards to withdraw immediately and to return all seized documentations to Xu (Xu 1987: 837). When Li Xiannian was accused by Red Guards of being "the Number One Traitor," Mao invited Li to watch Beijing opera with him, jokingly calling to Li as he was seated: "Number One Traitor is here! I want to watch the opera with Number One Traitor" (Huang et al. 2010). After the opera, Mao turned to Jiang Qing and told her, "Why do you want to overthrow Li Xiannian, even calling him a traitor. I know everything about Li Xiannian's history..." (Huang et al. 2010). Of course, after such a clear signal from Mao, Red Guard attacks on Li Xiannian subsided.

To be sure, not all FFA veterans emerged unscathed from the Wuhan incident. At a July 26 Central Military Commission meeting, Xu Xiangqian himself agreed to the purge of Li Yingxi and Zhang Guangcai, both senior officers in the Wuhan Military Region and FFA veterans (National Defense University Editorial Committee for *Xu Xiangqian Chronicle* 2016: 336). They never regained command, and

Zhang died in a work farm a few years later. Chen Changhao, the political commissar of the Western Legion, was dragged out by numerous Red Guard bands and was pressured to give up "criminal evidence" against Xu Xiangqian. He refused to do so and committed suicide after a few struggle sessions (Chen 2006). Perhaps Mao did not have a chance to save Chen before he committed suicide, but as a mid-level civilian official by that point, Chen also was strategically irrelevant to Mao.

On August 11, 1967, Mao suddenly ordered a stop to the campaign against "a small handful in the army" because it was "tactically inappropriate" (MacFarquhar and Schoenhals 2006: 232; Wang 2001: 810). Mao was in particular annoyed by two editorials in the *Red Flag*, the central committee's main publication, calling for the country to "drag out a small handful in the army" (MacFarquhar and Schoenhals 2006: 232). In the middle of August, he wrote a note saying that these editorials were "great, great, great poisonous weeds," a term he had applied to the writings by members in the doomed Liu Shaoqi faction (Chen 1988: 524). Also, when Lin Biao tried to get Mao to approve a document calling for the entire army to engage in a "drag out a small handful" campaign, Mao crossed out all mentions of the campaign and wrote on the margin "no need" (Chen 1988: 524). This caused a panic among the CCRG and Lin Biao; all mentions of "dragging out a small handful" were removed from the media, and Red Guards were told not to pursue this movement further (MacFarquhar and Schoenhals 2006: 232). As Chapter 4 discusses in detail, the junior ideologues responsible for writing these editorials were summarily purged, spending the subsequent decades in isolated confinement.

Although Lin Biao himself did not get into trouble for launching the campaign against FFA veterans, Mao now knew that he needed these tainted officers even more to counterbalance against Lin Biao, who clearly sought to dominate the military completely. Strangely, thirty years after Zhang Guotao had tried to usurp Mao's power during the Long March, the emerging cleavage was between Mao, followers of Zhang, and a group of upstart ideologues on one side and Mao's most loyal lieutenant and designated successor and his coterie of generals on the other side.

STATISTICAL ANALYSIS OF PURGE PATTERNS DURING
THE CULTURAL REVOLUTION

In the statistical analysis presented in Table 3.1, I examine whether Mao intervened systematically to protect and promote veterans of the FFA

TABLE 3.1 *The effect of being a FFA veteran on the likelihood of being purged during the Cultural Revolution*

	(1) CCPURGED	(2) CCPURGED	(3) CRPURGED	(4) CRPURGED
red4th	-1.717	-2.132	-0.620	-0.670
	(1.114)	(1.185)*	(0.334)*	(0.354)*
rank	-0.382	0.245	0.065	0.048
	(0.328)	(0.480)	(0.177)	(0.365)
birth	0.057	0.064		
	(0.075)	(0.036)*		
edu	-0.302	0.152		
	(0.407)	(0.173)		
korea	1.137	-0.300		
	(0.841)	(0.356)		
ptime	0.155	-0.018		
	(0.128)	(0.037)		
red2nd	-0.168	-0.076		
	(0.858)	(0.402)		
eightcc		0.127		
		(0.328)		
Constant	0.747	-407.813	-0.611	-87.416
	(0.840)	(252.473)	(0.302)*	(90.660)
Observations	54	54	244	238

during the Cultural Revolution. Although Mao saved FFA veterans from purges, the pattern was far from universal. For example, Gao Houliang, who had been Zhang Guotao's bodyguard in the 1930s and the political commissar of the air force in 1966, was accused by Lin Biao of trying to seize power in the air force and was removed in 1966 (Yu 2009: 408). Chen Changhao, the political commissar of the Western March, committed suicide after a few rounds of struggle at his work unit, the Central Translation Bureau.[8] More systematic analysis is needed to discern whether FFA veterans were systematically saved from purges. This analysis begins with the 1,058 generals appointed in 1955, the first and largest batch of generals appointed in the People's Republic. Almost all the generals had joined the Red Army before the end of the Long March in 1935 and thus were members of the various front armies (Editorial Staff of One Spark Lighting the Plains 2006). Due to the dearth of information about the political fate of brigadier generals during the Cultural

---

[8] Interview in Beijing February 12, 2015.

Revolution, I restrict my analysis to major generals or above, which total 253 generals.

The dependent variables are dichotomous variables that record three important political outcomes during the Cultural Revolution, when many civilian and military leaders were removed from power by the Red Guards (MacFarquhar and Schoenhals 2006). The first variable (CCPURGED) records whether a general who had been elected to the Central Committee at the 1956 8th Party Congress (PC) was removed from the Central Committee at the 9th Party Congress. This variable mainly pertains to higher-level officers who had been elected into the Central Committee in the first place. The second variable (CRPURGED) more broadly records whether a general was removed from his military post or was placed under extended custody during the Cultural Revolution. Because nearly every political figure underwent mass struggle during the Cultural Revolution, I did not use records of mass struggle as gauges of losing power. Instead, this variable records more permanent loss of power due to the Cultural Revolution. A little over one-third of all major generals or above appointed in 1955 were purged during the Cultural Revolution. Finally, a variable also captures whether these generals earned promotions or new appointments either in the civilian or the military apparatus during the Cultural Revolution (CRPROMOTE).

The main independent variable is also a dummy variable that simply records whether the general had served in the FFA of the Red Army before the First and the Fourth Front Army had joined together in 1935 (RED4TH).[9] If saving and promoting the tainted members of the FFA had indeed been a part of Mao's strategy, they should have faced a significantly lower probability of being purged during the Cultural Revolution and a significantly higher probability of being promoted during the Cultural Revolution. As a point of comparison, I also generate a dummy variable recording veterans of He Long's Second Front Army (RED2ND). If Mao somehow had systematically discriminated against his own followers in the First Front Army, He Long's men also should have benefited from a lower probability of being purged during the Cultural Revolution. Most of the remaining officers were members of Mao's First Front Army, who make up the null cases. Among the control variables, the most significant one is rank (RANK), which is an ordinal scale recording whether an officer was a major general (*zhongjiang*),

---

[9] This strict definition is used because the FFA after June 1935 also contained some units originally in the First Front Army.

lieutenant general (*shangjiang*), general (*dajiang*), or a marshal (*yuanshuai*). This is an important control variable because Cultural Revolution purges might have only applied to senior officers. I also control for the generals' birth year (BIRTH), year of joining the CCP (PTIME), and the level of education (EDU). Furthermore, at a time of great international threat from both the US and the Soviet Union, Mao might have wanted to preserve generals who had experience fighting a major modern army during the Korean War. Thus, I also created a dummy variable for command experience during the Korean war (KOREA). Since the dependent variables are all dichotomous variables, I use logistic regressions to carry out the analysis. For robustness sake, I include both simple regressions with just the main dependent and independent variables and only RANK as control, as well as regressions with all the other control variables.

In Table 3.1, it seems clear that having served in the FFA significantly reduced one's risk of being purged during the Cultural Revolution. This especially pertained to FFA veterans who had been elected to the Central Committee at the 8th Party Congress. They were much more likely to be reelected into the Central Committee at the 1969 9th PC than their counterparts in the other front armies. This pattern is even more striking when one considers that several non–Fourth Front Army veterans also committed "splittism" in 1935–1936 by going south with Zhang Guotao. In particular, Zhu De and Liu Bocheng both had supported Zhang's decision to go south, and both were reelected into the 9th Central Committee in 1969 (Li 2007: 223).

Table 3.2 shows that FFA officers were also more likely to obtain a promotion during the Cultural Revolution. When all Central Committee members at the 8th Party Congress were set aside on equation 4 of Table 3.2, however, FFA veteran status no longer had a positive effect on promotion during the Cultural Revolution. This result suggests that the promotion advantage mainly accrued to senior FFA veterans who had been elected into the CC in 1956, including Xu Xiangqian, Li Xiannian, and Xie Fuzhi. Together with the results on Table 3.1, they suggest that Mao pursued a strategy of preserving and promoting senior members of the FFA group in the military, while more junior members of the FFA group were maintained in their positions to balance against the rising influence of Lin Biao in the military. As we will see in Chapter 5, this strategy paid off handsomely as the relationship between Mao and Lin deteriorated after the 9th Party Congress.

In terms of the control variables, none of them is significant at the 0.1 level for those purged from the Central Committee. BIRTH strangely had

TABLE 3.2 *The effect of being a FFA veteran on the likelihood of being promoted during the Cultural Revolution*

	(1) CRPROMOTE	(2) CRPROMOTE	(3) CRPROMOTE	(4) CRPROMOTE
red4th	1.393 (0.813)*	1.526 (0.899)*	0.552 (0.322)*	0.316 (0.350)
rank	-0.399 (0.392)	-0.012 (0.556)	-0.198 (0.214)	-0.006 (0.430)
birth	0.057 (0.085)	0.125 (0.044)**		
edu	-0.196 (0.429)	0.168 (0.194)		
korea	-1.665 (1.193)	0.074 (0.368)		
ptime	0.093 (0.138)	-0.003 (0.046)		
red2nd	0.260 (0.979)	-1.074 (0.580)*		
eightcc		0.159 (0.386)		
Constant	-0.348 (0.952)	-287.989 (270.088)	-0.952 (0.348)**	-233.854 (107.987)*
Observations	54	54	244	238
Standard errors in parentheses				

a positive effect on both the likelihood of being purged and the likelihood of being promoted. This likely reflects a few trivial mechanisms. First, BIRTH is recorded as the year of a general's birth, so positive coefficients in the purge equations mean that younger officers were more likely to be purged. This may just be a reflection of the age structure of all the generals in question. In terms of younger officers having a greater chance of being promoted, the Cultural Revolution indeed saw the introduction of many younger officials into the Central Committee and other senior positions (Shih et al. 2010b).

In order to discern the effect of Mao's strategy on the careers of FFA veterans and their counterparts in the other factions more clearly, I calculate the predicted probability of their purges and promotions during the Cultural Revolution based on the logit results on Tables 3.1 and 3.2. In calculating predicted probabilities, the rank is set at the lieutenant general level, while the other control variables are set at their means.

TABLE 3.3 *Predicted probabilities of being purged and promoted during the CR for a lieutenant general in the First Front Army, Second Front Army, and Fourth Front Army*

	Removed from CC at 9th PC	Removed from Command during CR	Promoted Beyond CC during CR	Promoted During CR
First Front Army	0.43	0.38	0.18	0.25
	[0.23 0.64]	[0.26 0.51]	[0.03 0.32]	[0.13 0.36]
Second Front Army	0.39	0.37	0.22	0.10
	[0.02 0.76]	[0.17 0.56]	[-0.08 0.53]	[0 0.21]
Fourth Front Army	0.08	0.24	0.5	0.31
	[-0.1 0.26]	[0.12 0.37]	[0.07 0.9]	[0.16 0.46]

Note: 95 percent confidence intervals in []

For generals from the First Front Army who had been elected into the CC in 1956, their likelihood of being removed from the CC by the 9th Party Congress was 43 percent (Table 3.3). A Central Committee member lieutenant general from the Second Front Army had roughly the same risk of being removed by the 9th Party Congress. However, a lieutenant general from the FFA elected into the 8th CC only had an 8 percent chance of being removed from the Central Committee by the 9th PC, a significantly lower risk. This shows that Mao took particular care to protect the senior members of Zhang Guotao's remnant faction, who were members in elite selectorate bodies such as the Politburo and the Central Military Commission.

Similarly, a lieutenant general, including both CC and non-CC members, from the First and Second Front Armies had 38 and 37 percent chance of being removed from command or of being jailed, respectively, during the Cultural Revolution. An officer of the same rank from the FFA, however, was purged with only a 24 percent probability. To be sure, the 95 percent confidence intervals between Second Front Army officers and FFA officers overlap considerably, but FFA officers clearly had a higher chance of survival than their counterparts in the First Front Army. Although FFA veterans overall still fared better than their counterparts from the other front armies, junior veterans faced higher risks than their senior colleagues who were in the Central Committee. This likely had to do with the uneven impact of patronage by the senior veterans of the FFA. Xu Xiangqian, for example, tried to save several more junior FFA veterans, but he was only partly successful

(Xu 1987: 845). Meanwhile, Mao, who only focused on saving senior FFA veterans, had nearly 100 percent success rate in rescuing those he wanted to save.

The generals' promotion probability during the Cultural Revolution presents a similar picture. Among army veterans who had been elected into the 8th Central Committee in 1956, FFA veterans had a distinct advantage in obtaining promotion during the CR. While First and Second Front Army veterans in the Central Committee only had 18 and 22 percent chance of obtaining promotions during the CR, respectively, FFA veterans in the CC enjoyed a 50 percent chance of obtaining promotions. The effect for all the generals was weaker. A lieutenant general from the First Front Army was promoted either in the civilian bureaucracy or in the military with a probability of 25 percent. An officer of the same rank from the FFA was promoted with a slightly higher probability at 31 percent. However, an officer who served with He Long's Second Front Army was only promoted with a 10 percent probability during the Cultural Revolution. The much lower promotion probability of He Long's protégés is not surprising given that he was a target of ruthless struggle and ultimately died in custody (MacFarquhar and Schoenhals 2006: 281).

MAO'S USE OF OTHER TAINTED GROUPS

Although the FFA was the largest group of tainted officials used by Mao, they were by no means the only tainted group. Saiffudin, who had been a minister of education in the Soviet backed East Turkestan Republic, retained his position as the chairman of the Xinjiang Autonomous Region due to Mao's personal intervention (Mao 1987c). At the 10th Party Congress, Saiffudin, who did not speak Chinese, was further promoted as an alternate member of the Politburo, nominally elevating him to the pinnacles of power (Zhu 2007: 258). The retention of Saiffudin and the rehabilitation of Ulanfu after the Lin Biao incident suggest that Mao copied Stalin's trick of employing ostracized ethnic minorities in senior positions to some extent (Gregory 2009).

In addition, Kang Sheng, the main henchman behind the Central Case Examination Groups that compiled evidence of "counterrevolutionary crimes" against 220 senior cadres, was himself accused by many of betraying his comrades to the KMT in 1930, when he had been arrested in Shanghai (Central Committee 1982c). It is all but certain that Mao knew about these allegations, if not in possession of hard evidence of these indiscretions.[10] Because Mao knew of their vulnerabilities, he unleashed them to accuse others of being "traitors" and "spies." Kang Sheng, in particularly, personally concocted the infamous "Group of 61 Case," which led to the torture and purge of twenty-two survivors of a sixty-one-person group that had been accused of betraying the party in order to get out of KMT custody in the 1930s (Central Committee 1982d). As a deeply tainted individual himself, Kang Sheng was in no position to threaten Mao and zealously pursued his assigned tasks.

CONCLUSION

Examining historical and statistical evidence, Mao likely promoted and saved tainted members of the Zhang Guotao "splittist" line during the Cultural Revolution in order to preserve his own relative power and enhance his knowledge of the relative distribution of power in the Politburo and in the Central Military Commission. Core protégés of Zhang Guotao, including Xu Xiangqian, Li Xiannian, and even Xu Shiyou, were placed in important positions and wielded real power throughout Mao's reign. They prospered from their dishonored history because Mao could place them in important positions without elevating risks to his own power. The depth of Zhang Guotao's errors assured even Mao's suspicious mind that these besmirched individuals could never gain the capacity to betray him.

Mao's protection of FFA veterans during the first stage of the Cultural Revolution would have a profound influence on the evolution of elite politics in China in the subsequent two decades. As subsequent chapters show, Mao's instinct to preserve the FFA group in the initial months of the Cultural Revolution paid off handsomely, as they became a crucial ballast against Lin Biao's rising influence in the military. The purge of the Lin Biao faction in 1971 was carried out entirely by FFA veterans and led to the dominance of the tainted group in the PLA. The pervasiveness of FFA veterans in the military went a long way toward explaining the rise of Deng Xiaoping in the mid-1970s, as well as Deng's need to rehabilitate so many purged cadres. The wave of rehabilitation in the 1970s and 1980s in turn prevented Deng from dominating elite politics through his own coalitions of the weak.

---

[10] A 1978 Central Committee document, for example, claims that the government had "numerous testimonies" of Kang Sheng's betrayal of the party in 1930. It is all but certain that such "testimonies" had begun arriving in Zhongnanhai against the most hated official in China before Mao's death in 1976. See (Central Committee 1982c).

4

The Scribblers Mafia

Radical Ideologues in Mao's Coalition

Zhang Chunqiao helped Mao launch the Cultural Revolution and became a core member of the Central Cultural Revolution Group (CCRG). At the 10th Party Congress in 1973, Mao promoted him into the most powerful institution in the Chinese Communist Party, the Politburo Standing Committee, a rarely seen leap for a pre–Cultural Revolution vice-provincial-level official in the space of seven years. When his daughter asked him right after the congress whether he felt a sense of triumph, Zhang responded, "I don't feel much. Which revolutionary base area did I build? Which army did I lead? Which battle did I win?" (Zheng 2017: ix) Despite his formal power, Zhang knew that since he was a writer and an ideologue instead of someone with faction followers throughout the party and the military, he had very little informal power. Given their limited political experience and narrow political networks in the party, why did Mao elevate Zhang and others in the scribblers mafia (笔杆子) into senior offices during the Cultural Revolution?

The traditional literature on scribblers focuses on their ability to generate key polemics and policy documents to help launch important campaigns (MacFarquhar and Schoenhals 2006; Perry and Li 1997; Ye 2009). This book argues that these scribblers also served an important political purpose precisely because they were political novices with narrow networks. By replacing experienced veterans with the scribblers, the top leaders minimized the chance that a successful coup could be launched by other senior members of the regime. As our theoretical model presumes and as the post–Great Leap Forward case suggests, veteran cadres had greater confidence and capacity with which to oppose or even sideline Mao. In order to minimize elite opposition and to reduce agency problems, the incumbent dictator appointed inexperienced officials with little or no elite network.

The scribblers (笔杆子) fit this bill to the dot during the Cultural Revolution. Most of them had been junior and obscure cadres prior to the Cultural Revolution who had ridden the "helicopters" to important positions according to Mao's wishes. They then performed every task as instructed by Mao because they dreaded any deviation from the dictator's instructions. They also did not know the monitoring capacity of the dictator at first. Zhang Chunqiao's daughter remembered him often saying, "I listen to the Chairman on all things. If the Chairman asks me to move, I move; if the Chairman stays silent, I do not move" (Zheng 2017: 389).

Also, without a network of officials in the upper echelon with shared history, junior scribblers did not know whether forming a rival coalition against Mao would have been possible. This was knowledge that came with years of service in the upper echelon, which would have been unknown to a newly arrived official. As the biographer of Zhang Chunqiao observes (Zheng 2017: 519):

> Zhang Chunqiao felt that his opponents not only included Chen Pixian but also Chen Yi, Tan Zhenlin and others who were protected by the *guanxi* networks formed during the war. Mao Zedong controlled these *guanxi* networks and could observe and manipulate them at will. However, it was different for Zhang who lived under the shadow of these networks.

The ignorance of junior officials was especially useful for the dictator when ordering them to carry out risky undertakings on his behalf. A more experienced cadre would have known how to shirk from the risky action without being detected by the dictator. Alternatively, when asked to begin an attack on powerful opponents of the dictator, a veteran cadre might have defected from the dictator and formed a rival coalition (Egorov and Sonin 2011). A junior official, not having these options, would have carried out the dictator's instruction to the letter, serving as the sacrificial lamb if need be.

Finally, the strategy of promoting political neophytes into nominally important positions also reduced the costs of losing them, providing the dictator with greater strategic flexibility. First, losing an official without a dense political network of supporters incurred smaller costs to the dictator. Intuitively, because there were many others like them, replacing them would have been easy (Bueno de Mesquita et al. 2003). The dictator and his rival also could use them to engage in risky attacks on one another.

If a risky political undertaking failed, the junior official who carried out the task could be blamed and purged at relatively little costs to the dictator. This allowed the dictator to probe for weaknesses of his rivals much more aggressively. In a stroke of genius, Mao launched the Cultural Revolution by deploying a large number of low-level pawns, his wife included, to attack his political rivals. If an overpowering opposition had been formed against such probes, Mao could have laid the blame on the pawns, thus avoiding censure from his colleagues. This strategy worked wonderfully through much of the first year of the Cultural Revolution. One drawback of this strategy is that experienced rivals of the dictator soon copied this strategy and sent their own pawns to probe the dictator.

When pawns were deployed to probe the dictator, the relatively low costs of eliminating them allowed the dictator to purge them in order to send an unambiguous, credible signal to rivals. Although such purges were costly, the costs were small enough that the overall balance of power was largely undisturbed, thus negating the need to engage in an all-out fight with one another.[1] Unlike sacrificing core followers who served in the military, sacrificing scribblers allowed the dictator and his challenger to end a conflict without drastically upsetting the relative balance of power and exacerbating the commitment problem (Powell 2006). We will examine this logic in the cases of the Wang, Guan, Qi purge in 1967, as well as that of the 1970 Lushan Conference.

Assuming that inexperienced officials knew the enormous risks associated with serving as the dictator's pawns, why did they do it? In a hierarchical one-party state, moving up the administrative hierarchy of the party provided powerful incentives for junior officials to carry out risky tasks for the dictator (Svolik 2012). As the chapter outlines, an ordinary worker such as Wang Hongwen suddenly found himself just a few years later as the second highest official in all of China, entitled to the best luxury, comfort, and respect available in China at that time. Once elevated to high-level positions as pawns of their patrons, however, junior officials found themselves with very little agency. If they did not fully comply with their patrons' wishes, they faced near certainty of removal, followed by years in jail. If they complied fully, they still took the risk of being sacrificed, but they could expect a higher payoff, given the limited information they had. Again, Zhang Chunqiao provided this insight in his discussion with Xiao Mu, a young ideologue in his employ, "after the

---

[1] In a sense, sacrificing junior officials is akin to making international disputes more divisible and tractable for negotiations, as pointed out by (Fearon 1995).

Anting Incident, I have had no choice in anything" (Zheng 2017: 829). In late 1966, Zhang had a choice between backing his conservative colleagues in the Shanghai Municipal Government in quelling the Red Guards in Anting or backing the Red Guards in fulfillment of Mao's emerging radical vision for the Cultural Revolution. After he chose to back Mao's vision, he completely alienated the veterans who had tried to minimize the Cultural Revolution and embarked on a course of dutifully engaging in politics strictly according to Mao's instructions.

As mentioned in the Introduction chapter, the weak coalition theory expects the replacement of veteran cadres by young counterparts without extensive networks in large waves instead in a gradual fashion over time. Also, the theory suggests that the incumbent dictator would seek to assert absolute control over the "helicopters" instead of encouraging them to become autonomous leaders in their own right. These pawns, in this case the scribblers, also could be sacrificed for political expedience instead of being nurtured and protected as the future leaders of the regime. The Cultural Revolution illustrates that the promotion of the scribblers' mafia largely fits into the coalition of the weak logic.

IDEOLOGICAL TSARS IN THE MAKING: THE CCRG IN THE EARLY 1960S

The extant literature has gone into great details on how the Central Cultural Revolution Group (中央文化革命小组 CCRG), the extraordinary body formed by Mao on June 16, 1966 to circumvent the existing party hierarchy, helped Mao launch the Cultural Revolution (MacFarquhar and Schoenhals 2006; Perry and Li 1997; Walder 2009; Wang 1995). Yet one needs to emphasize how obscure and low level the core members of the CCRG had been prior to the Cultural Revolution. Also, although the CCRG was often conflated with the Gang of Four, the latter was mainly composed of the survivors among a coterie of professional ideologues Mao had used to launch the Cultural Revolution. The majority of the original CCRG group had been purged or sidelined by the time the Gang of Four emerged in the 1970s.

Most of the early CCRG members were indeed "nobody's" in the CCP upper echelon, which had been staffed in the mid-1960s with Long March veterans who had been in the party for four decades. Without Mao's intentional elevation of them during the Cultural Revolution, few if any of the CCRG members could have climbed to the highest level in the regime. To be sure, Chen Boda, the chairman of the CCRG, was a veteran revolutionary who had joined the party in the 1920s. Instead of serving in command positions, he mainly took ideological positions as Mao's tutor in Marxist–Leninist ideology and later as his ideological hatchet man during the Yan'an Rectification (Saich and Yang 1996: 1113). As a result, he only had been a Central Committee member prior to the Cultural Revolution instead of a Politburo member. Another veteran member of the CCRG was Kang Sheng, a Soviet-trained repression specialist who had nurtured two members of the CCRG. Kang had begun working with scribbler Wang Li in the early 1960s as the polemic against the Soviet Union heated up (Walder 2009: 16). Of course, Kang also had been Jiang Qing's protector in the party since the mid-1930s.

When Jiang Qing, the core member of the CCRG and later the Gang of Four, first arrived in the Communist base area Yan'an in 1937, she had been a disgraced and distrusted actress loosely affiliated with the party (Ye 2009: 190). After her mentor Kang Sheng introduced her to Mao, Jiang increasingly ingratiated herself into Mao's life – with Mao's willing cooperation. In order to marry her, Mao promised his party colleagues that Jiang Qing would refrain from politics for at least twenty years. By the early 1950s, Jiang finally was given a job as the head of the Central Propaganda Department movie section, giving her approval power over all movies shown in China (Ye 2009: 297). However, when Mao heard of her criticism of Zhou Yang and Hu Qiaomu, two well-known intellectuals in the party, he stripped her of her position (Ye 2009: 300). She then did not have any formal position until Mao instructed Lin Biao to help her organize the PLA Arts and Literature Forum in 1966. Even in 1975, when Jiang Qing was a Politburo member, Mao continued to see her as an inexperienced pawn at the elite level. Zhang Yaoci, Mao's bodyguard, recalls Mao's assessment of Jiang Qing at a Politburo meeting: "Jiang Qing did not participate in the vast majority of power struggles in the party...nor did she take part in the Long March. I think Jiang Qing is a young, young experientialist (小小的经验主义者)" (Zhang 2008b: 237).

Zhang Chunqiao, who ultimately became a standing committee member in charge of political work during the Cultural Revolution, had been a mid-ranking propaganda official prior to the movement. To be sure, of all the members of the Gang of Four, Zhang Chunqiao had had the highest credentials. Due to his relationship with Shanghai Party boss Ke Qingshi in the 1940s, Ke appointed him to a series of important positions in the Shanghai propaganda apparatus, culminating to his appointment as Shanghai's propaganda chief prior to the CR (Ye 2009: 280). He first met Mao in a personal setting in 1958 when Ke Qingshi had brought him to Hangzhou to see Mao, who was happy about Ke and Zhang's public support of Mao's Great Leap policy (Zheng 2017: 80). The seed was perhaps planted in Mao's mind to use Zhang as an ideological henchman in future political struggles.

Yao Wenyuan, another Politburo Standing Committee member during the Cultural Revolution, in 1955, was just a normal cadre in the propaganda department of the Luwan District of Shanghai (Ye 2009: 6). His rise to power in subsequent decades was puzzling, considering that it was fairly well known that his father, Yao Fengzi, had been a spy for the KMT in the 1930s against his circle of leftist intellectual friends (Chen 2000: 107; Ye 2009: 435). His criticism of Hu Feng in 1955, however, was noticed by his immediate superior Zhang Chunqiao, who sent it to Mao for review via Ke Qingshi. In 1957, Yao wrote a whole slew of sharply worded essays against the "rightists" during the Anti-Rightist Movement. Mao apparently liked these essays and praised Yao twice in 1957, including during a face-to-face meeting (Xia 2008). Even when Zhang Chunqiao entrusted Yao to author the highly secretive "Criticism of the Historical Play *Hairui Dismissed From Office*," which marked the beginning of the Cultural Revolution, Yao had only been the head of the arts and literature pages in the *Liberation Daily*, the premier party newspaper of Shanghai (Zhao 2011). When Jiang Qing nominated him to be a member of CCRG in 1966, Chen Boda, the chairman of CCRG, balked at it due to Yao Fengzi's checkered history. Mao, however, personally overturned Chen's decision and included him (Ye 2009: 609).

Other well-known members of the CCRG, including Wang Li, Guan Feng, and Qi Benyu, were obscure scribblers of attack polemics prior to the Cultural Revolution. Wang Li had been a talented writer for the party's flagship magazine *Hongqi* spotted by Mao in the late 1950s. Because he was in the international commentary department, Wang took a leading role in the Soviet "revisionism" polemics under the direction of Kang Sheng (Wang 2001: 28). His contribution to the polemics had been noticed by Mao and thus, before the Cultural Revolution, Wang was promoted to the vice head of the International Liaison Department of the Chinese Communist Party. Although Wang Li was a rising star even prior to the CR, given his thin revolutionary credentials, he likely would not have risen beyond ministerial level without the Cultural Revolution. Even during the Cultural Revolution, Wang Li's position was extremely vulnerable because the official who had inducted him into the party, Gu Mu, was under investigation for being a traitor in 1967 (Wang 2001: 21).

Guan Feng had been an ordinary writer for *Hongqi*, while Qi Benyu had been a low-level secretary in Mao's enormous secretarial staff (Qi 2016: 41). Thus, prior to the Cultural Revolution, they had had little chance of ever becoming powerful officials, at least not for decades more. They both attracted Mao's attention by writing essays that challenged the ideological establishment in the early 1960s. In the case of Qi Benyu, he wrote an obscure essay attacking the historical legacy of jailed Taiping rebel Li Xiucheng who had defected to the Qing Government after capture. This drew the ire of the history and propaganda establishment in the early 1960s because Li had been seen as a premodern "revolution-ary" much like Taiping leader Hong Xiuquan (Qi 2016: 149). Mao became drawn into the debate and even ordered a copy of Li Xiucheng's prison confession from Hong Kong to find evidence in sup-port of Qi's argument (Qi 2016: 150). After that, Qi was drawn into Mao's inner circle as he prepared to launch the Cultural Revolution.

Beyond these infamous figures, other early CCRG members were eliminated by the chaotic politics of the early Cultural Revolution soon after its formation. Yin Da, for example, was a professional historian who wrote an essay calling for the radicalization of historical studies. Although he was initially put on the CCRG, his past clashes with Chen Boda over ideological issues soon saw his expulsion from the organ (Qi 2016: 326). Another early CCRG member was Wang Renzhong, an experienced ideologue nominated by Mao to be on the CCRG. However, because he defended Deng and Liu in the summer of 1966, he was summarily removed and detained (Qi 2016: 237). Because they were dispensable, their removal was hardly remarkable to anyone, even to other CCRG members such as Qi Benyu (Qi 2016: 327).

Other radicals who rose to prominence during the Cultural Revolution also had led humble lives prior to the CR. Wang Hongwen, the junior member of the Gang of Four, had been nothing more than an ordinary worker prior to the Cultural Revolution. Only his steadfast implemen-tation of instructions by Zhang Chunqiao during the Anting incident earned him an entry into the political elite (Perry and Li 1997: 37). By the 10th Party Congress in 1973, he was appointed vice chairman of the Communist Party. Xu Jingxian had been a member of Zhang Chunqiao's political writing group, which had helped the Shanghai Municipal Government produce editorials matching the latest political fads from Beijing (Xu 2003: 5). Without the Cultural Revolution, he likely would have remained a local propaganda official. Yet Xu Jingxian became the second most powerful official in Shanghai during the Cultural Revolution.

Few of these officials had any administrative power prior to the Cultural Revolution, and, more importantly, few had any ties with the military. Wang Hongwen served as a foot soldier during the Korean War, which was a key reason why Mao had considered him a potential successor at the 10th Party Congress (Zheng 2017: 16). Even his meager military experience stood in sharp contrast to that of Long March veterans, most of whom had spent decades leading troops in the various guerilla bases and thus had deep historical ties with senior military officers in the various PLA departments and military regions. For Mao, their inexperience, ambition, and inability to ally with the military made these junior ideologues his perfect weapons during the Cultural Revolution. If Mao had wanted to nurture a group of younger successors with proven revolutionary fervor and political experience, he would have carefully nurtured and protected them. Yet, in 1967 and 1968, Mao and his allies casually casted away members of the scribbler mafia with scarcely a second thought, condemning some of them to years of solitary confinement and to wasted lives.

SCRIBBLERS IN ACTION: THE BEGINNING OF THE CULTURAL REVOLUTION

In the post–Cultural Revolution evaluation of Zhang Chunqiao, he was labeled as "the instigator and ultimate inciter and plotter of seizing the power of the people's government" (Supreme People's Court 1982). Yet Zhang and others in the scribblers mafia were pawns in Mao's risky gambit to overthrow much of the existing power structure. They served three key roles in the beginning stage of the Cultural Revolution. First, Zhang Chunqiao and Yao Wenyuan forged the literary weapon that allowed Mao to lure Peng Zhen into a political trap. Second, the scribblers mafia served as the main conduit between Mao and the emerging Red Guard movement. Finally, Zhang Chunqiao, Jiang Qing, and Kang Sheng, at times taking vague cues from Mao, took the risk to grant formal legitimacy to the Red Guard movement that violated key formal rules in both the party and the state. In all three instances, the radical ideologues took substantial risks on behalf of Mao and protected Mao from potential backlashes.

The literature has long pointed out that Mao instigated the Cultural Revolution by having Yao Wenyuan author the essay "Criticism of the

Historical Play *Hairui Dismissed From Office*," a play that had been authored by Peng Zhen's protégé Wu Han (Harding 1997; MacFarquhar 1997a; MacFarquhar and Schoenhals 2006). Yet the literature perhaps has not emphasized sufficiently the enormous risks that Yao and his mentor Zhang Chunqiao undertook in penning the essay. Mao got the idea of attacking *Hairui* in 1964 when Kang Sheng pointed out to him that the play was both a historical parallel to Peng Dehuai's purge in 1959 and an endorsement for private farming, a policy that Mao's challengers such as Liu Shaoqi and Deng Xiaoping had advocated after the 7000 Cadre Conference (Zheng 2017: 149). Mao soon put Jiang Qing in charge of the project of instigating a wave of criticism against Wu Han's play, likely with the initial aim of stopping any elite consensus on rehabilitating Peng and implementing household responsibility. At first, Jiang Qing approached Li Xifan, an established literature academic, to write a critical essay against *Hairui*, but Li, not wanting to offend an established figure such as Wu Han, wrote a narrowly focused, academic criticism of the play, which displeased Jiang Qing (Zheng 2017: 149). At the beginning of 1965, Jiang Qing sought out Zhang Chunqiao and Yao Wenyuan with Mao's blessings and gave them the mission of writing a polemic against *Hairui*, attacking not just the play's historical accuracy but also the ideological "line" errors embedded in the play (Xu 2003: 4). Yao and Zhang soon convened a crack team of historians and writers and set up a secret office at Number 2 Kangding Road, calling themselves by a code name, the "Luosiding Group" (Xu 2003: 4). The Luosiding Group worked for eight months and produced ten drafts, many of which were edited and revised by Mao personally (Xu 2003: 5).

Authoring an essay against the political correctness of Wu Han's play was not without risk. Wu Han had been an established literary figure and a senior official as the vice-mayor of Beijing. More important, he had the patronage of even higher-level figures such as Politburo member and Beijing secretary Peng Zhen, as well as Lu Dingyi, who headed the powerful Central Propaganda Department (Huang 2000: 279). Offending senior propaganda officials seriously jeopardized one's career. This was a lesson that Qi Benyu had learned in 1964, when he wrote an essay attacking a *historical* figure from the Taiping Rebellion approved by the Central Propaganda Department. Soon after Qi had circulated his polemic, Zhou Yang, the vice-head of the propaganda department, organized a conference to attack his essay (Qi 2016: 150). Without Mao's intervention to defend him, Qi's literary career likely would have ended.

Although Yao and Zhang had known all along through Jiang Qing that the essay had the backing of the "highest level," they likely were aware that Mao insisted on the secrecy of the project so that he could withdraw support if the tides had turned against him. This would have left Zhang, Yao, and others in the Luosiding team like Zhu Yongjia at the mercy of Wu Han and his powerful patrons. They likely would have been expelled from their positions, if not worse.

When "Criticism of the Historical Play *Hairui Dismissed From Office*" was officially published by the leading Shanghai newspaper *Wenhuibao* in November 10, 1965, a nervous Zhang had the *Wenhuibao* send reporters to major cities around China to gauge the reaction of scholars and officials to the essay (Zheng 2017: 163). For the next month or so, Zhang and Yao lived through a nervous period when they did not know whether Mao would publicly endorse their essay. Meanwhile, the Beijing Municipal Government, where Wu Han served as vice-mayor, refused to have its main news outlet *Beijing Ribao* carry the essay. Even after *Wenhuibao* printed "Criticism" as a pamphlet, Beijing refused to distribute it (Zheng 2017: 168). Finally, on December 21, 1965, Mao met with several senior officials in the propaganda realm, including his two former secretaries Tian Jiaying and Chen Boda, and revealed to them that he supported "Criticism" (Zheng 2017: 172). Word spread quickly that Mao himself was critical of the play by Wu Han. Astonishingly, Peng Zhen showed his true grits as a veteran cadre and argued with Mao about the political nature of Wu Han's play even after he had found out that Mao was behind "Criticism" (Zheng 2017: 173). He even sent a sharply worded warning to Zhang Chunqiao via Hu Sheng that Zhang should stop his criticism of Wu Han immediately (Dittmer 1998: 59). Perhaps wanting Peng Zhen to fall deeper into his political trap, Mao allowed Peng Zhen to convene a group of senior propaganda department officials, including Lu Dingyi, Zhou Yang, and Wu Lengxi, to investigate the issue of whether *Hairui* was a political or a historical play (MacFarquhar 1997a: 453). In retrospect, Peng Zhen's resistance to Mao seemed incomprehensible, but with the Four Cleans Movement still in full swing, Liu Shaoqi's faction was still in ascendance in late 1965. Given that Mao's errors during the Great Leap Forward were still fresh on everyone's mind, Peng Zhen might have gambled that Mao would not have wanted to launch an all-out attack on the Northern Bureau faction.

When Peng Zhen's group finished its assessment in February 1966, the document was dubbed the "February Outline" and presented to Mao. Not surprisingly, the "February Outline" argued that Wu Han's play had nothing to do with the politics surrounding Peng Dehuai's dismissal in 1959 and was merely a historical play (MacFarquhar 1997a: 460). An incensed Mao instructed Zhang Chunqiao days later to draft a document to "thoroughly attack" the "February Outline," while Jiang Qing instructed other junior scribblers such as Guan Feng and Wang Li to write similar polemics against Peng's report (Zheng 2017: 188). With Mao's backing, Zhang then rammed the attack on the "February Outline" through as an official document of the Shanghai Party Committee over the objection of Mayor Cao Diqiu (Zheng 2017: 188). By this point, the risk to Zhang and Yao was smaller because Mao had made public his displeasure with Peng, and to the surprise of Peng and others in his faction, the coalition of Mao and the group of junior ideologues created an inner party tide that overwhelmed them. By the May 6, 1966 enlarged Politburo meeting, which featured a long denunciation of Peng Zhen by Zhang Chunqiao, Liu Shaoqi was forced to sacrifice one of his top lieutenants and launched into a vitriolic attack on Peng Zhen, even accusing him of fomenting a "coup" against Chairman Mao (Zheng 2017: 192). The content of Zhang's attack of Peng Zhen was written up formally as a Central Committee circular published in the *People's Daily*, the famous "May 16th Circular" that marked the beginning of the Cultural Revolution. Two weeks later at the May 23 enlarged Politburo meeting, Peng Zhen, Luo Ruiqing, Lu Dingyi, and Yang Shangkun, all of whom had been accused by Mao of various plots, were summarily dismissed from their positions (Li and Shu 2009: 339).

Because Liu Shaoqi thoroughly denounced longtime comrades such as Peng Zhen and Lu Dingyi, Mao had no excuse with which to criticize him. If the Red Guard had not emerged, Liu might have remained a thorn in Mao's side for years to come. Fortunately for Mao, the Red Guards emerged with the encouragement of the scribblers mafia, which created opportunities for Mao to entrap Liu and Deng Xiaoping. In their barest form, Mao's maneuvers in the summer of 1966 were tantamount to enlarging the selectorate so that actors with preferences closer to his own constituted the winning majority, a move that Mao himself called "mixing in sand" (Bueno de Mesquita et al. 2003). Equally important, the emergence of a new group of political actors allowed Mao to create a new issue space, the support and opposition of the Red Guards, where the new actors, the Red Guards, were guaranteed to side with Mao.

In addition to a scathing denunciation of Peng Zhen and Wu Han, the May 16 Circular also gave rise to the Red Guards by warning readers of a continual threat from within the party: "people like Khrushchev are sleeping next to us" (Central Committee 1966). From this call for vigilance, bands of rebellious students at Beijing high schools and universities began to form into "Red Guards" to overthrow "people like Khrushchev" who had oppressed them (Walder 2015: 208). Teachers, department chairs, university presidents who had slighted students or colleagues became targets of ferocious verbal and even physical attacks by the rapidly developing Red Guard movement. At the prestigious Peking University (PKU), Kang Sheng, Mao's henchman with NKVD training, secretly sent his wife to encourage members of the philosophy department to post a poster attacking the university leadership (Walder 2015: 215). Nie Yuanzi, a mid-level university administrator who had engaged in a prolonged power struggle with her colleagues, responded with a handful of colleagues by penning the first big-character poster lambasting university president Lu Ping (Walder 2009: 36). When Mao signaled his support for Nie by publishing her poster in the party's major publications on June 1, Lu Ping and his supporters at PKU were summarily removed, thus setting the stage for similar power seizures in universities and high schools across China (Walder 2009: 37).

As the Red Guard movement engulfed campuses across Beijing in June 1966, Mao was ensconced in Hangzhou in a leisurely manner, so on June 9, Liu Shaoqi, Zhou Enlai, Deng Xiaoping, Chen Boda, Tao Zhu, and Kang Sheng went there to discuss the emerging Red Guard movement with Mao (Liu and Chen 1996: 330). Although Liu already had suffered defeats in losing close allies such as Peng Zhen and Yang Shangkun, he still was the patron of a powerful faction and still the second most powerful official in China. Thus, Liu argued with Mao on what to do with the Red Guards and suggested that the Cultural Revolution in the factories and in the countryside should be "merged with the Four Cleans Movement," which Liu had controlled through the work teams (Liu and Chen 1996: 330). The meeting did not decide on a strict course of action for the Red Guards, and the rest of the leadership returned to Beijing to ponder a plan to restore order on the campuses.

Upon returning to Beijing, Liu and Deng began to advocate for stricter control over the Cultural Revolution through the work teams (Walder 2009: 30). At a June enlarged Politburo Standing Committee meeting that he chaired, Liu Shaoqi laid out the rationale for imposing stricter control: "cutting off party leadership is no good because the vast majority of party committees are good, so we must not overthrow everything" (Liu and Chen 1996: 331). On June 20, Liu went one step further and endorsed as model the experience of the PKU work team, which had put an end to "chaotic struggling" on campus in "a speedy manner" (Liu and Chen 1996: 330). After the debate with Mao in Hangzhou, Liu almost certainly knew that the order to suppress the Red Guards went against Mao's wishes. Yet, for Liu, the Leninist discipline that required lower-level masses and party members to obey higher-level party authorities was much more important to preserve than the possible displeasure of Mao (Dittmer 1998: 71). With work teams occupying campuses around Beijing, the nascent Red Guard movement was on the verge of collapse.

In the midst of this crackdown, the scribbler mafia played the crucial role of cheerleading Red Guard rebels, letting them know that although the formal party channels had signaled repression, powerful leaders, including Mao himself, still supported Red Guard rebellion. When Kuai Dafu, a rebel leader at Tsinghua University, reported to the Central Cultural Revolution Group (CCRG) of work team suppression, Jiang Qing summoned Qi Benyu, Guan Feng, and Wang Li and told them to "rise up and resist" (Qi 2016: 215). According to Qi Benyu, he confessed to Jiang his fear that because they were "small figures with soft voices," they would be ignored, to which Jiang Qing replied, "[T]his is typical slave mentality" (Qi 2016: 215). Still, Qi, Guan, and Wang debated who would take the risk of going to Tsinghua to galvanize the rebels against the work team, which was led by none other than Liu Shaoqi's patrician wife, Wang Guangmei. Guan Feng finally agreed to go and publicly expressed support for the rebels at Tsinghua, which immediately led to an angry phone call from Wang Guangmei to the CCRG accusing Guan of "interfering with the Chairman Mao line" (Qi 2016: 215). Again, this was a very serious charge, and had Mao not later revealed his condemnation of the work teams, the scribblers who encouraged the Red Guards would have been severely criticized and punished for "interfering." In any event, after Guan Feng's visit to Tsinghua, the other scribblers also began to visit major campuses in Beijing on a regular basis to cheer on the rebels' resistance to the work teams and party authorities, where necessary (Qi 2016: 215).

Fortunately for the Red Guards and for the scribblers, Mao returned to Beijing on July 18 after watching Liu's handling of the Red Guards for some weeks. The next day, at a Politburo meeting presided over by Liu Shaoqi, Chen Boda proposed the withdrawal of the work teams, but the proposal was rebuked by Liu, Deng, and the majority at the meeting (Liu and Chen 1996: 335). Chen, who was the scribbler with the deepest ties to Mao, likely was sent by Mao to test the resolve of the pro-work team coalition and perhaps even to create an opportunity for Liu and Deng to further demonstrate their willingness to "obstruct the mass movement" (Liu and Chen 1996: 335). To be sure, work teams had not "obstruct(ed) the mass movement" in all cases (Walder 2009). Nonetheless, at the July 24 Central Secretariat-CCRG joint meeting chaired by Mao, he denounced Liu's decision to send the work teams as an obstruction to the CR and further charged that the work teams "necessarily helped the counter-revolutionaries and helped the black gang" (Liu and Chen 1996: 332). By the August 1, 1966 11th plenum, the work team line was completely repudiated, and Liu himself admitted that he had committed a "directional and line error" (Liu and Chen 1996: 333).

The one-year period between the August 1966 11th plenum and the 1967 Wuhan incident was the high watermark in the lives of the scribblers mafia. After the defeat of the work team line, they no longer faced the dread of being criticized and punished for supporting the Red Guards and for writing vitriolic polemics against senior leaders such as Liu, Peng, and Deng. Meanwhile, even relatively junior members of the CCRG such as Guan Feng and Wang Li had become the voices of Chairman Mao himself. They gave speeches and radio broadcasts to millions of Red Guards, providing specific instructions on how to carry out the revolution and whom to attack. For example, in an August 1966 broadcast, Guan Feng instructed students that "some while ago, some comrades committed an error of direction, mainly due to triggering some students to struggle against other students instead of unifying students to point the spear head against the capitalist authorities. This is completely wrong and causes disunity among the students" (Guan 1966).

Into 1967, as power seizures spread to numerous provinces, members of the CCRG were sent to the provinces to adjudicate power struggles between various Red Guard groups or to receive their delegations in Beijing. In one example, on being asked by Red Guards from the Beijing Hospital on whether former Red Guard messenger Gu Xichun should be detained, Qi Benyu answered, "[Y]ou don't have to detain him, just struggle against him...he is a minor figure, one of numerous dog legs. It's not worthwhile to hold a struggle session" (Wang and Qi 1966). The Red Guards in turn called members of the CCRG "central leading cadre" (中央首长), an exalted title typically bestowed upon top officials like Premier Zhou Enlai (Jiang et al. 1967). Their words became "central instructions" obeyed by the Red Guards, thus influencing the fate of millions of people in the middle of this maelstrom. Besides instructing the Red Guard, CCRG also instructed core party organs such as the Central Organization Department (Wang 1967). Instead of being locked up in secretive offices writing attack polemics, the scribblers enjoyed the limelight and the power that came with being senior party cadres.

To be sure, even during this triumphant year, the scribblers were asked to take great risks for Mao. For Zhang Chunqiao, a defining moment came in November 1966 when the CCRG asked him to return to Shanghai to deal with the sticky situation of a large group of worker rebels blocking the main railroad between Beijing and Shanghai. This came about after a large gathering of worker rebels organized themselves into the Workers' General Headquarters (WGH) and demanded an audience with the Shanghai Mayor Cao Diqiu (Perry and Li 1997: 33). After being ignored, thousands of worker rebels took over a Beijing-bound train, vowing to complain about the behavior of the Shanghai Municipal Government to the CCRG, but the Shanghai government pulled another trick on the newly formed WGH by ordering the train to go no further than the suburban station of Anting (Zheng 2017: 230). Frustrated and fearful of retribution, the WGH resorted to a sit-in on the most important railroad line in China at that time, stopping all rail traffic between China's two largest cities.

At this point, CCRG sent Zhang to Anting with the unenviable mission of unblocking the rail line, whatever it took. On the one hand, Zhang could have supported his colleagues in the Shanghai Party Committee, which likely would have ended in a crackdown on the Anting protestors. Such a move would have left Zhang vulnerable to charges of "obstructing the mass movement." On the other hand, he could have given in to the demands of the nascent WGH and recognized it as a "revolutionary organization," but that violated deeply held rules of obeying higher-level party authorities in the Communist Party and would have left Zhang vulnerable to a number of different charges. When he arrived on November 11, he immediately met with rebel leaders, including Wang Hongwen and Pan Guoping, who told Zhang that they wanted recognition as a "revolutionary and legal organization" and official acknowledgment that their action in Anting was made necessary by the actions of the Shanghai Party Committee (Perry and Li 1997: 33). Zhang, to his great credit, persuaded the workers to unblock the railroad after an intense bout of negotiations, and after further talks with the workers, he signed a document that granted the WGH their major requests (Perry and Li 1997: 33). Perhaps because of exhaustion, Zhang did not seek the permission of the CCRG leadership or of Mao before granting WGH its requests (Zheng 2017: 244). If his decision was wrong, he alone would have borne the brunt of the fallout. Fortunately for Zhang, Jiang Qing realized the enormity of the decision and immediately approached Mao, who gave his approval for Zhang's decision (Zheng 2017: 247). After this key episode, Zhang and Yao Wenyuan, who had become prominent in the Shanghai government by this point, began to sideline the existing Shanghai leadership, culminating to the January 1967 power seizure by these two and their support coalition of local scribblers and workers' rebels (Perry and Li 1997: 19).

PAWNS TO THE SACRIFICE: STRATEGIC PURGING OF SCRIBBLERS

In the first phase of the Cultural Revolution, the scribblers served the indispensable functions of laying risky traps for Mao's enemies and cheerleading the highly unorthodox Red Guard movement. However, by late 1967, a little over one year after the start of the Cultural Revolution, the majority of the founding members of the CCRG had fallen from power and were locked up in Qincheng Prison, some destined to stay there for decades to come. By the time they emerged from prison in the 1990s, they were old men trying to remember their brief glory days in the 1960s. Their loyalty to Mao, their ambition, and Mao's duplicity made them ready fodder in the emerging struggle between Mao and Lin Biao. The Wuhan incident and the 1970 Lushan Conference, which precipitated the downfall of several key scribblers, also illustrated a major pitfall of mobilizing ignorant pawns in political struggles – rivals also could exploit the pawns' ignorance and ambition and use them against the dictator.

Furthermore, the emerging split between Mao and Lin Biao serves as a controlled comparison between the behavior of the last remaining veteran faction, Lin Biao's First Front Army faction, and members of the scribblers mafia. Whereas the scribblers dared not coordinate with each other without clear support of either Mao or Lin Biao, Lin Biao's faction members coordinated on their own time and, again, at times even against the explicit wishes of Mao. Also, when one of them got into trouble, the scribblers did nothing to protect each other besides approaching Mao for greater clarity of his intentions. In contrast, Lin Biao spent much of the last year of his life defending key members of his faction, urging them to minimize the severity of their self-criticism in the aftermath of the 1970 Lushan Conference. The tendency of veterans to stage coordinated resistance against the dictator explains why Mao, in his twilight years, favored the coalition of the weak almost entirely.

As discussed toward the end of Chapter 3, the Wuhan incident was the first skirmish between Mao and his "dearest comrade" Lin Biao. While Mao wanted to preserve the Fourth Front Army (FFA) contingent to balance against Lin Biao, Lin saw an opportunity in the Wuhan incident to eradicate a major rival bloc in the military. However, scribblers had only the vaguest notion of the historical rupture between the First and the Fourth Front Army and failed to discern the different views on the FFA between Mao and Lin at the time. As a result, when Lin Biao issued instructions to attack FFA veterans, some scribblers readily agreed to do so, not knowing that this would bring down Mao's wrath.

Available recollection from the surviving scribblers suggests that Lin Biao took full advantage of the scribblers' ignorance to launch an all-out purge of FFA veterans. Immediately after the July 20 incident in Wuhan, when Mao's emissaries, Wang Li and Xie Fuzhi, were roughed up and kidnapped by workers' Red Guards close to the Wuhan Military Region, Lin Biao presided over the first meeting on the incident in Beijing, listening to the reports by Wang Li and Xie Fuzhi intently (Wang 2001: 132). The meeting quickly decided that the Wuhan incident was a "counterrevolutionary uprising" (反革命暴乱), a very serious charge and the same charge as the one laid on the escape incident orchestrated by FFA officer Xu Shiyou thirty years prior in Yan'an (Wang 2001: 132). On July 24, 1967, when Wuhan Military Region Commander Chen Zaidao was escorted to Beijing, Lin Biao ordered a mass rally the next day criticizing Chen and welcoming Wang Li, the hero of the Wuhan incident (Wang 2001: 133). In his speech at the rally, Lin Biao pointed out that Chen Zaidao and his allies constituted "a Liu-Deng line with guns" and that the party needed to "overthrow Chen Zaidao and a small handful in the military" (Wang 2001: 133). For weeks afterward, attacking "a small handful in the military" became a national movement carried out by radical scribblers and Red Guards in Wuhan, Nanjing, Beijing, and Chengdu, which were headquarters of military regions commanded by key FFA veterans (Wang 2001: 809). In his memoir, Wang Li recalls Lin Biao saying, "now we can make a big story out of Chen Zaidao," suggesting that Lin had meant for the "small handful" movement to be a widespread one to eradicate FFA veterans from the military (Wang 2001: 133). Without an understanding of the role that the "counterrevolutionary" FFA played in Mao's power strategy, ambitious radicals heeded Lin Biao's instructions with great zeal, believing that it was another opportunity to appease top leaders such as Mao and Lin Biao.

Lin Biao sent instructions through Wang Li that Red Guards were to "grasp the Wuhan Incident to resolve the problem of 'a small handful in the military'" (Chen 1988). Qi Benyu, by his own admission, heeded Lin Biao's order, conveyed through Ye Qun, and instructed Red Guard bands led by Kuai Dafu and Han Aijing to ransack the homes of Xu Xiangqian and Xu Haidong, two key FFA veterans (Qi 2016: 311). With direct encouragement from "central leaders," Red Guards ransacked Xu Xiangqian's home, looking for "criminal evidence" (Xu 1987: 837). Meanwhile, the CCRG sent a junior cadre to Nanjing to galvanize Red Guards into attacking another key FFA veteran and commander of the Nanjing Military Region, Xu Shiyou (Walder and Dong 2011). To be sure, Red Guards were not completely ignorant of Mao's desire to protect some FFA veterans. On one occasion, Kuai Dafu asked Wang Li, "Aren't some Fourth Front Army people obedient to Mao?" to which Wang answered, "some are; some are not" (Chen 1988). That apparently was sufficient assurance for Kuai to ransack the home of the second highest military officer in China at the time.

Scribblers also went into a feverish drive, producing dozens of editorials and articles in the major party and army newspapers linking the Wuhan incident with "a small handful in the military." In particular, on August 1, which was the founding day for the PLA, *Hongqi*, the lead journal for the Central Committee, published a headlining editorial entitled "The proletariat must tightly control the guns – commemorating the 40th anniversary of the founding of the PLA." After repeating harsh criticism against confirmed "plotters" in the military such as Peng Dehuai and Luo Ruiqing, the editorial further called for an attack on "a small handful in the party and in the military" (Hongqi Editorial Committee 1967):

Not long ago, a small handful of capitalist authorities in power in the party and in the military in Wuhan coalesced and repressed the proletariat revolutionary faction. Facts proved that we must further carry out great revolutionary critiques in order to thoroughly sweep capitalist authorities in power in the party and in the military into the trash heap.

The "a small handful in the military" campaign lasted well into August. On August 2, CCRG members summoned Red Guards from Wuhan and instructed them to spread their experience in purging "a small handful in the military" to other parts of the country so as to purge "other characters like Chen Zaidao" (Chen 1988: 523). As a result of this encouragement, many more rallies were held around China, especially in the headquarters of military regions dominated by FFA veterans.

Zhang Chunqiao prudently stayed out of the "a small handful in the military" campaign due to his position in the party hierarchy. The day after the Wuhan incident, Mao went to Shanghai to spend a few weeks. As the leader of Shanghai at the time, Zhang felt obligated to welcome Mao and to attend to his needs in Shanghai (Zheng 2017: 409). Soon after Mao's arrival, Zhang learned the true depth of Mao's desire to protect key FFA veterans. At a meeting with Zhang, Mao stated unambiguously, "I want to protect Xu Shiyou. If you want to overthrow Xu Shiyou, and Han Xianchu, and Chen Xilian, who will command the troops in battle?" (Zheng 2017: 410). Incidentally, the three names mentioned by Mao were FFA veterans who headed the Nanjing, Fuzhou, and Shenyang Military Regions, respectively. Nanjing and Fuzhou Military Regions were the ones targeted by Lin Biao in his remarks to radical scribblers. Zhang may have realized the emerging split between Mao and Lin and, in any event, carried out Mao's wishes to the letter and urged Jiangsu Red Guard to stop attacking Xu Shiyou (Zheng 2017: 410).

While Lin Biao pushed the "a small handful in the military" campaign into a feverish pitch, Mao was in Shanghai orchestrating the protection of key FFA veterans. He at first sent subtle hints to Lin Biao and others that he wanted the campaign stopped. For example, he ordered Yang Chengwu, the PLA chief of staff at the time, to not mention "a small handful in the military" during his remarks at the August 1, 1967 celebration in Beijing (Zheng 2017: 406). This subtle hint apparently had little effect, as the campaign continued to spread to military regions targeted by Lin due to Lin's continual encouragement of it. For example, on August 6, Lin Biao met with the new leaders of the Wuhan Military Regions, both First Front Army veterans, and told them, "Wuhan Incident was a very bad incident, but now it is very good...it thoroughly exposed the reactionary line of Chen Zaidao" (Li and Shu 2015b: 416).

Finally, upon hearing a report that Wang Li had instigated Red Guards to set fire to the British Embassy on August 22, 1967, Mao decided that the scribblers had to go. Curiously, instead of lambasting Guan and Wang for violating basic international law in ransacking the British embassy, Mao's wrath, expressed at a meeting with PLA Chief of Staff Yang Chengwu on August 25, was directed toward the August 1 editorial, which appeared annually to commemorate the founding of the PLA. Mao called the editorial, written under the supervision of Guan Feng but also Chen Boda, a "great, great, great poisonous weed," an extremely harsh label that automatically conferred guilt on authors and editors of the essay (Zheng 2017: 406). Also at the meeting with Yang Chengwu,

Mao uttered a puzzling phrase: "return to me my Great Wall" (还我长城) (Zheng 2017: 406). On the face of it, there was no need to restore the "Great Wall," a common metaphor for the PLA. Lin Biao, Mao's closest follower, had established dominance over the PLA by moving decision-making power to the Central Military Commission Administrative Office, populated by loyal First Front Army veterans. Instead, Mao's "Great Wall" likely was not the PLA per se but his strategy for controlling the PLA through balancing Lin Biao with FFA veterans.

Because they lacked their own power bases in the party, Jiang Qing and Chen Boda, who had enthusiastically supported the "a small handful in the military" campaign due to Lin Biao's encouragement, immediately laid the blame on the junior scribblers, including the hero of the Wuhan incident Wang Li, as well as Guan Feng. At an enlarged Politburo meeting on the night of August 26, Zhou Enlai read out the errors of the scribblers, including the ransacking of the British Embassy and support for the "a small handful in the military" campaign. When Chen Boda heard that Mao considered the August 1 *Hongqi* editorial to be a "great, great, great poisonous weed," he immediately pled that Guan Feng and Wang Li had published it without his sign-off, even though Chen was the chief editor of *Hongqi* (Qi 2016: 315). To his credit, Guan Feng engaged in a spirited defense of himself and his fellow scribblers, arguing that it would have been impossible for the editorial to be published without Chen Boda's sign-off and that Chen's signature was clearly on the final draft of the editorial (Qi 2016: 315). Zhou Enlai immediately verified that Guan's testimony was true, but Chen responded that because he had taken a sleeping pill at the time, he could not recall clearly what he had done. Zhou then sealed the fate of the junior scribblers by accepting Chen's excuse and putting the bulk of the blame for the *Hongqi* editorial on Wang Li and Guan Feng, resulting in their immediate arrests during the meeting (Qi 2016: 315). Zhou likely saw the emerging split between Mao and Lin and sought to bury the hatchet by sacrificing the scribblers. Although Jiang Qing and Zhang Chunqiao did not come to their defense, one account of the August 26 meeting had them sobbing after Guan and Wang had been detained (Qi 2016: 315).

The arrest of Guan and Wang led to a wave of arrests for junior scribblers under them, including Lin Jie, the deputy editor of *Hongqi* who had written the August 1 editorial; Mu Xin, the editor of *Guangming Daily*; Zhao Yiya, the editor of *Liberation Army Daily*; as well as prominent academic leftists such as Pan Zinian, Lin Yushi, and Wu Chuanqi (MacFarquhar and Schoenhals 2006: 233). Even Jiang

Qing's secretary Yan Changgui was arrested as a member of the "May 16th" group, as these junior scribblers were labeled, for having past ties with Guan Feng (Yang 2014: 23). Wang Li and Guan Feng soon found themselves accused of a long list of crimes, including spying for the KGB (MacFarquhar and Schoenhals 2006: 232). After several months of interrogation, they were transferred to Qincheng Prison, where they spent the next two and a half decades in solitary confinement. Qi Benyu, another key scribbler, survived the Guan-Wang purge, only to be purged at the end of 1967 because he had neglected to forward to Jiang Qing a cache of KMT propaganda gossip about Jiang Qing and Mao from the 1930s (Qi 2016: 350). By the end of the Wuhan incident, the first skirmish between Lin Biao and Mao, the majority of the scribblers who had helped Mao launch the Cultural Revolution had been purged.

The surviving scribblers did their best to pick up the pieces, but with the purge of so many propaganda cadres, key publications such as *Hongqi* could no longer function and had to suspend publication (Zheng 2017: 438). In July 1968, the scribblers' role was further marginalized when Mao officially disbanded the Red Guards, depriving the surviving CCRG members their key constituency and their eyes and ears in the provinces (MacFarquhar and Schoenhals 2006: 250). Zhang Chunqiao and Yao Wenyuan consolidated control in Shanghai by further repressing dissenting Red Guards and by forming their own scribbler team to author polemics and to gather intelligence across the country (Zheng 2017: 440).

THE CLASH ON LUSHAN

With his former enemies completely destroyed and the Red Guards disbursed to the countryside, Mao wanted to consolidate the gains of the Cultural Revolution by electing a new slate of formal leadership for the party. Thus, in 1968, Mao called on his coalition of Lin Biao and surviving scribblers to prepare for the 9th Party Congress. However, as Mao turned seventy-five, he realized that the new coalition formed after the first tumultuous year of the Cultural Revolution might not be lasting. To be sure, Lin Biao, who had served him loyally for decades and who had made the Cultural Revolution possible, was emerging as the obvious successor. The surviving scribblers such as Zhang Chunqiao and Yao Wenyuan meanwhile served as guardians of his radical legacy. Yet this was far from a stable equilibrium, as Mao's health deteriorated. The scribblers were so weak that a single utterance by Mao or Lin for that matter led to the wholesale purge of them. At the same time, Lin Biao had consolidated control over the military, which increased the odds of him usurping Mao's power before Mao's passing.

More troublesome for the relationship between Mao and Lin, "Mao's nature is to be suspicious," as observed by party historian Gao Wenqian (Gao 2003: 274). Thus, even if Lin had toed Mao's line absolutely in the run-up to the succession, Mao would have suspected a potential coup anyway and might have preemptively purged Lin Biao. Key Lin Biao follower Wu Faxian articulated this fear in the aftermath of the 1970 Lushan Conference: "Lin Biao followed Mao's instruction and sacrificed Chen Boda in order to save us, but that did not really save us and only allowed Mao to divide and conquer us. Such examples were numerous" (Wu 2006: 812). In response to that possible scenario, Lin did not want to sacrifice core followers, which would have weakened him substantially relative to Mao, allowing Mao to destroy him more easily. Lin Biao's uncertainty about the exact degree of Mao's suspicion instead created incentives for him to consolidate power in the party, thus triggering Mao's suspicion and paving the road for the eventual clash between the two. As the clash between Mao and Lin intensified, both sides used scribblers to spar with the other side, seeking to signal credibly while limiting potential costs. This created a highly risky situation for scribblers, even senior ones like Chen Boda, as they became the first casualties in the emerging conflict between Mao and Lin.

Chen Boda, the chairman of the Central Cultural Revolution Group, had been Mao's tutor of the Marxist ideological canons and secretary since the 1930s, but as Lin's role as the designated successor became clear, he increasingly shifted his allegiance to Lin. A key episode that sealed his alienation from Mao came when the chairman assigned him the task to write the 9th Party Congress political report in 1969, a key document that was expected to shape policies for years to come (Gao 2003: 269). At first, Chen's draft focused on the importance of economic construction, an agenda that Lin Biao had supported, but after reviewing it, Mao thought that Chen's draft neglected the accomplishments of the Cultural Revolution and reassigned the drafting to Zhang Chunqiao, Yao Wenyuan, and Kang Sheng (Wu 2006: 740). Also, Chen was tasked with finishing the report by the scheduled start date of the congress – March 15, 1969 – but he failed to deliver a draft on time so that the congress had to be postponed to April 1 (Zheng 2017: 521). The drafting team led by Zhang Chunqiao, meanwhile, began to deliver completed drafts to Mao for review within a few days of receiving the assignment (Zheng 2017: 521). The reassignment was enormously embarrassing for a key scribbler such as Chen Boda, whose power derived largely from his ability to deliver key polemics and documents to the top leadership. After this embarrassing episode, Chen threw in his lot with Lin Biao because Mao increasingly favored Zhang Chunqiao as the main scribbler (Zheng 2017: 531).

Regardless of this unpleasant episode, Mao was able to consolidate his control over the upper echelon of the party at the 9th Party Congress. Officials with historical ties to Liu Shaoqi were largely removed from the Central Committee, although a handful of veteran cadres survived as figureheads in the Central Committee (Liu et al. 2018). Beyond being enshrined as the designated successor to Mao, Lin Biao also secured Politburo seats for his followers, including his wife Ye Qun and also Wu Faxian, Qiu Huizuo, Huang Yongsheng, and Li Zuopeng (Shih et al. 2015). Chen Boda remained the most powerful scribbler in the party hierarchy as an official Politburo Standing Committee member, while other radical scribblers such as Zhang, Yao, and even Jiang Qing secured promotions into the Politburo. The purging of Mao's rivals required the systematic "investigation" of "counterrevolutionary crimes" by the police and military bureaucracies (Schoenhals 1996). The key enforcers in those bureaucracies, Xie Fuzhi and Kang Sheng, received seats in the Politburo, with Kang Sheng moving to the Standing Committee. Finally, to balance against Lin Biao in the military, Mao insisted on Politburo seats for senior FFA officers – Xu Shiyou, Chen Xilian, Li Xiannian, and Li Desheng (Zhu 2007: 81).

Through the promotion of Lin Biao's faction and the scribblers at the 9th Party Congress, Mao formally put in place a ruling coalition mainly composed of the "victors" of the Cultural Revolution, but this was not a complete coalition of the weak. As such, the logic of mutual distrust accelerated with the formal designation of Lin Biao as the successor. Mao's suspicion of Lin's rising influence and Lin's desire to credibly signal his power set the stage for the 1970 Lushan Conference, a medium-intensity clash that led to the purge of the veteran scribbler Chen Boda. The conflict began over a seemingly trivial debate about whether Maoist development of Marxism was a work of "genius" and whether Mao should be given the largely ceremonial position of state chairman (MacFarquhar and Schoenhals 2006: 328). The first skirmish was actually between Zhang Chunqiao and Lin Biao follower Wu Faxian at a preparatory meeting of the Lushan Conference on August 13, 1970. At the meeting, Wu Faxian proposed adding "with genius, creativity, and wholeness" to describe Mao's contribution to Marxism, but Zhang, noting that Mao had earlier rejected similar hyperboles, argued that such exaggeration made a mockery of Mao's contribution to Marxism and that only buffoons like Khrushchev would use such wordings (Li and Shu 2015b: 485). Zhang and Kang also had a debate with Wu over whether the position of state chairman should be written into the new state constitution and whether Mao should serve in it. Mao had repeatedly rejected this proposal at this point, but Wu, with the urging of Lin Biao, still defended Mao as the state chairman (MacFarquhar and Schoenhals 2006: 328). According to evidence gathered by Lin Biao's secretary, Lin approved of Wu's debate with Zhang and urged Wu not to back down on that issue during the Lushan Conference, scheduled to take place just a few days later (Li and Shu 2015b: 489).

These debates came to a head at the August 1970 Lushan Conference. At the opening meeting, Lin Biao made a speech that criticized those who opposed the notion of Mao's "genius" contribution to Marxism (Wu 2006: 793). Wary of Mao's political traps, Lin even asked Mao for his permission to raise the "genius" issue prior to his speech, and Mao approved Lin's remarks but urged him to not mention Zhang Chunqiao by name (Wu 2006: 793). After Lin set the tone, Chen Boda and Lin's followers in the military began to criticize Zhang Chunqiao and Kang Sheng for their opposition of the creation of a state chairman position and of enshrining Mao's "genius" thoughts in the state constitution (MacFarquhar and Schoenhals 2006: 340). According to a participant of the conference, Lin Biao further mobilized Chen Boda and Wu Faxian to circulate a list of "genius" mentions by Marx, Engel, and Mao to conference participants (Chen 2007: 366). For the first part of the conference, Zhang and Kang faced a barrage of attack by Chen Boda at the northern China discussion group.[2] Veterans like Yang Dezhi, Han Xianchu, and Chen Yi, who had resented Zhang Chunqiao's meteoric rise since the Cultural Revolution, took the opportunity to attack him (Miao 2011). Chen Boda then printed a summary of the criticism at the northern China discussion group and distributed it to the conference attendees, which labeled those who opposed Mao's "genius" thoughts as "power grabbers, plotters, and reactionaries" (Wu 2006: 799).

In a panic, Zhang Chunqiao, Yao Wenyuan, and Jiang Qing ran to Mao for help, and Mao assured them of his support (Wu 2006: 800).

---

[2] At the 1970 Lushan Conference, participants were divided into regional groups to discuss the main issues of the conference. Heads of the discussion groups then regularly conveyed the summaries of the discussion to Chairman Mao and Zhou Enlai. See (Wu 2006).

Mao also revealed his true preference to another key group – members of the FFA. According to Xu Shiyou's biographers, Mao summoned Xu in the middle of a discussion held by the East China Group that Xu chaired in Lushan and told him in no uncertain terms that he did not want to be state chairman. As a result of Mao's clear signal, the Eastern China discussion group did not pursue the state chairmanship issue, which protected them from the subsequent political fallout (Wen and Li 1998).

Similar to the 1959 Lushan Conference, Mao revealed his real intentions halfway through the conference, which completely changed the tone of the conference and put Chen Boda and Lin Biao on the defensive. On August 25, 1970, Mao suddenly informed Lin Biao and the other participants that the meeting would reconvene in two days and that issues of state chairmanship and the "genius" theory should not be mentioned again (Wu 2006: 801). At a tense Politburo meeting on August 26, Mao told his audience that those who wished him to be state chairman clearly also wished for his death. He then turned to Lin Biao and sarcastically offered him the job: "[I]f you want the position, go ahead and have it" (Li and Shu 2009: 1187). The split between Mao and Lin could barely be disguised, and those in attendance knew that Mao saw Lin's backing of the state chairmanship issue as a power grab. On August 31, just after the Lushan Conference, Mao summoned his former bodyguard Wang Dongxing and FFA veterans Xu Shiyou and Han Xianchu to a secret meeting in Nanchang and told them in no uncertain terms that he considered Lin Biao the main culprit of the "plot" at the Lushan Conference (Li 2002: 201). After the meeting, Xu Shiyou ordered another FFA veteran Xiao Yongyin to send trusted troops to guard the major rail lines between Nanjing and Shanghai and between Shanghai and Beijing. Xu's secretary also began to carry around a scrambler for all of Xu's telephone calls (Li 2002: 203).

Once again, Zhou Enlai, who stood between Mao and Lin, saw that the only way to smooth things over was to sacrifice a scribbler, in this case Chen Boda. To be sure, Chen Boda spearheaded the debate on the chairmanship issue and the genius issue, especially at the north China group meeting during the Lushan Conference. However, without Lin Biao's private and public endorsement of those issues and without Wu Faxian's forceful interventions, Chen would not have raised these issues. Even a senior scribbler like Chen would not have dared to defend an issue so forcefully without clear backing from Mao or from Lin. Yet, like Guan Feng and Wang Li before him, Chen soon found himself accused by the Politburo of starting a "military club" and for being a traitor and a

Trotskyite (Miao 2011; Wu 2006). Chen tried to salvage himself by admitting in written self-criticism that he "sang a tune that clashed with Chairman Mao," but still Mao opted for the much more serious charges raised by Kang Sheng (Miao 2011). He was soon arrested and put into jail, where he stayed until one year before his death in 1989. By sacrificing his own former secretary, Mao sent an unambiguous signal to Lin Biao about his displeasure of Lin's power plays. At the same time, despite Chen's seniority, his relatively small network in the party made him a relatively low-cost sacrifice for both Lin and Mao.

After the Lushan Conference, Mao did not immediately press for the purge of other members of Lin Biao's camp, but they all had to write and deliver self-criticism for supporting erroneous lines (Gao 2003: 325; Wu 2006: 803). Kang Sheng and Jiang Qing tried to minimize the guilt of Lin's core followers by accusing Chen Boda of "fooling" the participants of the Lushan Conference (Li and Shu 2015b: 496). Although Lin Biao sacrificed Chen Boda without a second thought, he initially called on his followers in the military to resist writing self-criticisms as Mao and Zhou Enlai had requested (Wu 2006: 807). This kind of coordination and resistance would have been impossible among the scribblers, especially given Mao's explicit condemnation of their actions. When pressure from Zhou Enlai to write self-criticism increased, Lin's followers had no choice but to write them but agreed to not mention Lin Biao, Ye Qun, or each other in their self-critiques (Wu 2006: 809).

Again, Lin Biao supported the limited self-criticism of his followers in the military but urged Ye Qun and others in his coterie to visit Jiang Qing to make informal apologies to Mao through his wife (Li and Shu 2015b: 496). Just after the Lushan Conference, Mao opened a door for Lin to save himself by asking him whether Wu Faxian should be replaced, but according to one account, Lin defended Wu's performance in running the air force (Wu 2006: 827). Lin continued to protect Wu Faxian even after Mao had expressed deep displeasure over a tepid self-criticism submitted by Wu in mid-September, calling the self-criticism "yet another lie told to save himself" (Mao 1987d). Arguably, had Lin Biao been willing to sacrifice a few of his key followers in the military, especially Wu Faxian, Mao might have spared him.

However, as Wu Faxian pointed out in his memoir, "in reality (sacrificing Chen Boda) did not save us, and we would have been divided and conquered by Mao" (Wu 2006: 827). Certainly for Lin Biao, sacrificing core followers high up in the military would have run into the classic commitment problem in war, wherein ceding key resources to a stronger enemy would have increased the asymmetry in capacity and enticed the enemy, in this case Mao, to further encroach on one's power (Powell 2006). For Lin Biao, the stakes were even higher than in relations between two countries because Lin Biao, as the designated successor, also had to nurse the strength of his faction against all future enemies in the party after Mao's passing. Thus, throughout much of 1971, Lin fought a defensive warfare of only heeding Mao's calls for self-criticism nominally in order to save key followers and to maintain the status quo relative power (Li and Shu 2015b: 508). Even months after Mao had passed words to Lin and his followers that a sincere and thorough self-criticism would have pleased him, none of Lin's followers did so, and they only wrote perfunctory self-criticism (Zhang 2008a: 316). For Lin's followers, if they had betrayed Lin Biao after the Lushan Conference by naming Lin as the instigator of the "genius" debate, Lin would have immediately fallen from power, most likely bringing the entire faction down with him. As the son of Lin Biao follower Huang Yongsheng puts it, "at the time...if my father had gone over to the side of the Chairman, the charges against Lin would have been much heavier" (Huang and Mi 2013: 43). According to Mao's bodyguard, who heard the story from Zhou Enlai, Mao tried to give Lin Biao a final chance to clear his name in early 1971 by having him chair a meeting aimed at "rectifying" the errors of Chen Boda, but Lin Biao found an excuse to evade that task (Zhang 2008b: 178).

Lin's reluctance to show contrition to Mao and, more importantly, to break up his power base in the military further placed him on a path toward a final confrontation with Mao. At the 1971 May First parade, Lin did not take his usual seat next to Mao, which was an unusual signal to the attending foreign dignitaries, including Prince Sihanouk (Chang and Halliday 2005: 545). After hearing a report on the meeting to criticize Chen Boda in the PLA General Staff Department in July 1971, Mao muttered that "their confessions are fake; the affairs on Lushan have not ended" (Li and Shu 2015b: 512). With that sentiment, both Lin and Mao in the summer of 1971 planned the elimination of each other. Mao, besides signaling clearly that Lin had to go, also finally put into place a coalition of the weak that ultimately helped him govern China in the twilight of his life.

CONCLUSION

Although lacking in political experience and in extensive networks in the party, scribblers who specialized in ideological polemics played important roles in Mao's power strategies in the twilight of his life. First, they undertook the risky task of setting up ideological traps against Mao's enemies in a way that protected Mao's own stature had things gone wrong. If other veterans had united in defense of Wu Han against Zhang and Yao's criticism, Mao would have sacrificed these junior scribblers at little cost to himself. Once the Red Guard movement had emerged, the scribblers also encouraged rebel students to maintain their attacks on the authorities even in the midst of crackdowns by central work teams, again an endeavor fraught with potential risks. If the Liu–Deng alliance had been triumphant in their attempt to restore order, the scribblers would have been sacrificed by Mao so as to preserve his own standing in the party. Once the Northern Bureau faction and Mao's other enemies had been purged after the first year of the Cultural Revolution, the scribblers found themselves occupying senior positions in Shanghai and in the propaganda apparatus. Here, they also served Mao's strategy in that their weakness assured Mao of their absolute obedience.

Their weakness and ignorance, however, also constituted a problem for Mao because Mao's emerging rival, Lin Biao, also learned that he could manipulate the scribblers into doing his biddings against Mao's wishes. Lin Biao mobilized the scribblers and the Red Guards in a nation-wide movement to eradicate veterans of the Red Fourth Front Army, which would have undermined Mao's emerging strategy of using the tainted faction to balance against Lin Biao. Not being fully aware of the tortuous history of the FFA, several of the scribblers naively thought that eradicating proven "counterrevolutionaries" for Lin Biao also would have served Mao's purpose and enthusiastically contributed to the "grab a small handful in the military" campaign. Mao, however, saw through Lin Biao's ploy and ordered a stop to the campaign in order to preserve his check against Lin Biao. Furthermore, to credibly show Lin Biao his displeasure, Mao purged several senior scribblers, condemning them to a life of solitary confinement, even though they had been loyal executioners of Mao's wishes up to that point. The surviving scribblers were in no position to defend each other and could only weep as Mao and Lin sparred with one another with the scribblers as fodder. The emerging clash between Lin Biao and Mao came to a head in 1971, with Mao and Lin each retrenching in their respective positions. As Chapter 5 shows, one of Mao's pawns, the besmirched FFA group, would play an important role in the final showdown between Mao and Lin, while the surviving scribblers completed Mao's coalition of the weak.

5

Realizing the Coalition of the Weak

Politics in the Late-Mao Period

Even at an abstract theoretical level, the power configuration in China after the 1969 9th Party Congress was highly unstable. On the one hand, Mao continued to be an active and powerful chairman of the party. On the other hand, Lin Biao, the anointed successor, had a great deal of control over the military. Without the possibility of other powerful factions in the party to check a potential fight between Mao and Lin, both sides had much temptation to eliminate the other if they believed they had sufficient power to do so (Acemoglu et al. 2008: 162). Fortunately for Mao, he had cultivated two disparate groups to help him govern China in the event of a purge of Lin Biao: the Fourth Front Army (FFA) and the surviving scribblers. Mao's strategy of cultivating the tainted FFA paid off handsomely. Instead of having to concede to Lin Biao's reluctance to carry out self-criticism or being forced to rely on Lin's followers, Mao forced Lin's hand, knowing that he could credibly threaten Lin with replacing the Lin Biao faction with FFA veterans. After Lin Biao fled, Mao carried out his threat and eradicated close associates of Lin Biao wholesale from the military, replacing them with veterans of the FFA. The Lin Biao incident on September 13, 1971, finally led to the full installation of the coalition of the weak.

Between the Lin Biao incident in 1971 and Mao's death in 1976, veterans of the Red Fourth Front Army came to dominate the People's Liberation Army (PLA). At the same time, with Zhou Enlai falling increasingly ill, propaganda work and even administration fell more and more onto the shoulders of the surviving scribblers and their allies, most of whom had come out of the workers' rebel movement in Shanghai and other workers' and peasants' mass representatives. This coalition of the weak removed any intraparty threat that could have jeopardized Mao's rule as his health deteriorated. Even if members of the weak coalition had joined forces, the FFA veterans and the scribblers could not have come close to defeating Mao due to their historical problems and weak networks. Mao made sure that a loose collection of surviving and rehabilitated veterans from the First Front Army could resist them. The ongoing low-intensity conflict between the scribblers and the rehabilitated veterans allowed Mao to rule without fearing a loss of power in the twilight of his life.

The coalition of the weak strategy was successful for Mao. The succession dilemma largely disappeared because no potential successor, except for Deng Xiaoping, could threaten Mao's power even as Mao's health failed him. The trade-off of this policy-making style was that high-level party and state institutions degenerated to meetings where participants competed with each other on who truly knew Mao's wishes. Larger institutions for enacting laws and policies, such as the National People's Congress and the Central Committee, stopped meeting altogether. Politics became endless squabbling between members of the weak coalitions in a competition to obtain Mao's favor, putting central policy making into a stasis. This meant that the coalition of the weak did not fundamentally solve the agency problem, especially as Mao's health began to fail. With his monitoring capacity failing, even members of the weak coalition began to deviate from his wishes, opting to maximize their own agenda for the post-Mao era.

The coalition of the weak strategy also failed to uphold Mao's legacy after his death. After his death, the staunchest defenders of his radical vision were arrested within weeks, while his anointed successor was sidelined within two years. Deng and his colleagues then pursued economic policies and ideological lines that were markedly different from those pursued in the late-Mao period. An important legacy of Mao's coalition strategy was the continual importance of the FFA group into the 1980s, who, along with other rehabilitated veterans, prevented Deng from ruling as a dictator. This led to a sustained period of collective leadership in the post-Mao era.

THE LIN BIAO INCIDENT AND FUSION OF THE COALITION OF THE WEAK

As early as the Wuhan incident in 1967, Mao had revealed his desire for the FFA and the scribblers to be important members, if not the keys, to his coalition. When Xu Shiyou ran off to the Dabie Mountains in a panic, Mao ordered Zhang Chunqiao personally to go to the mountain to persuade Xu to return to Shanghai (Zhu and Gu 2011). Zhang even offered to stay behind as a hostage while Xu went to Shanghai to see Mao. After Mao revealed that he wanted to protect Xu, a grateful Xu, an avid hunter, gave Zhang the pelt of a leopard that he had shot (Zhu and Gu 2011).

Prior to the Lin Biao incident, however, Lin Biao and his wife actively wooed Jiang Qing, the leader of the scribblers. Jiang Qing, likewise, paid homage to Lin Biao in anticipation of his ascent to the throne. According to Jiang Qing's personal secretary, between 1969 and the Lin Biao incident in September 1971, Jiang Qing directly called Lin's office 470 times (Yang 2014: 111). Even after the 1970 Lushan Conference, Ye Qun sought guidance from Jiang Qing on how to navigate Mao's wrath while still saving Lin Biao's standing in the party (Yang 2014: 155). For her part, Jiang Qing reciprocated the overtures by inviting Lin and Ye Qun for a photograph portrait session at her residence in Diaoyutai just three months before Lin Biao's flight (Yang 2014: 112).

As Lin Biao's assertion of authority independently of Mao became clear around the time of the Lushan Conference, however, Mao began to consolidate his ties with veterans of the FFA, especially those who were deeply stained by the "armed counterrevolutionary plot" at the Anti-Japan University. They were placed in positions of great formal authority and led the purge of Lin Biao followers in the military. Had this group been untainted, Mao would have been very vulnerable to a power seizure and would never have used them so extensively, which would have prevented him from purging Lin's followers wholesale from the military. As it turned out, after the purge of Chen Boda at Lushan, Mao signaled clearly to the remaining scribblers that they were to work closely with FFA veterans rather than with Lin Biao's coterie.

On the eve of Lin Biao's flight, Mao revealed his strategy against Lin during his southern tour, where he met with FFA veterans in key military regions:

I used three methods – the first was throwing stones; another one was mixing in sand; another one was digging up the corner stone ... I take some stones, add my comments, and generate some discussion, which is called throwing stones ... if the earth is so packed that it can't breathe, one must add some sand to let it breath. I added some people to the Military Affairs Commission Administrative Group as well as add some other officials, which is called mixing in sand. I rotated officers in the Beijing Military Region, which was digging up the corner stone.

(Mao 1987b: 387)

According to Li Desheng's recollection, which differs from the official version, Mao's remarks pertained specifically to FFA veterans: "[I]f the earth is so packed that it can't breathe, one must add some sand to let it breath. Li Xiannian led troops in the past, so why can't he participate in the Central Military Commission Administrative Group. I also sent Li Desheng and Ji Dengkui to the Beijing Military Region, which is called digging at the cornerstone" (Zhu 2007: 190). Both Li Xiannian and Li Desheng were FFA veterans. In this rare instance, Mao explicitly revealed his political strategy against a potential opponent.

The heart of Mao's strategy against an increasingly disobedient Lin was "mixing in sand," which involved diluting Lin Biao's dominance in the military with new appointments. Although the Central Military Commission (CMC) nominally still existed, daily business of the CMC was carried out by the Central Military Commission Administrative Group (CMCAG, 军委办公组) after 1968. Until the Lushan Conference, the CMCAG was dominated by Lin Biao followers, including Huang Yongsheng, Wu Faxian, Qiu Huizuo, and Ye Qun (Central Organization Department et al. 1997a: 7). Mao, however, began to add FFA veterans into CMCAG after the 9th Party Congress, first with Li Desheng and Xie Fuzhi, followed by Zhang Caiqian and Li Xiannian in April 1971, even though Li had had nothing to do with the military since the early 1950s (Zhu 2007: 81). Among the military regions (MRs), which controlled all of China's land forces, FFA veterans Xu Shiyou and Han Xianchu had commanded for years the Nanjing and Fuzhou Military Regions, respectively. Likewise, Chen Xilian and Qin Jiwei, also from the tainted faction, had commanded Shenyang MR and Kunming MR, respectively, for years (He et al. 1993). After the 9th Party Congress, Mao rotated Pi Dingjun, another FFA alumnus, to command the Lanzhou MR. In 1971, Mao further secured control over the vital Beijing Military Region through Li Desheng.

Most significantly, Mao placed two FFA veterans, Wu Zhong and Xie Fuzhi, in the commander and political commissar positions, respectively, of the Beijing Capital Garrison, which directly protected Beijing (He et al. 1993). Even at lower levels, Mao was carefully putting in place officers who were in the FFA camp instead of the Lin Biao group. In March 1971, Chi Haotian, who had served under Xu Shiyou for two decades in the Nanjing Military Region, was suddenly ordered to join the leadership group of the *Liberation Army Daily*, the main newspaper of the military (Editorial Committee 2009a: 146). Although he was puzzled by the appointment initially, after Lin Biao's flight, Chi immediately took overall charge of the publication.

The meteoric rise of Li Desheng illustrates Mao's strategy of "mixing in sand" to dilute Lin Biao's dominance over the military. A junior member of the FFA group, Li Desheng had been only an army-level commander, but at the 1969 9th Party Congress, Li suddenly found himself catapulted into an alternate seat in the Politburo, as well as a member of the CMCAG, the secretary of the Anhui Revolutionary Committee, and the vice commander of the Nanjing Military Region. When Mao had asked for a young comrade in the army to be elevated to the Politburo, Xu Shiyou and Chen Xilian, two of the most senior survivors of the FFA, had recommended Li Desheng because he had served under Chen and Xu since his teenage years in the early 1930s (Gao 2003: 276; Zhu 2007: 96). Li soon found himself in charge of the General Political Department, one of the three major departments in the PLA. At the 1973 10th Party Congress, Li was ultimately elected vice chairman of the Chinese Communist Party, where he served for one year until Mao demoted him during the Anti-Lin, Anti-Confucius campaign (Zhu 2007: 403). Amazingly, even after Deng's rise to power, Li Desheng continued to serve in senior positions in the army. He ended his career in 1990 as a standing committee member of the Central Advisory Committee and the political commissar of the National Defense University (Zhu 2007: 425). Among the relatively large cohort of military officers who had joined the party in the mid-1930s, Li's meteoric rise certainly stood out and would have been impossible without Mao's active orchestration.

Another official who greatly benefited from Mao's "mixing in sand" strategy was Li Xiannian, whose rise in this period resulted in him becoming a permanent fixture among the power brokers of Beijing for the rest of his life. At the 1969 9th Party Congress, Mao personally insisted that Li Xiannian be included in the new Politburo despite Li's own objection (Wu 2006: 746). Because the Cultural Revolution had paralyzed the State Council bureaucracy, Li Xiannian, one of a handful of State Council officials allowed to continue working, came to acquire an enlarging portfolio of policy power, especially as Zhou Enlai's health declined. With Lin Biao's threat rising, Li for a time gained formal control over the army for the first time since 1949 as a member of the CMCAG and its successor organ, the Central Military Commission Administrative Conference (CMCAC, 军委办事会议) (Zhu 2007: 247). Since that point, Li, more so than the other FFA veterans, became the chief representative of the tainted group. To the extent that Mao and his successors relied on FFA veterans to oversee key units in the military, they had to include

Li Xiannian in important decisions, thus making Li a vital member of all ruling coalitions in China until his death in 1992.

By August 1971, Mao had given up on a scenario whereby Lin Biao conducted a thorough self-criticism and announced voluntary retirement. Instead, Mao embarked on a tour of southern China to rally a mixed support coalition in case an inner-party struggle or even a violent clash occurred with Lin Biao. During the tour, which included key southern cities such as Wuhan, Changsha, Nanchang, Hangzhou, and Shanghai, Mao told his audience of senior military and civilian officials that the struggle with Lin Biao likely would come to a head and that, although reconciliation was still possible, "the leading figures committing line error are hard to change" (Gao 2003: 326). Similar to what Mao had done in 1966 to rally support for his purge of Liu Shaoqi, Mao's description of the events in Lushan left no doubt of Lin's duplicity:

> [A]t the 1970 Lushan Conference, they engaged in surprise attack and underground activities. Why didn't they dare to be open about it? ... Someone is eager to be state chairman and would like to split the party and seize power quickly ... the struggle against Liu Shaoqi was a struggle between two headquarters. This time at the Lushan Conference, it was also a struggle between two headquarters.
> (Mao 1987b: 387)

According to the recollection of Mao's bodyguard Zhang Yaoci, of the fifteen senior military officers that Mao met on the southern tour, seven had been FFA veterans (Zhang 2008b: 178). The remaining officers were either more junior officers who had joined the party after the Long March or members of the disgruntled Jiangxi wing of the First Front Army, who had been the targets of a bloody internal purge carried out by Mao and Lin Biao in the late 1920s (Gao 2000: 16–17). In Hangzhou and Wuhan, Mao met with FFA veterans, including Xiong Yingtang (Zhu 2007: 190). As Mao had expected, the tainted faction showed absolute loyalty to him. Just in case, though, on his stop in Changsha, Mao met with Liu Xingyuan, Ding Sheng, and Wei Guoqing, veterans of the First Front Army who were not core members of Lin Biao's coterie, and told them to obey Ye Jianying because of his great contribution in foiling Zhang Guotao's plot to eliminate the Central Committee during the Long March (Zhang 2008a: 318). This was an obscure historical issue to raise on the eve of a major struggle with Lin Biao, but Mao was likely cultivating an insurance policy against FFA veterans. If the FFA had dared to challenge Mao's power, Ye Jianying, the sole witness to the FFA's most heinous crime of plotting to eliminate the Central Committee, could lead the charge against them with the remaining officers of the First and Second Front Army, as well as more junior officers.

Before returning to Beijing, Mao's last stop was in Shanghai a few days later, where he met with Xu Shiyou alone. When Wang Weiguo, a follower of Wu Faxian in the air force, tried to join the meeting, Mao stopped him from entering his personal carriage (Zhu 2007: 185). At the meeting, Mao asked Xu, "[W]hat would you do if someone launched a coup?" Without hesitation, Xu answered, "[L]ead troops on a Northern Expedition," to which Mao responded with a big grin (Wen and Li 1998: 34). Mao was apparently delighted that the insurance policy he had cultivated for decades was coming to fruition.

Finally, at the end of his tour and just before Lin's flight, Mao had a meeting arranged at the last minute just outside of Beijing with the top four officers of the Beijing Military Region, two of whom, Li Desheng and Wu Zhong, had served in the FFA (Li and Shu 2009: 1202). At the meeting, Mao once again emphasized the deep contradiction between him and Lin Biao and told his audience to prepare for the upcoming struggle. Mao further ordered Li Desheng to move the 38th Army closer to Beijing, just in case the struggle with Lin Biao became violent (Zhu 2007: 187).

By September 6, 1971, Lin Biao had heard from various sources that Mao was preparing for his removal from power. Although he himself did not want to fight his inevitable purge, his wife Ye Qun and his son Lin Liguo, both of whom had enjoyed enormous power and prestige as family members of Mao's "closest comrade," wanted to avoid the inevitable purge (Teiwes and Sun 1996). In the case of Lin Liguo, he hastily put together some plans with a few confidants in the air force to assassinate Mao, but none of the plans worked out (Chang and Halliday 2005: 547; MacFarquhar and Schoenhals 2006). Also, by this time, Mao had heard reports that Lin Liguo was organizing unusual activities in the air force. Mao then notified the Central Committee Office that he would not return to Beijing until right before the October First celebrations, but in reality he immediately commenced his journey back to Beijing via Shanghai, where he met again with Xu Shiyou to ensure his loyalty (Gao 2003: 334).

On September 12, a dejected Lin Liguo returned to Beidaihe, where he told his parents that the only course now laid in an escape to Guangdong or to the Soviet Union (Chang and Halliday 2005: 549). The Lins had planned on leaving for the Soviet Union on the morning of September 13, but Lin Biao's daughter, Lin Liheng, reported her parents' plans to an officer of the Central Guard Unit, who reported the news to Zhou Enlai.

Here, Mao and Zhou could have immediately ordered the arrest of the Lin family, but Zhou instead made inquiries to verify the story, which gave Lin Biao and his family time to make their escape to the Shanhaiguan Airport late on the night of the twelfth (Zhang 2008b: 199). When Mao found out that Lin's plane had taken off and was asked by Zhou Enlai whether he wanted to shoot it down, Mao answered, "[I]f the sky wants to rain, or a woman wants to find a new husband, these are events beyond our control. Let them go" (Zhang 2008b: 199). Because Lin's plane was not sufficiently refueled, it ran out of fuel in the middle of Mongolia, where the plane crashed, killing Lin Biao, Ye Qun, Lin Liguo, a few close associates of Lin Biao, as well as the crew (Chang and Halliday 2005: 549). Lin Liheng stayed behind and was the only survivor of the Lin family.

The night of September 12–13, 1971 was the tensest political time that China had seen since the CCP took control of the country in 1949. If Lin had landed safely in Mongolia, then a Soviet protectorate, Lin might have rallied his supporters in China to launch a coup against Mao. For all Mao knew, Lin might have already put in motion a plan to launch a coup. Mao was awoken on the night of the 12th and remained up until the 14th, when the Mongolian government officially notified China of the crash of Lin Biao's plane (Chang and Halliday 2005: 550). In this tense period, Mao and Zhou Enlai relied almost exclusively on FFA veterans to secure the armed forces and to arrest Lin's associates for questioning. Meanwhile, the scribblers were in Beijing and Shanghai helping Zhou Enlai stabilize the civilian government. Zhang Chunqiao and Yao Wenyuan stayed in the Great Hall of the People as Zhou Enlai's assistants, helping Zhou issue orders to various units in the government (Zheng 2017: 556). After the Mongolian embassy notified China that Lin's plane and the bodies had been recovered in Mongolia, Zhou had Yao and Zhang draft a notice to the party on Lin's "traitorous escape" (Zheng 2017: 557).

On the military side, Zhou Enlai ordered Li Desheng to take overall control of the entire air force of China, and Zhou's first order was to ground all airplanes in China (Zhu 2007: 206). In subsequent days, Li Desheng organized work teams composed of officers from the General Political Department to take command of all key air force units around Beijing, especially those that Lin Liguo had frequented, including the Air Force Academy, the West Suburb Airport, Shahe Airport, and the air force guesthouse (Zhu 2007: 219). When the plot against Mao was revealed, Li Desheng, the junior FFA veteran, was put in charge of investigating it. His interrogation of Lu Min, a Lin Liguo crony in the air force, led to Lu's confession of the shocking plot to assassinate Mao (Zhu 2007: 219). Li then followed up by seizing control of several more air force units and arresting all those who had been involved in the plot. At the Air Force Academy, Li uncovered a booklet outlining the entire "Plan 571," the code name for the plot against Mao, which was homophonic with the words "armed uprising" (Zhu 2007: 235). Li then proceeded to interrogate the core followers of Lin Biao, including Wu Faxian, Li Zuopeng, Huang Yongsheng, and Qiu Huizuo, who were still senior officers and Politburo members. On September 24, Mao made the decision to have them all arrested (Zhu 2007: 247).

Meanwhile, the man who had been the condemned leader of the "armed counterrevolutionary plot" at the Anti-Japan University, Xu Shiyou, was entrusted by Mao to seize control of air force organs in the Nanjing Military Region and to arrest Lin Biao associates (Zhao 2006). On September 13, Zhou Enlai called Xu Shiyou to have him shut down all the airports and ports around Shanghai (Zhao 2006). Assisting Xu was another FFA veteran and longtime Xu protégé, Xiao Yongyin, then the vice commander of the Nanjing MR. Two days later, Xu was summoned to Beijing and received orders from Chairman Mao to arrest two of Lin's close associates in the air force, Wang Weiguo and Chen Liyun (Leng 2009). In Shanghai, junior radical Wang Hongwen cooperated with Xu and invited Wang Weiguo to a meeting at the Jinjiang Hotel, where Xu and Xiao waited with a battalion of army troops for the arrests (Leng 2009; Zhao 2006). Wang Hongwen and junior scribbler Xiao Mu further helped Xu to take over the 5th divisions of the PLA air force, which had been a Lin Liguo stronghold (Zheng 2017: 639). In Hangzhou, Xu Shiyou called on Xiong Yingtang, who had served under Xu for decades, to arrest Chen Liyun, a close Lin Biao associate (Zhao 2006).

Since Huang Yongsheng, a core member of Lin's coterie, had served as the commander of the Guangzhou MR for over a decade, Mao sent Li Xiannian and Hunan Party Secretary Hua Guofeng to take control of the MR (Ding 2008: 207). Upon arrival, Li Xiannian convened a meeting of senior officials in the MR and told them no one who was not directly involved in the plot would be arrested, including the children of those who were involved in the plot (Ding 2008: 207). This immediately dialed down the level of panic among the officers in the Guangzhou MR. In other key army units across the country, trusted officers dominated by FFA veterans or junior officers cultivated by them commenced a rectification campaign that involved investigating and removing close followers of

Lin Biao and Lin Liguo. At the *Liberation Army Daily*, Chi Haotian, an officer who had served under Xu Shiyou in the Nanjing MR for two decades, suddenly found himself in charge of the rectification campaign at the paper (Editorial Committee 2009a: 152). Chi took this opportunity to build up political capital by rehabilitating officers who had been purged in the earlier part of the Cultural Revolution (Editorial Committee 2009a: 155). This likely helped his eventual rise to the position of minister of defense.

For weeks after the Lin Biao incident, Mao fell ill, leaving Zhou Enlai, Ye Jianying, veterans of the FFA, and key scribblers to run the entire country (Gao 2003: 356). The first order of business was the restructuring of the military command structure. Since Lin Biao and his followers had dominated the CMCAG, it needed to be disbanded and replaced by a new organ, the CMCAC (Zhang 2008a: 321). CMCAC was chaired by none other than Ye Jianying, and its members included Xie Fuzhi, Zhang Chunqiao, Li Xiannian, Li Desheng, Ji Dengkui, Wang Dongxing, Chen Shiyu, Zhang Caiqian, and Liu Xianquan (Zhu 2007: 247). Of the ten members, four – Xie Fuzhi, Li Xiannian, Li Desheng, and Zhang Caiqian – came from the FFA, making up the single largest bloc in the CMCAC. In early October, Mao also decided to form a special case group to investigate the crimes of Chen Boda and Lin Biao. Although this group was dominated by party veterans such as Zhou Enlai and Kang Sheng and junior radicals such as Jiang Qing, Zhang Chunqiao, and Yao Wenyuan, it also included FFA veterans such as Li Desheng and Wu Zhong (Zhang 2008b: 208).

As Table 5.1 shows, FFA occupied the majority of the key positions in the PLA in early 1972. In all three of the PLA's major departments, FFA veterans took up at least one of the two command positions. In the case of the General Logistics Department, they occupied both the secretary and vice secretary positions. Even the Second Artillery, China's nascent missile force, was commanded by Xiang Shouzhi and Chen Heqiao, both FFA veterans (Xiang 2006: 344). In the regional command, they occupied at least one of the two command positions in six of the ten military regions. In the all-important Beijing Capital Garrison, Wu Zhong, a FFA veteran, retained the commander position until after Mao's death (He et al. 1993: 589). First Front Army veterans only dominated in Jinan, Guangzhou, Chengdu, and Wuhan Military Regions. In the case of Guangzhou, although Ding Sheng and Wei Guoqing nominally retained command, Mao sent Li Xiannian, the head of the Fourth Front Army group, to check on the loyalty of officers in the military region (Ding 2008). Likely in an

TABLE 5.1 *Major military units, commanding officers, and their affiliations prior to the Long March and with Deng Xiaoping: 1972*

Unit and Position	Name	Experience prior to the Long March	Prior ties with Deng Xiaoping
General Staff Department			
Secretary	Vacant		
Vice Secretary	Zhang Caiqian	Fourth Front Army	Yes
General Political Department			
Secretary	Li Desheng	Fourth Front Army	Yes
Vice Secretary	Tian Weixin	None	No
General Logistics Department			
Secretary	Zhang Chiming	Fourth Front Army	No
Vice Secretary	Zhang Tianyun	Fourth Front Army	No
Beijing Capital Garrison			
Commander	Wu Zhong	Fourth Front Army	Yes
Political Commissar	Xie Fuzhi	Fourth Front Army	Yes
Beijing Military Region			
Commander	Li Desheng	Fourth Front Army	Yes
Political Commissar	Ji Dengkui	None	Yes
Shenyang Military Region			
Commander	Chen Xilian	Fourth Front Army	Yes
Political Commissar	Zeng Shaoshan	Fourth Front Army	Yes
Jinan Military Region			
Commander	Yang Dezhi	First Front Army	No
Political Commissar	Wang Xiaoyu	None	No
Nanjing Military Region			
Commander	Xu Shiyou	Fourth Front Army	Yes
Political Commissar	Zhang Chunqiao	None	No
Fuzhou Military Region			
Commander	Han Xianchu	Fourth Front Army	No
Political Commissar	Li Zhimin	First Front Army	No
Guangzhou Military Region			
Commander	Ding Sheng	First Front Army	No
Political Commissar	Wei Guoqing	First Front Army	Yes
Wuhan Military Region			
Commander	Zeng Siyu	First Front Army	No
Political Commissar	Wang Liusheng	First Front Army	No

(*continued*)

TABLE 5.1 (*continued*)

Unit and Position	Name	Experience prior to the Long March	Prior ties with Deng Xiaoping
Kunming Military Region			
Commander	Wang Bicheng	Fourth Front Army	No
Political Commissar	Zhou Xing	First Front Army	No
Chengdu Military Region			
Commander	Liang Xingchu	First Front Army	No
Political Commissar	Liu Xingyuan	First Front Army	No
Lanzhou Military Region			
Commander	Pi Dingjun	Fourth Front Army	Yes
Political Commissar	Li Ruishan	Shaanxi Base Area	No

Source: He et al. (1993).

attempt to prevent any MR from falling completely under the control of the FFA group, Mao left the Wuhan Military Region, where many junior veterans of the tainted group had served, in the hands of First Front Army veterans. When Mao and Deng shuffled the commanders of the military regions in 1973, the influence of the FFA bloc did not diminish because they still served either as commander or political commissars in the majority of the MRs. FFA veterans like Xu Shiyou, Qin Jiwei, Xu Liqing, Wang Bicheng, Li Desheng, Pi Dingjun, and Han Xianchu all remained MR level commanders; only their positions changed (He et al. 1993).

Meanwhile, the scribblers and their underlings also enjoyed a significant boost in their standing and authority in the party. In the immediate aftermath of the Lin Biao incident, Zhang helped Zhou Enlai run the entire State Council apparatus. Meanwhile, Wang Hongwen and Ma Tianshui, both Zhang Chunqiao loyalists in Shanghai, played key roles in helping Xu Shiyou purge the air force contingents loyal to Lin Liguo in the Nanjing Military Region (Zhao 2006). Jiang Qing loyalist Chi Qun and Xie Jingyi, who had been minor functionaries in the party prior to the Cultural Revolution, were put in charge of ransacking Lin Biao's former residence in Maojiawan for any evidence of a plot against Mao (Gao 2003: 485). At their highest point of power, Chi Qun served as the equivalent of vice minister of education, while Xie Jingyi became a secretary (equivalent to today's vice secretary) in the Beijing party committee (Ye 2009: 1226).

In the run-up to the Lin Biao incident, Zhang also consolidated control over two key institutions: the propaganda apparatus and the Shanghai Municipal Government. Instead of reviving the propaganda department, previously a giant bureaucracy staffed by thousands, Zhang exerted control over propaganda through the formation of writing groups, staffed by dozens of trusted scribblers such as Mu Xin. These writing groups scoured the country for intelligence on local political development and authored essays that reflected the latest "spirit" from Beijing, as instructed by Zhang Chunqiao and Yao Wenyuan (Zheng 2017: 597). Instead of rebuilding the core organ of the Central Propaganda Department, Zhang's incentive was to build sufficient intelligence and writing capacity to survive without waking Mao's suspicion with major institution building efforts.

Meanwhile, even before 1971, Zhang and Yao had consolidated almost total control over the Shanghai Municipal Government (SMG). In 1968, a visiting Zhang Chunqiao ordered Wang Hongwen and other workers' rebels to install 140–150 worker representatives into leadership positions in the various departments of the SMG (Perry and Li 1997). Zhang and Yao further consolidated power with the formation of the Workers' Mao Zedong Thought Propaganda Teams in July 1968, as these teams, filled with workers' rebels loyal to Wang Hongwen, Chen Ada, and Wang Xiuzhen, essentially took over decision-making power in all schools, districts, counties, municipal departments, and party bureaus (Perry and Li 1997: 155). The ultimate triumph of the scribblers' control over Shanghai, also a key justification for their undoing, was the formation of a three-million-strong workers' militia with 226,000 guns and thousands of cannons and rocket launchers (Perry and Li 1997: 162). An important political backdrop for the arming of the Shanghai militia was the replacement of FFA veteran Xu Shiyou with Ding Sheng in the Nanjing Military Region. Unlike the ascendant members of the FFA faction, Ding was a vulnerable former protégé of Lin Biao who ingratiated himself with the scribblers by helping them arm and train the militia, thus laying the foundation for the most serious charge against the Gang of Four after their 1976 arrest (Ye 2009: 1298).

With the coalition of the weak in charge of daily decisions in the party-state, Mao could rule the entire country without consultation with other senior leaders in the party. His words, whether written or conveyed orally, became the law. Meetings by formal bodies of decision making such as the State Council, the National People's Congress, or even the party Central Committee ground to a halt or only occurred very rarely

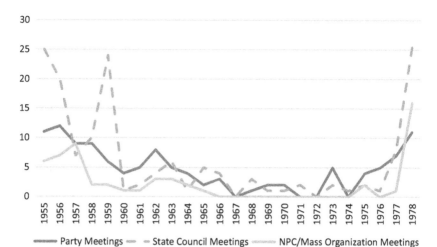

FIGURE 5.1 The number of Central Party, State Council, and National People's
Congress or mass organization meetings by year: 1955–1978
Source: Author's data

compared to the pre–Cultural Revolution period. In place of formal meetings, different factions competed with one another to get the ear of Mao.
Those who had access to Mao, such as junior translators Tang Wensheng
and Wang Hairong and nephew Mao Yuanxin, gained enormous informal
power as gatekeepers to Mao and conveyors of his wishes (Ye 2009: 1148).

To be sure, Figure 5.1 shows that the number of State Council and
Central Party meetings, as reported by the *People's Daily*, had been in
decline even after the Great Leap Forward, which saw Mao's personal
prestige plummet. After 1966, however, the number of formal Central
Party and State Council meetings further plummeted to just one or two
per year. In 1971, 1972, and 1974, no formal party meeting took place,
and major decisions in the party were made in a purely informal manner
with Mao issuing fiats (Figure 5.1). The State Council, including the
ministries, held no meeting in 1971 and only had one formal meeting in
1974 and 1976, respectively (Figure 5.1). In the meantime, the National
People's Congress and other mass organizations had no meeting throughout the entire Cultural Revolution period, except for a couple of mass
meetings on the Dazhai model toward the end of Mao's life (Figure 5.1).

Thus, if Mao had intended for the purge of revolutionary veterans and
the elevation of the coalition of the weak to eradicate the need to consult
with formal collective decision-making bodies, he was highly successful in
that endeavor toward the end of his life. As the following section shows, it

did not mean that he became the perfect dictator because of his failing health and because of information asymmetry. However, it meant that no credible institution or person within the party could challenge his power directly or change major decisions against his wishes.

FROM WEAK COALITION TO WEAK SUCCESSORS

The installation of the coalition of the weak after Lin Biao's fall brought with it its own problems. To be sure, these problems were much less formidable than the ones faced by Mao prior to the Cultural Revolution or prior to the Lin Biao incident, when high-level officials had threatened to marginalize or remove Mao. Nonetheless, even with a selectorate of weaklings, Mao did not govern over a perfect dictatorship. First, agency problems still abounded, which became more severe as Mao's health failed him. That is, as Mao got sicker, all the relatively weak players placed consolidating their own power after the passing of Mao as the highest priority, at times forgoing absolute obedience to Mao. For the scribblers, that meant blindly accusing rehabilitated veterans like Deng Xiaoping of ideological deviation so that they could be removed prior to Mao's death. Mao expressed displeasure about this tendency on more than one occasion. For the veterans, including FFA veterans, it meant placing as many faction members in high-level party and military positions prior to the transition. Thus, although no one challenged Mao's position as the head of the party, policy-making was volatile and beset by constant political squabbling among members of the weak coalition.

As was the case with the 9th Party Congress, the 10th Party Congress in August 1973 formalized the status of the new coalition. Scribblers Zhang Chunqiao and Yao Wenyuan took over drafting of the congress' political report, while Wang Hongwen, an ordinary worker just a few years ago, took charge of revising the party constitution to eradicate all traces of Lin Biao (Ye 2009: 1136). More importantly, as the person sitting next to Mao on the rostrum at the opening of the congress, Wang Hongwen became the unspoken designated successor to Mao (Ye 2009: 1137). When the new slate of leadership was announced, Wang found himself named the vice chairman of the party after Zhou Enlai. However, he also had to contend with a potential challenger. Li Desheng, a junior member of the FFA group, was made the fifth vice chairman of the party (Li 2007: 236). In terms of military experience and network, Li was vastly more prepared to lead China than Wang, making Li a formidable challenger. Of course, Li, along with all FFA veterans, took part in "counterrevolutionary splittism" as a foot soldier in 1935. The Politburo Standing Committee at the 10th Party Congress also included senior scribbler Zhang Chunqiao, as well as Zhu De and Dong Biwu, two aging veterans who had retired from active politics already (Li 2007: 236). Mao vetoed Jiang Qing's bid to enter the PSC, thus continuing the precedence of excluding women from the PSC that remains unbroken today (Zhang 2008a: 346). Hua Guofeng, who eventually became Mao's successor, was only inducted into the Politburo, not the standing committee, at the 10th Party Congress.

Beyond the scribblers and Hua Guofeng, several "mass representatives" were also inducted to the top elite at the 10th Party Congress. Ni Zhifu, a worker credited with several inventions; Chen Yonggui, a peasant leader at the model Dazhai Commune; and Wu Guixian, a model worker were all inducted into the Politburo, although none of them had extensive leadership experience. One sees the impact of this "mixing in sand" strategy at the 10th Party Congress (Figure 5.2). Whereas the least networked member of the Politburo at the 8th Party Congress still had ties with over 10 percent of the Central Committee, the least networked seven Politburo members at the 10th PC had ties with just one or two colleagues in the Central Committee (Figure 5.2). Although it was natural for the networks of revolutionary veterans to degenerate over time due to deaths and purges, Mao's appointment of multiple Politburo members with little experience and nonexisting elite networks suggested a deliberate strategy

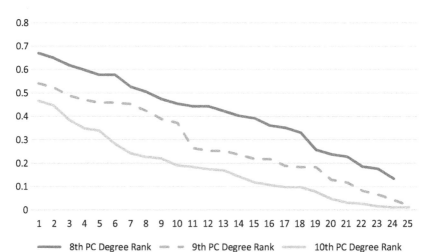

FIGURE 5.2 Ranked ordering of degree centrality of Politburo members: 8th, 9th, and 10th Party Congress

that averted officials with deep elite political experience. Meanwhile, scribblers and junior officials made up the rest of the lower half of Politburo members in terms of the number of connections they had with other Central Committee members (degree centrality) at the 10th Party Congress. Yet they only had ties with less than 20 percent of the Central Committee, whereas their counterparts at the 8th Party Congress had ties with around 40 percent of the Central Committee. Among younger generations of officials, Mao did not pick anyone with a high degree of influence and network among his peers.

By the end of the 10th PC, FFA veterans controlled much of the military and influenced much of State Council operation through Vice Premier Li Xiannian, and a faction member also became a runner-up successor after heavy lobbying by Xu Shiyou (Zheng 2017: 649). Only loyalty to the Communist Party and fear of Mao stood in the way between the FFA and ultimate power. To ensure FFA loyalty, Mao retained and rehabilitated several key veterans who could help Mao resist any potential power seizure by the FFA group. First, Ye Jianying, the "witness" to Zhang Guotao's damning cable in 1935, was now in charge of daily affairs of the PLA as chairman of the CMCAC (Zhang 2008a: 331). Because of the historical animosity between Ye and the FFA, Ye could be trusted with the task of monitoring FFA officers.

Several veterans with their own historical guilt were also rehabilitated at the 10th Party Congress to check the rising influence of the FFA. Ulanfu, an ethnic Mongol Communist who had been accused of forming a splittist ethnic party in Inner Mongolia, was rehabilitated without his guilt being removed. Wang Jiaxiang, accused of being too conciliatory toward imperialism and revisionism even before the Cultural Revolution, also was rehabilitated and rejoined the Central Committee. Most tellingly, Liao Chengzhi, a man who had been accused by Zhang Guotao for being an enemy spy and nearly had been executed in the 1930s, also regained his Central Committee seat at the 10th Party Congress (Sun 2013; Zhang 2008a: 328). Having been wrongly imprisoned by the FFA and a close associate of Ye Jianying as a fellow Cantonese, Liao doubtless was no friend of the FFA faction.

The main person Mao designated to check the rise of the FFA, however, was Deng Xiaoping. Events in the 1930s and 1940s allowed Deng to divide the loyalty of FFA veterans, thus rendering FFA leaders such as Li Xiannian and Xu Shiyou much less threatening to Mao. Like many ambitious early Communists, Deng had had his own base area and a sizable army, but he lost nearly all his troops when his base area had been overrun by KMT general Li Zongren (Vogel 2011: 27). As a result of this devastation, the Baise Base Area only produced a handful of PLA generals who had survived into the 1960s, including Deng, Mo Wenhua, and Wei Guoqing (Editorial Staff of One Spark Lighting the Plains 2006). After Deng's arrival in Jiangxi in 1931, he fell in with Mao and stood with him while he was attacked for following the "Luo Ming line" (Saich and Yang 1996: 1009).

Thus, when Mao casted for someone trustworthy and respectable to take charge of the volatile FFA group in 1937, it was natural that he thought of Deng. In 1937, the FFA contingent had just gone through the traumas of losing their comrades in the Western Legion death march and of undergoing harsh criticism at the Anti-Japan University. With the war against Japan heating up, the CCP soon reconstituted much of the surviving FFA into the 129th Division of the Eighth Route Army, nominally a KMT unit in the new united front against Japan (Chen 2007: 63). Over the subsequent thirteen years of warfare, the 129th Division grew and transformed into larger units, culminating in the formation of the half million strong Second Field Army in the latter part of the Civil War period (1946–1949) (Whitson and Huang 1973). Although the rapid expansion of the 129th division meant that rank-and-file members were new recruits, the senior officer corps was still dominated by veterans of the FFA (Chen 2007: 96). Thus, Deng, as the political commissar of the 129th division, had a chance to work closely with numerous veterans of the FFA who served in the 129th Division and its successors, including Xie Fuzhi, Xu Shiyou, Qin Jiwei, Wang Xinting, Xiang Shouzhi, Wang Hongkun, Kong Qingde, Li Chengfang, and Chen Xilian (Chen 2007: 63). As Table 5.1 shows, of the thirteen FFA veterans holding key PLA positions in 1972, nine of them had served under Deng Xiaoping in the 1930s or the 1940s.

Although the disgraced officers of the FFA had all been demoted by multiple ranks in 1937, under Deng's mentorship, many of them regained or even surpassed their former status by 1945 (Huang 2000: 203). Chen Xilian, who had been the divisional commander of the 10th division of the FFA, was initially demoted to battalion commander in the 129th Division (Xia and Su 2010). One year after Deng took command of the 129th Division, he entrusted Chen to command two battalions in a battle, putting him in charge of a unit headed by First Front Army veteran Zeng Guohua (Xia and Su 2010). Decades later, Chen remembered that "Deng encouraged us, and also trusted us" (Xia and Su 2010: 28). By 1943, Chen was promoted to be the commander of a subdistrict in the Taiheng

Military Region (Xia and Su 2010). By 1945, Deng had bestowed FFA veterans such as Chen Xilian, Chen Zaidao, and Xie Fuzhi commander or political commissar positions at the main column level (*zongdui*), equivalent to corps. The key role that Deng had played in rehabilitating the careers (although not the political records) of FFA veterans allowed Mao to use Deng as a wedge between FFA stalwarts like Li Xiannian and Xu Shiyou and the rest of the FFA faction.

Mao's plan to rehabilitate Deng went into motion at Chen Yi's funeral in January 1972, three months after the Lin Biao incident. At the funeral, Mao told Chen Yi's widow that Deng's problem should be viewed separately from Liu Shaoqi's problem because Deng's problem was one of "contradiction among the people" (MacFarquhar and Schoenhals 2006: 340). For Jiang Qing and her coterie of radicals, however, Deng represented an existential threat to them after Mao's passing. Unlike FFA veterans, Mao himself acknowledged that Deng had sided with him consistently through all of the party's internal struggles prior to the Cultural Revolution (Ye 2009: 1123). At the same time, he also commanded the loyalty of many FFA veterans and was a very capable administrator widely respected by revolutionary veterans and even many younger officials. If Deng was still in power after Mao's passing, he would have had the capacity to remove the Gang of Four. Deng's rehabilitation also clearly diminished Xu Shiyou and Li Xiannian's influence over the FFA. Yet, unlike Lin Biao or other unsullied veterans who could have maneuvered against Mao's wishes, the scribblers and senior FFA commanders could do little to stop Deng's rehabilitation because of their fear of Mao's wrath.

By March 1973, the Politburo formally had passed a resolution to reinstate Deng Xiaoping as the vice premier of China and an attendee of Politburo meetings (Zhu 2007: 309). By the end of 1973, Mao had put Deng in charge of implementing the rotation of military region commanders as the vice-chairman of the Central Military Commission, which aimed at weakening the power bases of FFA veterans in several military regions (Gao 2003: 472; MacFarquhar and Schoenhals 2006: 379). Most important, the leader of the "counterrevolutionary uprising" Xu Shiyou lost his longtime stronghold in the Nanjing Military Region, although the new commander Ding Sheng complained even in 1976 that units in the military region did not obey him, presumably due to residual loyalty to Xu (Ye 2009: 1298). Be that as it may, Deng, with Mao's blessing, reassigned the command positions of the major military regions with hardly a murmur from the commanders; the coalition of the weak was in no position to resist Mao's wishes.

To the scribblers' dismay, although many surviving and rehabilitated veterans came from disparate and often rival factions prior to the Cultural Revolution, suddenly they all gravitated toward Deng, who previously had little affinity with them. Perhaps his revolutionary pedigree, record as a strong administrator, and the backing of key members of the military were enough to cause the majority of the veterans to rally around Deng. Also, they gravitated toward Deng because the alternatives, the scribblers, simply lacked the connections and political savvy to become true leaders of China. As scribbler Xiao Mu observed, "to be sure there were all kinds of contradiction between the different front armies and the field armies, but the veterans all had a deep distain for us scribblers relative to other veterans" (Zheng 2017: 841). In a famous anecdote, when Wang Hongwen, by then the vice chairman of the party, called roll call at a Central Military Commission meeting, some of the commanders, starting with Xu Shiyou, did not answer it, even as Mao looked on (Zheng 2017: 660). Sensing the scribblers' inability to govern the regime, Mao had allowed Deng to chair Politburo Standing Committee meetings by mid-1975, which had put Deng in effective charge of daily affairs in the party, the State Council, and the military (MacFarquhar and Schoenhals 2006: 381).

In response to Deng's rising power and an emerging alliance between Deng and key FFA veterans, Jiang Qing and the scribblers pursued two tactics to salvage their positions in the run-up to Mao's death. The conventional narratives in China portray Jiang Qing as a hysteric, often accusing her Politburo colleagues of being plotters in wild conspiracies. In retrospect, this mudslinging tactic was not a manifestation of hysteria. Strategically, the more veterans were rehabilitated and were in positions of power, the weaker the Gang of Four, as the surviving scribblers were called, would have been after Mao's death. Because they lacked the ability to remove the veterans themselves, they had a strong incentive to hurl one accusation after another on the veterans, hoping that an increasingly ill Mao would believe some of these conspiracies and remove veterans from power, thus increasing the scribblers' relative power after the transition.

One of the most infamous cases of such mudslinging was the *Fengqing* incident, which saw Jiang Qing accusing the newly rehabilitated Ministry of Transportation of engaging in "betraying and selling out China" after senior cadres in the ministry advocated buying more foreign ships even after the successful testing of a domestically produced passenger ship (Mao 1987a; Pantsov and Levine 2015: 286). In reality, this campaign likely was a ploy to undermine the veteran group because the newly appointed minister of transportation at the time, Ye Fei, had been a military veteran and a subordinate of Chen Yi in the New Fourth Army. Given his appointment as the head of the PLA Navy in the Deng Era, one can infer that he had been a trusted lieutenant of Deng all along and thus a sensible target for Jiang Qing's attack (Chen 2018). Jiang also launched attacks against Zhou Enlai and ultimately Deng Xiaoping, which successfully removed Deng from power after the Gang of Four and Mao's nephew Mao Yuanxin persuaded a sickly Mao that Deng had aimed at undoing Cultural Revolution policies (MacFarquhar and Schoenhals 2006: 416; Vogel 2011: 145).

Related, the scribblers did their best to place even more junior followers into important party and state positions so that they could control more of the formal hierarchy when Mao passed. The scribblers were very clear that they had nothing to lose as Mao's life ebbed. In the summer of 1976, just before Mao's death, Zhang Chunqiao's daughter heard her father, then still a member of the powerful Politburo Standing Committee, declare morosely, "What can I do but to await disaster" (Zheng 2017: 745).

Of course, the scribblers were not as fatalist as Zhang's quote implies and fought tooth and nail against the rehabilitation of key veteran cadres. When Zhou Enlai proposed the rehabilitation of Chen Pixian, Zhang's predecessor, as the head of Shanghai, and received Mao's preliminary backing, Zhang and Yao dragged their feet by highlighting the dubious history of Chen's close associate, Cao Diqiu, who had been accused of being a traitor prior to 1949 (Perry and Li 1997: 183). The scribblers wanted to delay Chen's rehabilitation as much as possible because it would have quickly galvanized all surviving veteran cadres in Shanghai around Chen, ending the scribblers' total control of Shanghai. Finally, when Mao asked again about the status of Chen in the fall of 1974, Wang Hongwen, by then vice chairman of the party, could no longer delay Chen's rehabilitation but asked Wang Xiuzhen, a key Zhang lieutenant in Shanghai, to quickly put together a list of ousted rebel leaders in Shanghai who could be rehabilitated and presumably inserted into important positions in Shanghai (Perry and Li 1997: 183). Far from engaging in hysterics, the scribblers engaged in a calculated game of maximizing relative power before Mao's death, at times even delaying implementation of Mao's instructions.

At the national level, Zhang and Wang Hongwen prepared lists of worker rebels who could potentially serve as vice ministers in the State Council, but a coalition of rehabilitated veterans rejected most of them (Perry and Li 1997: 170). As Mao sent word that he wanted to revive the

National People's Congress in late 1974, Jiang Qing repeatedly sent proposed lists of State Council leadership to Mao, including recommendations for high-level positions for her close acolytes Chi Qun and Xie Jingyi, but Mao rebuked her and urged her to "not show your face too much, do not approve documents, do not take part in forming governments because you have accumulated much ill will so must try to unify the majority" (Ye 2009: 1172; Zhang 2008b). The advice to "unify the majority" suggests that Mao did not want Jiang and her fellow radicals to withdraw from politics altogether but to take a more nuanced approach, as Mao had done time and again, to unify the majority against the most threatening enemies. However, as Mao became increasingly ill in 1975, the scribblers felt increasingly out of time and thus had to pursue their plans of appointing as many trusted followers to formal positions as possible against Mao's advice.

Likewise, Deng was no blind executioner of Mao's will. Throughout 1975, Deng pursued his agenda of getting the economy on its footing, criticizing the promotion of young radicals, and rehabilitating veteran cadres (Pantsov and Levine 2015: 289; Vogel 2011: 121). In doing so, Deng likely had two objectives in mind. First, his actions made obvious and credible his desire to rehabilitate veteran cadres who had been purged during the Cultural Revolution, thus garnering him support from these veterans. As Mao's death drew closer, the rehabilitations were tantamount to a down payment to his "voters" for the coming political struggle. Second, in pursuing economic reform and an alternative ideological vision even before Mao had passed away, he sent veterans a credible signal that after Mao's death, Deng would not share power with the radicals, knowing that the radical scribblers' basis of legitimacy after Mao's death would have been the continuation of Mao's legacy.

Similar to the scribblers, Deng also pursued a strategy of filling positions with rehabilitated veterans. However, he ingeniously did so by "creating" new positions in revived central ministries and by clearing military officers from civilian positions. State Council ministries, which had been in stasis since the beginning of the Cultural Revolution, were revived by Deng, who also restored grateful veterans to their former positions (Zheng 2017: 702). In the summer of 1975, Deng, who by then was running the Central Military Commission as its executive vice chairman, ordered the withdrawal of military officers from civilian positions, thus freeing up many positions for rehabilitated veterans (Vogel 2011: 121). Indeed, the number of military officers in the Central Committee plummeted by the 11th Party Congress (Liu et al. 2018). This wave of rehabilitation greatly helped his own political revival after Mao's death.

The most daring political maneuver by Deng in this period was the formation of the State Council Political Research Office, which had a mandate to "produce some theoretical documents against the Gang of Four," according to a founding member, Deng Liqun (Deng 2005: 10). Although most contemporary studies see this as a natural beginning of Deng's reform drive, it in fact was a very risky gamble in the late-Mao period. Mao had made clear time and again that he had wanted the legacy of the Cultural Revolution preserved. Mao clearly trusted Zhang Chunqiao and his coterie of scribblers with ideological work in this period, as shown in his appointment of Zhang as the head of the powerful General Political Department of the PLA (Zheng 2017: 679). Yet Deng dared to meddle in ideological work by forming a new organ for it and appointing disgruntled veteran scribblers to it, most of whom were newly rehabilitated from hard labor. Among those rehabilitated to work at the Research Office were Deng Liqun and Hu Sheng, both loyalists of Liu Shaoqi (Deng 2005: 10). At a theory study meeting for senior party officials in mid-1975, Deng Xiaoping further deviated from the Maoist line by calling for a new round of vetting for the millions of new party members who had joined the party in the wake of the Cultural Revolution (Vogel 2011: 121). This call was clearly aimed at the radical scribblers who had rushed many workers' rebels through the party initiation process in order to appoint them to positions.

If Deng had wanted to ingratiate himself to Mao, he never would have started such an organ or called for a revetting of party members. At least he would have filled the Research Office with radical scribblers approved by Mao and Zhang Chunqiao. Instead, he risked Mao's wrath, which eventually came, to form such an organ and to have it produce ideological polemics against Mao's radical vision. Deng likely calculated that even if it had resulted in his purge in the last months of Mao's life, the surviving veterans would have clamored for his rehabilitation after Mao's death because he credibly showed that he would dismantle Mao's radical ideological line after his death. As events in the late 1970s showed, his calculation paid off handsomely.

Of course, such a daring move soon attracted the ire of the scribblers, who soon submitted report after report of Deng's duplicity to Mao. Mao Yuanxin, Mao's nephew who by then was a key bridge between a sickly Mao and the party, whispered to Mao reports on Deng's reluctance to praise the Cultural Revolution and his refusal to criticize Liu Shaoqi

(Vogel 2011: 145). Like for Lin Biao, Mao offered Deng a final chance to repent and to acknowledge that the Cultural Revolution was at least 70 percent good, but Deng refused to do so (Vogel 2011: 147). By November 1975, Mao had ordered a Politburo meeting aimed at criticizing Deng for his "rightist reversal of verdicts" (Vogel 2011: 149). Unlike the purges of Liu Shaoqi and Lin Biao, Mao no longer needed to spend months plotting Deng's downfall. Instead, he simply ordered a Politburo meeting criticizing him, which was immediately executed by the coalition of the weak. After the Politburo meeting, Deng was promptly removed from power (MacFarquhar and Schoenhals 2006: 411).

Because the other members of the elite were all in the coalition of the weak, they had no choice but to participate in Deng's downfall. According to Li Xiannian's official biographer, Li took part in the Politburo meeting that criticized Deng, chiming in that Deng "should still try harder to deepen his understanding of the Cultural Revolution" (Editorial Committee 2009b: 880). At a December 29, 1975 Politburo meeting, Li again criticized Deng for not seeking Mao's approval for his remarks and for not following proper procedures (Editorial Committee 2009b: 883). Although relatively mild, Li nonetheless took part in Deng's criticism. Still, Li survived in high politics after the 12th Party Congress when none of his Politburo colleagues at the time did because of his role as the head of the FFA faction.

In February 1976, Chen Xilian, Deng's former subordinate in the 129th Division, was again put in charge of the daily affairs of the Central Military Commission (Chen 2007: 384). Along with Wang Dongxing, Chen was the only old guard still serving in the CMC because Ye Jianying fell ill at this time. Chen's hold over the military continued until after Mao's death. Meanwhile, although Hua Guofeng became the premier, Li Xiannian was put in charge of the daily operation of the State Council after Zhou's death in January 1976 (Teiwes and Sun 2007: 13). Thus, in the transition period from Mao to Hua Guofeng to Deng, Chen Xilian and his mentors Li Xiannian and Xu Shiyou, as well as his protégé Li Desheng, played a pivotal role as the largest single bloc in the party and in the army. Without the tacit approval, if not active support, of FFA veterans, Deng's rise to power would have been impossible.

Between Deng's fall and Mao's death in September 1976, FFA veterans held the most important positions in the regime but tried as much as possible to remain neutral and to survive the coming upheaval. An untainted faction would have taken advantage of the situation to position itself for ultimate power after Mao's death. In an alternate universe, Li Xiannian, instead of Deng, would have been China's titular leader in the 1980s. Senior members of the FFA, however, stayed away from any overt alliances. So long as the Gang of Four had Mao's blessing, FFA veterans cooperated with them. However, they also fell short of backing the Gang of Four outright. In the spring of 1976, when Li Xiannian ran into his old comrade Chen Xilian at Beihai Park, Chen, who worked with Zhang Chunqiao, then the vice premier and the head of PLA Political Department, told Li, "[Y]ou must be careful with those four (the Gang of Four); they are not to be trifled with" (Editorial Committee 2009b: 896). There is also no evidence that Chen Xilian or Li Xiannian did or said anything in favor of Deng's rehabilitation before Mao's death.

CONCLUSION

In the run-up to Lin Biao's doomed attempt to usurp Mao's power, Mao's coalition of the weak strategy proved its worth. The vulnerable FFA group faithfully executed Mao's order to first rotate troops to protect his safety and then to arrest and purge military officers loyal to Lin Biao. Without a large contingent in the military whom he could count on with high certainty, Mao could not have carried out a thorough purge of Lin's faction. He would have worried about a potential resurgence of Lin Biao's faction for the rest of his life. In the meantime, the scribblers also faithfully executed Mao and Zhou Enlai's orders to maintain calm and some semblance of normal operation on the civilian side of the regime. After the Lin Biao incident, FFA veterans and the scribblers faithfully executed major decisions made by Mao, and more importantly for an increasingly sickly Mao, they had no capacity to usurp his power.

Despite successes in realizing the major outcome of ensuring Mao's supremacy in the party, important institutions for policy decisions lapsed into stasis, while Politburo meetings degenerated into arguments on who understood Mao's wishes better. The main mode of politics involved members of the weak coalition each reporting on each other's failings to Mao. Yet, for Mao, agency problems still abounded. As Mao's health began to fail, the scribblers began to prioritize promoting their own followers into senior party positions over maintaining elite harmony, as Mao had desired. The newly rehabilitated Deng, meanwhile, also focused his effort on the post-succession game instead of on faithfully executing

Mao's instructions. Instead of preserving the legacy of the Cultural Revolution, Deng sought to credibly signal his preference for rehabilitating purged veteran cadres and in focusing on economic construction by reviving numerous economic agencies, staffed with veteran cadres. His deviation from Mao's wishes finally caused his downfall again on the eve of Mao's own death. Deng's credible signaling to the elite, however, set the stage for his return to power after Mao's death.

6

The Collapse of the Coalition of the Weak and Power Sharing in the 1980s

After Mao's passing in September 1976, the coalition that Mao had put in place at the end of his life, which was composed Cultural Revolution radicals with little revolutionary experience, even more junior officials like Wu De and mass representatives, the tainted Fourth Front Army (FFA) group, and a handful of trusted First Front Army veterans like Ye Jianying and Wang Dongxing, took over the People's Republic of China. An uneasy truce persisted for a very short time before the Gang of Four had alarmed Hua Guofeng by challenging his role as the anointed successor, which compelled him to seek more drastic solutions (Zhang 2008b: 263). In this decisive moment, the FFA swung behind Hua, thus sealing the Gang of Four's fate, but Hua also became very dependent on FFA veterans. His dependence on military veterans with vastly more experience and greater networks ultimately also brought about his downfall. Within two years of Mao's death, *none* of the potential successors Mao had put into place just prior to his death survived as powerful figures in the party. The Gang of Four had ended in jail, while Hua was sidelined at the third plenum in 1978. Even FFA veteran Li Desheng, who had served as vice chairman of the party for a short while, ended his career in the 1980s as the head of the National Defense University (Zhu 2007: 425). Except for key members of the FFA group, the vast majority of Mao's coalition of the weak had ended in jail or in retirement by the early 1980s. His legacy of continuous revolution also was completely expunged from the party ideology in favor of a single-minded focus on economic development.

The death of Mao also represented a critical juncture that determined the power balance in China for the next three decades. Because of the continual role played by the FFA in the PLA, Deng emerged as a pivotal figure. As an outside patron of many FFA veterans, he remained the lone figure who could control the FFA bloc without being a member of the group. In the meantime, his policies of rehabilitation and economic reconstruction, which he credibly signaled in the late Mao years, drew other revolutionary veterans to him. Thus, soon after Mao's death and the arrests of the Gang of Four, the remaining veterans began to clamor for his rehabilitation, which occurred in short order. For the newly reempowered Deng, he was incentivized to rehabilitate hundreds of Long March veterans, especially in the PLA, because he did not want to rely solely on the FFA in the military. To fill civilian positions formerly occupied by the scribblers, Deng and the other surviving veterans at first rehabilitated scores of purged veterans from the Northern Bureau and the other factions. The mass rehabilitation of veterans set elite politics in the 1980s on a course of power sharing, where Deng, even as the first among equals, had to consult with representatives of the major factions on key decisions. Power sharing encouraged institution building for the regime as rehabilitated veterans competed with each other to increase resources to and define the authorities of the bureaucracies they controlled. As Chapter 7 details, the power-sharing arrangement of the 1980s also shaped succession arrangements in that period, which provided the preconditions for political outcomes in the run-up to the post–Hu Jintao transition.

SCRIBBLERS TO THE DUSTBIN OF HISTORY

After the arrest of the Gang of Four, they were accused of being a part of a "counterrevolutionary group" and of plotting an "armed rebellion in Shanghai" after Mao's death (Supreme People's Court 1982). To be sure, the scribblers sought a politically advantageous arrangement for themselves, but there were few signs that they actually had designs for complete power. Nonetheless, the Gang of Four's strategy had aimed at isolating Hua Guofeng, Mao's designated successor, which backfired on them within weeks of Mao's passing. Immediately after Mao's death, both Wang Hongwen, then a vice chairman of the party, and Hua Guofeng, the first vice chairman of the party, phoned all the provinces in the name of the party center, each competing to appear as the voice of the party center at that crucial moment (Ye 2009: 1315). At the first Politburo meeting after Mao's death, Jiang Qing criticized Hua Guofeng for being incompetent, which later was interpreted as proof of Jiang's naked ambition. However, Yao Wenyuan and Zhang Chunqiao followed with pleas to strengthen collective leadership, which suggested that the Gang of Four had merely wanted to undermine Hua's emerging status as "first among equals" (Zheng 2017: 755). Regardless, these initial attacks on Hua hardened his attitude toward the scribblers and laid the foundation to Hua's plan to arrest them.

Another charge against the Gang of Four was that they had armed the militia in Shanghai, thus making them guilty of fomenting an "armed uprising" (Supreme People's Court 1982). To be sure, members of the Gang of Four were in regular contact with Nanjing Military Region Commander Ding Sheng, who was a remnant member of Lin Biao's coterie, and Ding was "guilty" of notifying Zhang Chunqiao of Xu Shiyou's threat of "preparing for war" against the Gang of Four (Zheng 2017: 748). According to Ding Sheng, conversations he had with Zhang Chunqiao had taken place in accordance with standard procedures considering that Zhang had been the head of the General Political Department of the PLA, a position that had allowed him to rotate military units and to distribute arms to militia (Ding 2008: 278). If Ding had heard rumors of another member of the military threatening civil war, it was his duty to notify Zhang Chunqiao, who was in charge of political control of the military. In other words, later charges of an "armed uprising" were on shaky ground given the enormous formal power Zhang Chunqiao had in the PLA. Meanwhile, in September 1976, Hua Guofeng had multiple conversations with representatives of the FFA and with Ye Jianying to plot the arrests of his duly elected Politburo colleagues (Zhang 2004).

As Hua contemplated a move against the Gang of Four after Mao's death, he knew he needed the military's cooperation and devised a clever maneuver. In September 1976, he asked Li Xiannian, the head of the FFA faction, to approach Ye Jianying about removing the Gang of Four (New fourth Army research society et al. 2009: 201; Xiong 2008). If Ye had reported the request to Jiang Qing, Hua could have blamed it on the lone act of a former renegade. The entire FFA group would have been purged, but Hua likely would have survived it because he was Mao's anointed successor. On the other hand, if Ye confessed his willingness to betray Jiang Qing, Hua, knowing the historical animosity between Ye and the FFA, would have been more certain of the sincerity of Ye's willingness to cooperate. The meeting went according to the second scenario, and Ye only had one question for Li, which he wrote on a piece of paper for fear of listening devices: "Chen Xilian?" to which Li replied "completely reliable, please ease your heart" (Liang 2010: 12). After this crucial meeting, Ye and Wang Dongxing began to set in motion plans to arrest the Gang of Four. Just in case, though, Wang and Ye did not share the exact plans with Chen Xilian or Li Xiannian (MacFarquhar and Schoenhals 2006: 445; Xia 2005a). This episode reveals that even a weak successor like Hua Guofeng could make use of the historical guilt of the FFA.

Although FFA veterans did not take an active part in the arrest of the Gang of Four on October 6, 1976, it could not have proceeded smoothly without their cooperation. For one, the Beijing Garrison and the Beijing Military Region were both controlled by them. Chen Xilian, who was the commander of the Beijing Military Region, recalled that Wang Dongxing had approached him about moving troops in the Beijing Garrison, and without a second thought, Chen told Wang that he could move troops without his permission (Chen 2007: 390). Had Chen ordered troops to resist the Central Guard Unit in charge of the arrests, civil war would have erupted in China. Immediately after the arrests, Xu Shiyou was summoned to Beijing, where he guaranteed that troops in Shanghai would resist any Gang of Four attempt to co-opt the army (Vogel 2011: 179). By 1976, Xu Shiyou had no formal authority over any troops in Shanghai because he was no longer the commander of the Nanjing Military Region, which encompassed Shanghai. Yet his cooperation was crucial. The cooperation of Chen in Beijing and Xu in Shanghai ensured that the Gang of Four's removal went off without bloodshed.

On September 26, 1976, Hua Guofeng had one last meeting with Li Xiannian and Wu De to discuss the method of removing the Gang of Four. Wu De, a Politburo member, got cold feet and suggested a Politburo vote to remove the Gang of Four, but Li Xiannian's reply was "do you know how Khrushchev came to power?" (Ye 2009: 53). This reference likely was a slight misunderstanding on Li's part of the attempted ousting of Khrushchev by the Presidium of the CPSU in 1957, which Khrushchev defeated by mobilizing votes in his favor from Central Committee members (Taubman 2003: 275). Because of the infusion of numerous mass representatives into the Central Committee at the 10th Party Congress, Li and the other plotters were afraid of a similar scenario if they had attempted to oust the Gang of Four through a Politburo vote. They thus made up their minds about a military solution.

Politically, the main plotters were Hua Guofeng, Ye Jianying, Li Xiannian, and Mao's longtime bodyguard Wang Dongxing. After the political decision was made, Wang Dongxing took charge and organized four teams of seasoned guards in the Central Guard Unit to carry out the arrests (Ye 2009: 36; Zhang 2008b: 269). Under the pretext of summoning them to a meeting at Zhongnanhai, the leadership compound at the center of Beijing, the members of the Gang of Four – Jiang Qing, Yao Wenyuan, Zhang Chunqiao, and Wang Hongwen – were arrested in turn without bloodshed. The next day, thirty or so Gang of Four followers were arrested, including Mao's nephew Mao Yuanxin (Vogel 2011: 181). As Kong Dan, the son of security minister Kong Yuan, observes about the arrest of the scribblers: "[I]n the end, weaponizing criticism could not stand up to criticism by weapons" (Kong and Mi 2013: 140). Every member of the Gang of Four would spend at least ten years in prison, with Jiang Qing and Wang Hongwen dying in captivity.

THE RISE OF DENG AND POWER SHARING IN THE 1980S

A by-product of Mao's coalition of the weak strategy was that no one could completely dominate the party after the coalition of the weak had collapsed. The FFA bloc and the surviving veterans, however, agreed on one thing: that Deng Xiaoping would be first among equals in the new ruling coalition. After his rehabilitation, Deng himself also had incentives to maintain the power-sharing arrangement, thus inaugurating an era of power sharing between Deng and a handful of "immortals." The ruling coalition in the 1980s included Deng and his core followers, FFA veterans, key party figures with ties to the FFA bloc, and rehabilitated First and Second Front Army veterans (Huang 2000). The subsequent decades of policy oscillation due to disagreement between the "immortals" doubtless frustrated Deng, but it also institutionalized politics within the party to some extent (Miller 2008). Finally, the relatively decentralized pattern of power in the party led to a decentralized pattern of promoting successors, which, as Chapter 7 reveals, would have an impact on contemporary politics in China.

Soon after the arrest of the Gang of Four, revolutionary veterans who had survived the last round of Maoist purge began advocating Deng's rehabilitation, partly in an effort to rehabilitate their own power bases. For Li Xiannian, he probably would have been happy with not rehabilitating Deng because Chairman Hua depended almost exclusively on the support of FFA veterans. This gave Li and other FFA veterans enormous power. However, Hua's insistence on the "Two Whatevers" line, a pledge to adhere to Mao's dictums from the Cultural Revolution, limited his policy options and prevented him from rehabilitating too many veterans who had been purged by Mao. Also, Hua could not have rehabilitated too many veterans because his ruling coalition included a number of junior cadres promoted during the Cultural Revolution. These cadres, including Ji Dengkui, Wu De, Ni Zhifu, Chen Yonggui, and Li Xin, would have been displaced by rehabilitated veterans (Vogel 2011: 240). This limited Hua's support coalition and gave rise to an opposition that advocated large-scale rehabilitation of veterans, starting with Deng. When Ye Jianying himself signaled that he preferred Deng's rehabilitation (Document Research Center of the CCP CC 2004), Li Xiannian and others in the tainted group likely realized that they gained more by bargaining with Deng for positions in the new leadership than from backing a likely loser.

In late February 1977, before his rehabilitation, Deng and Ye met for a long talk, likely working out the future ruling coalition of China (Document Research Center of the CCP CC 2004). Then, at a crucial March 1977 Politburo meeting, most of the veterans who had been in power then – Ye Jianying, Wang Zhen, Chen Yun, Hu Yaobang, Li Xiannian – called for Deng's rehabilitation, whereas Hua Guofeng and Wang Dongxing opposed it (Deng 2005: 85; Vogel 2011: 193). By July 1977, an official CC document was issued, which restored Deng to the Standing Committee of the Politburo, vice chairman of the party, vice chairman of the Central Military Commission, and vice premier (Document Research Center of the CCP CC 2004). After that, Deng, Hua, Ye, Chen Yun, and Li Xiannian began to appear in public together as the collective leadership of China.

Deng's alliance with Li was clearly motivated: Li represented the largest single bloc in the military that had close historical ties with Deng. For his own part, Li likely saw little choice besides supporting Deng because so many in the FFA had their allegiance to Deng (Table 5.1). Moreover, even under a Deng leadership, Li knew that his role as the representative of the tainted faction remained indispensable. Thus, even before he publicly supported Deng's rehabilitation in March 1977, Li had met Deng and had suggested to Deng that he should at least come back to serve as vice premier (Huang et al. 2010). He also supported Chen Yun occupying a senior position partly because Chen was the only elite witness to the legitimacy of the Western Legion, which was the formative experience in Li's life (Zhang and Hu 2010). Also, Li and Chen had worked closely together in the 1950s and 1960s to manage economic affairs.

But what motivated the mutual support between Deng and Ye Jianying, who was still a strong supporter of Hua Guofeng? Besides isolating Wang Dongxing and Ji Dengkui, Deng likely retained Ye

Jianying at the highest level because Ye remained a trump card against FFA veterans. Until the end of his life, Ye continued to insist that he had received the telegram sent by Zhang Guotao, which urged Xu Xiangqian and Chen Changhao to "thoroughly struggle" against the Central Committee during the last stage of the Long March (Zhang 2008a). If FFA veterans had dared to challenge Deng's power, Ye would have made an appearance again as a witness to their treachery, as he did in 1935. Ye likely acceded to Deng's rehabilitation because so many cadres in his limited faction had supported Deng. For one, Hu Yaobang, whom Ye had rehabilitated two days after the Gang of Four's arrest, began clamoring for Deng's rehabilitation as soon as he had been reinstated (Man 2005: 202). Chen Yun, expecting Deng to revive the State Council bureaucracy, also supported Deng's rehabilitation (Document Research Center of the CCP CC 2000). Ye also mistakenly thought that Deng and Hua would continue to corule in tension, which would have given Ye an important pivotal role. However, Deng formed a powerful coalition with rehabilitated cadres and FFA veterans to sideline Hua within a year. In the emerging debate between the "Two Whatever" line championed by Hua and the "Practice" line favored by Deng, Li Xiannian took a clear stance supporting the "Practice" line (Hu 1998: 48). As the tide turned against Hua in the fall of 1978, Ye tried to resist Hua's removal, but it merely delayed the inevitable (Deng 2005: 170; Vogel 2011: 240).

After his restoration to power, Deng clearly did not want to solely rely on the support of the FFA faction and pursued two main strategies to balance against FFA veterans. First and foremost, Deng rehabilitated officers from the other front armies who had been purged by Mao. Second, in the midst of wholesale reversal of verdicts on large groups of cadres with "historical problems," Deng did not reappraise the sins of the FFA, thus leaving them vulnerable to charges of "counterrevolutionary splittism" for the remainder of their lives. FFA veterans continued to play an important role in commanding the Chinese military throughout the 1980s and even into the 1990s with historical stains on their records.

In the 1978–1982 period, Deng rehabilitated scores of Long Marchers from the other front armies and thousands of more junior revolutionary veterans, who filled high-level positions in newly reconstituted party and state organs, including members of Liu Shaoqi's doomed faction such as Peng Zhen, Lu Dingyi, and Bo Yibo. As shown in Table 6.1, new entrants into the Politburo in the 1956 8th Party Congress, as well as new and existing CC members, had similar profiles, having joined the party around the time of the CCP-KMT split in 1927. As outlined in Chapters 4 and 5,

TABLE 6.1 *Average party tenure of new Politburo and Central Committee entrants: 8th Party Congress to 14th Party Congress*

	8th PC	9th PC	10th PC	11th PC	12th PC	13th PC	14th PC
Average Party Tenure of Politburo Entrants	30.7	35	28.5	44	47.8	36.5	42.4
Average Party Tenure of CC Entrants	28.4	29.4	30.5	37	38.5	36.1	38.4

the Cultural Revolution led to the rejuvenation of the Chinese leadership with the introduction of scribblers' mafia and mass representatives into both the Politburo and the Central Committee, thus arresting the rise of average party tenures of new Politburo and Central Committee members, even though thirteen years had passed between the 8th and the 9th Congress (Table 6.1). The wave of rehabilitation that began after the purge of Lin Biao and continued with the Dengist rehabilitation produced a Politburo leadership cohort dominated by revolutionary veterans with an average of forty-seven years of party membership and an average of 38.5 years of party membership at the CC level by the 12th Party Congress. Below the top level, thousands of officials, most of whom with revolutionary credentials, were rehabilitated to central-level party and State Council positions in 1978 alone (Central Organization Department et al. 1997b: 3).

This wave of rehabilitation was accompanied by large-scale institutional rebuilding and creation matched only by the decade after 1949. On the party side, dozens of major units such as the Central Party School were reconstituted, staffed by revolutionary veterans (Central Organization Department et al. 1997b: 282). On the State Council side, in addition to the revival of dozens of traditional ministries, new ministerial organizations were also formed to meet the challenges of a reforming economy. The late 1970s and early 1980s saw the creation of the State Economic Systems Reform Commission, State Science and Technology Commission, State Council Export-Import Commission, the Ministry of Urban Construction and Environmental Protection, and scores of other ministerial and vice-ministerial organs, headed mainly by Long March veterans and younger revolutionary veterans (Central Organization Department et al. 1997b: 285). Followers of the different factions staffed the thousands of new positions these ministries created in this period.

In the military, FFA veterans continued to feature prominently in the leadership, but they increasingly had to share power with rehabilitated veterans from the other front armies. Between 1977 and 1982, Xu Xiangqian, Li Xiannian, and Chen Xilian served as standing committee members in the Central Military Commission, making them a major bloc in this thirteen-person body. Of the forty members of the Central Military Commission (CMC) in this period, one-fourth came from the FFA. When the CMC was reconstituted and vastly shrunken in 1983, FFA officers, including Xu Xiangqian and Hong Xuezhi, took two of the nine seats, while the other seats were filled by rehabilitated veterans such as Zhang Aiping, Nie Rongzhen, and Yang Shangkun (He et al. 1993). Ye Jianying also continued as vice chairman of the CMC. On a daily basis, Deng maintained this balanced coalition by consulting senior representatives of the major factions on important decisions, including the appointment of senior civilian and military officials. For example, when Deng considered appointing Yu Qiuli the head of the PLA General Political Department in 1982, he instructed his secretary to consult "the three marshals," that is, Ye Jianying, Xu Xiangqian, and Nie Rongzhen, as well as Li Xiannian and Chen Yun (Document Research Center of the CCP CC 2004). The "three marshals" who represented the First Front Army and the FFA, also became vice chairmen of the Central Military Commission from 1982 to 1987 (He et al. 1993).

Although the FFA was a part of the ruling coalition and was consulted on all major decisions, its tainted past meant that it was the weaker partner. Zhao Ziyang, for example, recalled routinely ignoring Li Xiannian's wishes, forcing Li to exert influence through more junior officials such as Deng Liqun (Zhao 2009: 247). Vogel (2011: 353) also heard from elite informants that the ruling coalition in the 1980s was "two and a half – Deng and Chen were roughly equal and Li was one step behind." On economic matters, Li Xiannian exerted greater influence, but only if he made policies with Chen Yun's blessing. For example, because both Chen Yun and Li Xiannian supported Li Peng's appointment as the Premier in 1988, this appointment moved forward (Zhao 2009: 211). In contrast, Li Xiannian alone had backed Deng Liqun's promotion to the Politburo, but without Chen Yun or Deng Xiaoping's support, he watched helplessly as Zhao Ziyang orchestrated a campaign to eliminate Deng Liqun from even the alternate list of the Central Committee at the 1987 13th Party Congress (Deng 2005: 472; Zhao 2009: 201). Even fifty years after their crimes, veterans of the FFA still had little ability to exert independent power at the highest level, even though they held senior positions in both the civilian and the military spheres.

Clearly, the wave of rehabilitation starting in 1977 diminished the dominance of the FFA, but the new collective leadership had no intention

TABLE 6.2 *Predicted probability of a 1955 lieutenant general holding a position of real power after 1982*

	Probability of Holding a Command or a CC Seat Among post-1978 Survivors	Probability of Holding a Command or a CC Seat
First Front Army	0.63 [0.44 0.82]	0.42 [0.29 0.56]
Second Front Army	0.72 [0.49 0.95]	0.46 [0.25 0.67]
Fourth Front Army	0.76 [0.61 0.92]	0.54 [0.38 0.7]

of eradicating the influence of the FFA. To show that the new leadership did not seek to eradicate the influence of FFA veterans, I conduct logit analysis on 253 brigadier generals or above who had been ranked in 1955. The dependent variable is whether a general continued to hold either a Central Committee position or an active command after the 12th Party Congress in 1982. The independent variables are dummy variables for FFA and Second Front Army, with membership in the First Front Army being the null case. Control variables include rank, birth year, year of joining the party, education level, and fighting experience in Korea. Instead of presenting the regression coefficients, Table 6.2 presents the predicted probability of a lieutenant general holding either a CC seat or an active military command after 1982. The third column shows higher probability of a FFA veteran holding an active command than First Front Army veterans after 1982. However, that may have been a by-product of fewer of them undergoing the physical and mental torment of purges during the Cultural Revolution. Indeed, this seems to be the case. When we only examine the survivors of the Cultural Revolution in 1978 on the second column, FFA veterans had roughly the same chance of receiving an active command as their counterparts in the First and Second Front Army. This result, however, shows that Deng and the other leaders did not discriminate against FFA veterans in the 1980s. They just did not receive the preferential treatment that Mao had bestowed on them.

The resulting political equilibrium was relatively stable because even as Deng and Hu Yaobang removed criminal labels from hundreds of veterans, Deng never rehabilitated the history of the FFA. Thus, the FFA's loyalty to the incumbent continued to be a condition of their occupying important positions in the new leadership. When Deng Xiaoping reassessed history after the Cultural Revolution, the central leadership still voted to label the Zhang Guotao line as "splittism" (Document Research Center of CCP Central Committee 1983). Chen Yun, perhaps delivering on promises he had made to Li, began to clamor for a rehabilitation of the Western Legion's history in 1981, arguing that the Western Legion's march west had been approved by the Central Committee and therefore was not a product of "Zhang Guotao opportunism" as Mao had argued in the 1930s (Zhang and Hu 2010). However, Chen Yun knew that the full rehabilitation of the Western Legion would have diminished Li Xiannian's dependence on him. Thus, after Li Xiannian had written a detailed account of the Western Legion in 1983, instead of using this document as the basis of a full rehabilitation of the Western Legion, Chen Yun recommended the document be stored in the party archive, a move that was approved by Deng (Zhang and Hu 2010). Although storing the document in the party archive meant that Li Xiannian's account of the Western Legion was acknowledged by the Central Committee, it was far from a full rehabilitation, which would have involved the issuance of a Central Committee document explicitly refuting the "Zhang Guotao opportunism" label on the Western Legion. This was a slap on the face for Li and the other survivors of the Western Legion at a time when thousands of others were exonerated of their historical crimes.

In addition to large-scale institutional rehabilitation, rule by coalition also compelled Deng to sequence the implementation of reform to favor measures with widespread support within the ruling coalition, such as decollectivization and forming the special economic zones (SEZs) (Shirk 1993). For decollectivization, it was such a widely supported policy in the elite circle that Deng quickly implemented it after the removal of its final obstacle, Chairman Hua Guofeng (Fewsmith 1994: 115). Meanwhile, although Chen Yun remained uncomfortable about the SEZs in the early 1980s, Deng supported it because Ye Jianying, a crucial ally in the military to balance against the FFA bloc, had strongly backed liberal investment policies for his native Guangdong Province (Gao 1999:133). Because these low-hanging fruits had such major economic payoffs, Deng's political strategy born of necessity led to massive productivity gains that fueled decades of growth in China (Lin 1992).

THE FFA IN TIANANMEN AND BEYOND

Deng's strategy of using the tainted faction to balance against the other factions in the PLA continued into the late 1980s and formed the foundation of his succession strategy. By preserving the FFA bloc in the military, Deng ensured that the party survived the biggest political shock since the Cultural Revolution, the Tiananmen Protests.

The 13th Party Congress in 1987 resulted in a major wave of retirement as well as a substantial reshuffling of the Central Military Commission. Instead of the "three marshals" system, Ye Jianying had passed away in 1986, while Xu Xiangqian and Nie Rongzhen had stepped down from the CMC. In their place, general secretary Zhao Ziyang became the first vice chairman of the CMC, signifying him as Deng's successor at the time. Meanwhile, Yang Shangkun, a First Front Army veteran who had never led troops, became the secretariat of CMC, which put him in charge of its daily operation. FFA veterans and their protégés Liu Huaqing, Hong Xuezhi, and Chi Haotian, however, took vice secretariat and membership positions in the CMC (Central Organization Department et al. 1997b).

Besides being a fellow Sichuanese who had worked closely with Deng in the 1950s and a capable administrator, Yang also was a total stranger to the FFA bloc. In his meticulously kept diary, Yang recorded only three perfunctory meetings with Li Xiannian during his fifteen-year tenure in the 1950s and the 1960s as head of the Administrative Office of the Central Committee, the nerve center of the party (Yang 2001b). There were no personal meetings with Li or any other member of the FFA despite daily meetings with scores of other revolutionary veterans. This was not surprising as Yang was preoccupied with running a network of spies in the "white" areas occupied by the Japanese and the KMT for much of the thirties and forties (Central Organization Department and Party History Research Center of CCP CC 2004). In the 1950s and the first half of the 1960s, Li Xiannian, who had been the vice premier in charge of food supply, was the only high-level FFA veteran in the civilian sphere, and he only met with Yang when Yang wanted to know about food supplies (Yang 2001b). Yang was placed in detention in late 1965 for twelve years and had no interaction with FFA veterans who came to occupy high-level military positions during the Cultural Revolution. The complete absence of friendship between Yang and veterans of the tainted faction made an alliance between them against Deng unlikely.

By maintaining the FFA's vulnerability and by appointing an outsider to monitor FFA veterans, Deng controlled the military through the Tiananmen crisis. The Tiananmen Square protests and subsequent massacre were nothing short of a political crisis in the CCP. The formal head of the party, Zhao Ziyang, favored negotiations with the student protest-ors, while the de facto head of the party, Deng Xiaoping, turned to a hardline solution of military crackdown. The FFA bloc still maintained enormous influence over land forces in China because FFA veterans had commanded numerous military regions for decades prior to 1989. Had the FFA bloc sided with Zhao Ziyang in 1989, history would have had a very different outcome. Yet they remained politically vulnerable to charges of "splittism" and, further, were internally divided by varying degrees of loyalty they owed to Deng Xiaoping personally. FFA veterans thus had little choice but to back the military crackdown favored by Deng.

As the students escalated the protests on May 12, 1989, with hunger strikes, the leadership began to divide over how to end the protests. While Zhao Ziyang advocated negotiations with more moderate students, sev-eral surviving elders from the Long March generation, including Peng Zhen, Li Xiannian, and Chen Yun, called for a decisive response (Deng et al. 2001). By May 17, 1989, Deng had made up his mind to move troops into Beijing to finally quell the protests (Zhao 2009: 28). Although Li Xiannian clearly took a hardline position, he only did so because Chen Yun, Wang Zhen, and other Long March veterans also took a hard stance. Had Deng supported a moderate position, Li likely would have stayed out of the debate. As for the FFA veterans in the PLA, available evidence suggests that they largely stayed out of the debate while First Front Army colleagues like Yang Shangkun were at the heart of the political scheming (Zhao 2009: 23–36). This was remarkable considering that both Hong Xuezhi and Liu Huaqing were vice chairmen of the CMC and were from the Long March generation. Without their historical guilt, they could have played a pivotal role in the debate about the crackdown and the debate on Zhao Ziyang's successor. Instead, the key decision makers in that period included Deng, Yang Shangkun, Li Xiannian, Chen Yun, Bo Yibo, Peng Zhen, Wang Zhen, and Deng Yingchao, Zhou Enlai's widow (Party Central Office Secretariat 2001a). Li Xiannian was the lone voice representing the FFA faction, again remarkable considering that it had been over fifty years since the disbanding of the FFA. When the decision on imposing the martial law was made, Hong Xuezhi only said, "[F]or a soldier, duty is paramount. I will resolutely carry out the order to put Beijing under martial law" (Yang 2001a).

Once the decision was made, the army, led by many FFA veterans and their protégés, swung into action. On May 18, Yang Shangkun chaired an enlarged meeting of the CMC, attended by Hong Xuezhi, Qin Jiwei, Liu

Huaqing, Chi Haotian – all in the FFA bloc – as well as Yang Baibing and Zhao Nanqi. Not surprisingly, the meeting decided to resolutely carry out the decision by veteran revolutionaries, many of whom were already in retirement, to implement martial law and to clear the square (Yang 2001a). By that point, of course, Zhao Ziyang, the general secretary of the party, was excluded from such meetings. Yang Shangkun made the plans, and a martial law headquarters was set up, which was commanded by Liu Huaqing; Chi Haotian, then the PLA chief of staff; and Zhou Yibing, the commander of the Beijing Military Region (Yang 2001a).

After consulting with his FFA colleagues, Yang Shangkun decided to deploy troops from the Beijing, Shenyang, and Jinan Military Regions (Yang 2001a). To be sure, in the interest of proximity, it made sense to deploy troops from the Beijing Military Region, but it also happened to be a main stronghold of FFA veterans, as they had held the commander position there from 1969 to 1987 without interruption (Central Organization Department et al. 1997b). Although Zhou Yibing, the commander of Beijing MR in 1989, was from a younger generation, he had spent the bulk of his officer career in the Beijing MR under the command of FFA veterans (Baidu 2014b). Had that not been the case, it might have taken much longer to move sufficient number of troops into Beijing. Likewise, the Shenyang Military Region had been a FFA stronghold from 1959 to 1985. The commander of the Shenyang MR at the time, Li Jingsong, was a protégé of Li Desheng who spent the bulk of his career under the command of FFA veterans (Baidu 2014a). Meanwhile, the Jinan MR had been dominated by First Front Army veterans from Jiangxi. With the exception of one army level commander refusing to carry out the order (Wu 2007), troops from these three military regions brutally executed the order of the elders and quashed the nascent democracy movement on Tiananmen Square on the night of June 3, 1989 (Calhoun 1994).

In the aftermath of the Tiananmen massacre, Deng Xiaoping had to rethink his succession strategy from scratch. Already, two of his proposed successors, Hu Yaobang and Zhao Ziyang, had failed. To salvage his political legacy, Deng made two crucial decisions. First, he would consult with the surviving revolutionary elders about a successor. Second, he would retire from the chairmanship of the Central Military Commission and hand the baton over to his successor. Yet the informal power configuration he left to his successor, Jiang Zemin, was the same one that Mao himself had devised – competitive tension between First and Fourth Front Army veterans in the military. This tension allowed a junior upstart like

Jiang Zemin to survive two major political crises and established himself as China's ruler even after Deng's passing.

Almost immediately after the June 4 crackdown, Deng began to signal that he wanted to retire from the chairmanship of the Central Military Commission (Li 2007: 321; Vogel 2011: 645). Despite some initial opposition, Deng got his way, and at the November 1989 Fifth Plenum, Jiang Zemin was elected as the new chairman of the Central Military Commission with Yang Shangkun as the first vice chairman and his brother Yang Baibing as the CMC secretary general (Vogel 2011: 647). Just in case, though, Liu Huaqing, a FFA stalwart and a Deng protégé, also became CMC vice chairman. Although Yang Shangkun participated in the Long March as a member of the First Front Army, he never led troops directly or formed his own guerilla base, which limited the size of his power base (Central Organization Department and Party History Research Center of CCP CC 2004). Rather, he had been a lifelong political commissar and a spymaster for the military (Yang 2001b). His brother, who didn't even join the party until 1938, had a similar profile (Central Organization Department and Party History Research Center of CCP CC 2004). Deng might have chosen the Yang Brothers to run the military on his behalf after his retirement precisely because of their relatively weak power base.

Nonetheless, after 1989, the collective leadership of Deng and a handful of revolutionary elders broke down as many of them had passed away in rapid succession. In 1992, Deng Yingchao, Chen Yun, Li Xiannian, and Nie Rongzhen all passed away in rapid succession, and many of them had been infirmed in the previous two years and could no longer participate in major decisions (Central Organization Department and Party History Research Center of CCP CC 2004). Thus, the Yang Brothers had fewer and fewer checks against their actions.

When Deng embarked on his 1992 Southern Tour to signal to the new leadership his displeasure with the slow pace of reform, the Yang Brothers saw a chance to be the new kingmakers. Yang Baibing, who controlled the propaganda apparatus in the army, published articles vowing that the PLA would serve as the "protective escort" of reform, which deepened the implicit threat against the new civilian rulers of China, Jiang Zemin and Li Peng (Gilley 1998: 151). Moreover, after hearing that Deng had a minor stroke just before the 14th Party Congress, Yang Baibing convened a series of meetings discussing succession arrangements and may have suggested Qiao Shi as an alternative to Jiang (Lam 1995: 212). Yang Baibing also drafted a list of 100 officers to promote after the 14th Party

Congress, showing his ambition to control the entire military (Nathan and Gilley 2002: 153).

Jiang Zemin, who had only been in power for a little more than two years, saw bad omens in the Yangs' activities. Fortunately, his most trusted advisor was Zeng Qinghong, a princeling with extensive ties with the various factions in Beijing. Partly through Zeng's lobbying and deal-making, Jiang got the backing of Liu Huaqing as well as that of the other Long March stalwarts such as Chen Yun and Zhang Aiping (Gilley 1998: 195; Nathan and Gilley 2002: 153). With the support of various elders, but especially those from the FFA contingent in the military, Jiang asked Deng's son Deng Pufang to broach the subject of the ambitious Yang to his father (Nathan and Gilley 2002: 153). In wanting to establish Jiang's ability to govern as the strongest leader in the party, Deng concurred with Jiang's request and forced both of the Yang brothers into retirement at the 14th Party Congress (Gilley 1998: 195; Lam 1995: 212; Vogel 2011: 685).

Clearly, giving too much power to any significant bloc in the military was too dangerous for junior politicians with no military experience like Jiang Zemin. Deng's final gift to Jiang was a reversion to the power structure in the military from the 1970s – a balance between the surviving First Front Army faction and the FFA faction. At the 1992 14th Party Congress, Deng appointed two of the last survivors of the Long March as vice chairmen of the Central Military Commission: Zhang Zhen, a First Front Army veteran, and Liu Huaqing, a FFA veteran. Liu Huaqing, who also had worked closely with Deng at the 129th Division of the Eighth Route Army in the late 1930s, was further named a member of the Politburo Standing Committee, the highest governing body of the Chinese Communist Party. Yet Deng left a counterweight against Liu Huaqing at the last minute. Days before the 14th Party Congress, Zhang Zhen, a First Front Army veteran who had been preparing to retire from the National Defense University, found out that he would join the new Central Military Commission as a vice chairman, but not a member of the new Politburo Standing Committee (Zhang 2007: 357).

As Deng's health failed in the mid-1990s, Jiang was increasingly on his own. Also, with the passing of most of the high-level veterans of the Long March, Liu Huaqing increasingly had the run of the military, a first for FFA veterans in sixty years. When Jiang wanted to firm up the party's control over the economy by having the PLA divest some of its businesses, he had to send Vice Premier Zhu Rongji to negotiate directly with Liu Huaqing, but Liu only handed a small share of PLA businesses over in

1993 (Lam 1995: 233). Furthermore, Liu Huaqing, who had been an officer in the PLA Navy since the 1950s, used his influence in the navy to protect an enormous smuggling racket organized by the Yuanhua Corporation based in Fujian (Pomfret 2000). Navy ships were even used as escorts for the smuggle ships, and firefights broke out between naval and customs vessels (Inside Mainland China 1998). As Chapter 7 discusses, Jiang was in the generation of "always nice people" (*laohaoren*) that the founding generation had promoted in the 1980s, who found it difficult to overcome even a tainted veteran of the FFA.

Finally, in the run-up to the 15th Party Congress in 1997, Jiang managed to dislodge the unruly Liu Huaqing. First, he split the surviving FFA bloc by promoting Chi Haotian, a longtime Xu Shiyou protégé from the Nanjing Military Region, into a CMC vice chairman position in September 1995. This effectively diluted Liu's power in the military because Chi represented the remnant Xu Shiyou faction. According to one account, although Liu Huaqing opposed this promotion, Deng Xiaoping, in one of his final acts as a politician, supported Jiang's maneuver (Lam 1999: 184). Second, in the middle of the 15th Party Congress in 1997, Jiang suddenly called an enlarged Politburo meeting to discuss whether he himself, Qiao Shi, or Liu Huaqing should retire at the end of the congress. Likely having made a deal with Jiang ahead of time, Northern Bureau veteran Bo Yibo suddenly chimed in to argue that while Jiang, as the head of the leadership, should stay in power for another five years, the other two should retire (Lam 1999: 333). With the retirement of Liu Huaqing from the Central Military Commission at the end of 1998, original members of the "counterrevolutionary splittist" group finally withdrew from high-level political intrigues, over sixty years after their original crime had made them useful tools for China's rulers.

CONCLUSION

Deng's own policy of mass rehabilitation limited his ability to achieve absolute power. With veterans from various "mountaintops" once again dominating the Central Committee at the 1982 12th Party Congress, they also began to clamor for institutional changes to prevent the rise of another Mao. As Fewsmith puts it, Deng "both made a virtue of necessity and rallied the veteran party leaders to his cause by turning away from the personality cult" (Fewsmith 1994: 6). In the revision of the Party Constitution at the 12th Party Congress, a clause forbidding cults of personality was added, while the wording "continuous revolution" was removed (Li 2007: 289). In the early 1980s, mandatory retirement age was also imposed on most party officials, followed by a revision of the state constitution that placed a two-term limit on the head of the state (Manion 1993). Although these institutional changes did not eliminate fundamental uncertainties in authoritarian politics, they reinforced power sharing among successive generations of collective leadership for the next three decades.

With the rise of a relatively balanced coalition at the top of the Communist Party, the leadership also began to consider successors to the revolution. As Chapter 7 shows, far from cultivating capable and powerful successors, the surviving Long Marchers cultivated figures who were weak and obedient, giving rise to a generation of educated but poorly networked leadership. The relatively narrow experience and factional makeup of these leaders created a power vacuum that a small group of princelings took advantage of as they competed with nonprincelings and each other for ultimate power.

7

Weak Successors

The Final Calculus of the Founding Generation and the Rise of Xi Jinping

Although much of this book concerns political dynamics in the Mao Era, the tumults of the Cultural Revolution and the coalition rule that resulted from late-Mao politics indirectly led to an important political outcome by the 2010s, the survival of Xi Jinping as one of the few princelings among political leaders on the civilian side of the CCP. This created one of the preconditions for Xi to dominate the party soon after taking office as the head of the party in late 2012 – the relative absence of competition and oversight from other highly networked princelings. In the 1980s, two forces drove the selection of future leaders in the party. First, founding leaders such as Chen Yun and Deng Xiaoping had a genuine desire to promote a new generation of well-educated, loyal potential successors as their health began to fail them. Second, as the rest of the book has argued, the top leadership and even mid-level officials at the ministerial level did not want serious competitors to their power bases, and each pursued a coalition of the weak strategy within his own jurisdiction. Thus, besides a few senior veterans who had placed their children on accelerated paths for promotion, the vast majority of revolutionary veterans resisted the promotion of princelings due to their Red Guard activism during the Cultural Revolution and to fear of interference by well-networked princelings.

This had consequences on two important outcomes today. First, after the Tiananmen Square crisis forced the Long March generation to select a new generation of top leaders ahead of succession plans, they opted for a group of technically competent but narrowly networked officials, who then held leadership positions in the 1990s and 2000s. Second, the vast majority of princelings had been eliminated from consideration for top CCP positions after the 1990s. By the early 2010s, only a handful of princelings had survived as senior leaders in the party, but they could count on vast networks of princeling supporters in the commercial world and in the PLA. For the surviving princelings, they only had limited competition from each other, while they could draw on the vast princeling networks to trump officials from outside of the revolutionary "bloodline" group. The decades of coalitions of the weak strategy pursued by senior CCP politicians laid the groundwork for complete domination by a princeling politician, Xi Jinping, over his nonprinceling colleagues.

PROMOTING YOUNG CADRES IN THE DENG ERA

After the death of Mao and the arrest of the Gang of Four, the subsequent two party congresses (11th and 12th) saw the rehabilitation of the old guard into the top leadership, thus reversing the rejuvenation of the top leadership seen in the late-Mao years. However, in the early 1980s, surviving veterans like Chen Yun and Deng Xiaoping realized that nature would soon force their hands in choosing successors. After a post-Mao assessment of the backwardness of China's economy, the surviving veterans opted to select a cohort of substantially younger and significantly better-educated "reserve cadres" as potential successors, who were better equipped technically to deal with China's rise in an increasingly complex global economy. The decision to cultivate technocrats as potential successors shaped the makeup of the CCP leadership in the 1990s and 2000s. On the one hand, senior leaders became much more educated than their predecessors within short order, some with highly specialized skills such as nuclear physics (Shih et al. 2010b). On the other hand, the veteran sponsors of these younger leaders preferred those who readily took guidance and orders from their patrons. This produced a cohort of leaders who were described by a Central Organization Department cadre as "a cadre group of 'always nice people'" (老好人) (Cui 2003: 488). In other words, "these cadres will not cause much trouble, but they will not have any outstanding achievements either. They lack in energy and vitality, like bottle stoppers" (Cui 2003: 488). Although the promotion of this generation of technocrats was an integral step in the institutionalization of the vast machinery of the party-state, crucial to governing over an increasingly complex economy, these technocrats proved relatively helpless in the face of resourceful and daring internal challengers.

By 1980, the average age of Central Committee members had reached 64.6 (Figure 7.1), while senior veterans like Chen Yun, Deng Xiaoping, and Ye Jianying were all above 70. As much as they enjoyed returning to

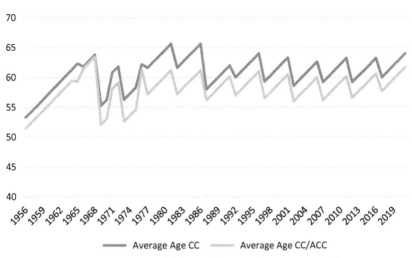

FIGURE 7.1 The average age of full and full and alternate Central Committee members: 1956–2021
Source: (Shih et al. 2015)

power after the deluge of the Cultural Revolution, they also realized that time was not on their side. As Chen Yun chastised his fellow veterans at a 1981 conference for senior cadres, "Your face has some colors, and you have put on some weight. But internally, your structure and your parts have aged" (Chen 1982b: 1165). Meanwhile, Deng also exerted pressure on his colleagues to retire and to promote young officials: "[A]mong those of us here, I am afraid only a small handful is relatively young; most of us are around 60 with the majority above 60. In 7 or 8 years, we will be 70 or over 70. This won't do" (Deng 1994a: 386). In early 1982, Deng successfully pushed through a Central Committee resolution on retirement, which imposed mandatory retirement age of sixty-five on provincial and ministerial officials (Central Committee 1982b). The newly selected secretary general, Hu Yaobang, also supported rapid promotions for younger cadres because he wanted to replace Maoist stalwarts with younger, more open-minded scribblers in the propaganda apparatus (Deng 2005: 365). To be sure, given that rehabilitation had just occurred a few years ago, provisions were made to "preserve a small number of veteran revolutionaries who had exceeded the retirement age," thus preserving the power sharing between Long March veterans (Central Committee 1982b). The revised party constitution at the 12th Party Congress made room for advisory committees staffed with retiring officials to be set up both at the central level and at the provincial level, thus making way for younger cadres to take over leadership positions (Manion 1993).

Discussions of potential successors quickly focused on college graduates with specialized skills, especially in the sciences and engineering. To be sure, a hidden motive in preferring young successors with this profile was that many children of senior leaders had enjoyed preferential admissions into elite Chinese universities in the early 1960s, and most of them opted to major in the sciences and engineering. Well-known princelings such as Chen Yuan, Chen Weilan (children of Chen Yun), Liu Tao (daughter of Liu Shaoqi), Liu Yandong (daughter of Liu Ruilong), Qiao Zonghuai (son of Qiao Guanhua), and He Pengfei (son of He Long) were all graduates of Tsinghua University in the sciences or engineering (Yan 2017: 99, 206). In the early 1980s, Chen Yun set the precedent for promoting specialists with his insistence that Li Peng, the son of a revolutionary martyr and an adoptee of Zhou Enlai, be promoted to a full ministerial-level position because "he is young, and he specializes in electricity...why are we still arguing about him?" (Chen 1982b: 1168).

After Chen Yun called for the formation of a specialized bureau to evaluate and compile lists of young cadres, the Central Organization Department (COD) formally instituted the Youth Cadre Bureau (*Qingnian Ganbuju*), headed by former Mao secretary and Chen Yun ally Li Rui (Yan 2017: 182). Almost immediately upon its formation, the Youth Cadre Bureau (YCB) began to compile a list of "third tier group" (*disan tidui*), commonly known as the reserve cadre list (*houbei ganbu mingdan*) (Yan 2017: 212). By late 1983, the Central Organization Department decreed the selection of some 1,000 cadres with college degrees and between the age of forty-five and fifty into a "reserve" for ministerial-level positions, making them potential future leaders of China (Yan 2017: 212). In accordance to the decision made at the 12th Party Congress, cadres on that list had to be "more revolutionary, younger, more knowledgeable, and more specialized" (Li 2016b).

The establishment of the YCB and the creation of the "third tier group" were major steps in the institutionalization of cadre promotion in the party, as they created a reservoir of senior cadres for decades to come (Cui 2003: 614). After the issuance of the guidance document, hundreds of COD cadres fanned out across China to interview reserve cadre candidates proposed by the provinces, as well as their colleagues and superiors (Cui 2003: 92). In total, over 4,000 senior cadres were consulted in the dozens of ministerial-level organs in Beijing and across China's provinces (Cui 2003: 93). According to Yan Huai, a key YCB cadre heavily involved in compiling the reserve cadre list, the provinces proposed either favorite subordinates of the incumbent provincial leaders or princelings, that is, children of ministerial level or above revolutionary veterans, although some in the former category were rejected due to either insufficient education credentials or Red Guard activism during the Cultural Revolution (Yan 2017: 226). Many Politburo members in the 1990s and 2000s were selected out of the 1984 reserve cadre list, including Wu Yi, Hui Liangyu, Zhang Dejiang, Li Tieying, Liu Yandong, and Xi Jinping (Yan 2017: 220–227).

The formal criteria for the reserve cadre list seemed to accord with the institution of a meritocratic system of promotion, often attributed as the key to high growth in China and across East Asia (Bell 2016; Lee 1991: 3; Wade 1990). However, the way in which China's "technocrats" came to power was not conducive to cultivating well-educated leaders who could stand on their own feet politically. Instead of appointing officials to important local positions or to mid-level central positions for long trial periods before giving them important responsibilities, some among the newly promoted were thrust into positions of great authority without any preparation. For example, Deng personally promoted Wang Zhaoguo, a manager at a car factory in the early 1980s, to the head of the General Office of the Central Committee, the nerve center of the party, in 1984 (Deng 2005). Likewise, Wen Jiabao and Hu Qili enjoyed meteoric rise in the mid-1980s that catapulted them from obscure positions into senior offices over numerous cadres with richer experience and better education. Such "helicoptering" stood in sharp contrast to the orderly promotion of younger cohorts of technocrats seen in other Asian developmental states (Evans 1995; Johnson 1982). A coalition of the weak strategy, instead of nurturing successors, provides better explanation to the rapid promotions of junior officials in the 1980s.

As Chapter 6 points out, new members of both the Politburo and the CC at the 11th and 12th PC were surviving or rehabilitated party veterans. Thus, the average age of Politburo members rose from 61 at the 10th Party Congress to 69.4 by the 12th Party Congress, while their party membership tenure rose to nearly half a century. The sharp increase in the age and party experience of the CC and Politburo members compared with the 10th Party Congress suggests that Deng had indeed fulfilled his "campaign" promise to rehabilitate veteran cadres. However, the rehabilitation of hundreds of cadres with extensive networks meant that the healthier ones demanded positions with some authority and a say in important policies, including policies on promoting younger cadres.

Thus, when the call for the reserve cadre list came out in late 1983, these rehabilitated veterans quickly swung into action to advocate for their favorite underlings. Instead of choosing the most experienced and capable officials, they chose their personal secretaries or those with a special talent for appeasing veteran revolutionaries. In this way, these veterans could have one or more up-and-coming young cadres whom they could count on for favors as they transitioned into retirement. Jiang Zemin, the future party secretary general of the Communist Party, was a major beneficiary of this logic. As a young cadre in the First Ministry of Machinery, Jiang befriended several veteran cadres who had also been assigned there, including minister Zhou Jiannan and Yan Wen, a senior cadre with New Fourth Army and Fourth Field Army ties (Yan 2017: 69). He already had had a reliable patron in New Fourth Army stalwart Wang Daohan, who had served with Jiang's martyred uncle and also had held a senior position in the First Ministry of Machinery (Gilley 1998: 35).

As Jiang's fortune rose, he continued to signal his loyalty to his patrons by visiting them regularly, bringing along lavish gifts of food and traditional Chinese medicine, and helping the children of his patrons land desirable jobs in jurisdictions under his control (Yan 2017: 273). His persistent effort to be the "always nice person" paid off repeatedly. At the 12th Party Congress, Zhou Jiannan recommended him for a seat in the Central Committee, and, in 1985, Wang Daohan strongly recommended him for the mayoral post in Shanghai (Gilley 1998: 83; Yan 2017: 274). These positions paved the way for his eventual appointment to the highest office in the Party. In other words, for officials who obtained ministerial rank in the 1980s and the early 1990s, they had to be adept at appeasing aging veterans, in addition to having technocratic qualifications.

Although revolutionary veterans remained in office for a few more years, Deng, and especially Hu Yaobang, enthusiastically paved the way for their retirement at the 1985 National Representative Conference (全国代表会议) and at the 1987 13th Party Congress. The 1985 National Representative Conference clearly aimed at speeding up cadre retirement before the 13th Party Congress. Sixty-four full and alternate CC members, including a few Politburo members, retired, replaced by sixty-four new full and alternate CC members; another twenty-seven alternate CC members were elevated to full membership (Central Committee 2010). Indeed, Deng expressed his gratitude at the conference to "a group of elderly comrades who through concrete action took the lead to abolish lifetime tenure" (Deng 1993c: 145). Younger cadres catapulted into the

Politburo Standing Committee included Li Peng and Hu Qili, both in their fifties.

To select new cadres for full and alternate CC membership, Hu Yaobang convened a personnel small group in Zhongnanhai composed of his trusted advisors to draw up lists of cadres to promote into ministerial and provincial positions. Deng Liqun claims that Hu dominated the initial step of drawing up lists of candidates, although the lists needed Central Organization Department vetting and approval by the Politburo Standing Committee (Deng 2005: 442). When Zhao Ziyang took over as party secretary general, he continued to convene a personnel small group in the central office to come up with candidates for important positions (Wu 1997: 142).

With the mass retirement of CC members at the 1985 Party Representative Conference, the tone of rejuvenation was set for the 13th Party Congress. Deng and the new party secretary general Zhao Ziyang ensured the rejuvenation of the elite by mandating that 58.5 percent of the delegates had to be below the age of 55 (Li 2007: 304). Relative to the 12th Party Congress, the average age of a CC member at the 13th PC was 2.5 years younger at 57.8, which again is impressive because five years had passed (Figure 7.1). The average "party age" of a CC member dropped by over three years relative to the 12th PC, again signifying a substantial degree of turnover. At the Politburo level, the average age of a new Politburo member dropped dramatically to 59.3 from 66 at the 12th PC, which led to a decrease in the average Politburo age to 64 from 69 at the 12th PC. Deng's gentler method of encouraging retirement with benefits and honorary positions in advisory bodies essentially served the same purpose as the bloody purges of the Cultural Revolution (Manion 1993). Elite institutions like the Politburo and the Central Committee were increasingly filled with cadres with relatively little experience in elite politics and thus shallow elite networks, thus giving surviving veterans greater power, as the model in Chapter 1 suggests. This was especially the case because a group of well-networked younger officials, the princelings, were systematically prevented from rising to senior offices in the 1980s.

THE LOST GENERATION: WHY PRINCELINGS DID NOT DOMINATE POLITICS IN THE 1990S

China observers today talk much about the "princeling advantage" in Chinese politics, and indeed, China's top politicians in the past ten years included several notable princelings: Xi Jinping, Yu Zhengsheng, Liu Yandong, Bo Xilai, and Li Yuanchao (He and Gao 2000; Li 2016a; Wedeman 2003). Yet given the large cohort of children of ministerial or above level officials who came of age in the 1960s, they were surprisingly absent from high-level politics in the 2000s. Although princelings still had much better odds than ordinary people in their cohorts in achieving high political offices, their odds likely did not stand out compared to their peers who had matriculated in China's top high schools and universities in the 1950s and 1960s. This was evident in the modest stations of many children of elite families. PLA Chief of Staff Luo Ruiqing, for example, had eight children born in the baby boom years between 1938 and 1960, but none of them had made it to full ministerial level by 2010. Bo Yibo, a powerful politician in the 1980s, likewise had seven children, but only one eventually made it to full ministerial level before being purged as a Politburo member. In addition to the narrow power base of the nonprinceling technocrats, the elimination of a whole generation of princelings from the highest level of power by the 2000s also allowed the surviving princelings to thrive after the mid-2000s.

The elimination of a large cohort of princelings from elite politics largely stemmed from three sources. First, despite their rehabilitation in the 1980s, many of them continued to live with the stain of their Red Guard activism at the beginning of the Cultural Revolution. Their activities during the Cultural Revolution fundamentally altered their career trajectories and stymied many of their careers during the 1980s, when they needed rapid promotions in order to enter the competition for top positions in the 1990s and 2000s. Second, many of the former conservative Red Guards opted to go into business in the 1980s when it became clear to them that their connections with the political elite gave them major advantages in China's nascent market economy. Third, perhaps most important, besides a few veterans with ambitious children and their close friends, most of the revolutionary veterans were resistant to promoting princeling officials beyond the division or bureau (司局) level because they did not want these princelings to meddle with top-level decisions in their jurisdictions. This led to surprisingly few princelings from the baby boom of the 1940s and 1950s becoming full ministerial-level officials. These three mechanisms of attrition allowed the few princelings who had made it into the Politburo by the early 2000s to have disproportionate influence in the party.

The relatively large cohort of princelings attending high school and college in the 1960s was shaped by the trajectory of the Chinese revolution. In essence, only a handful of top leaders in the CCP had been allowed to bring along with them their spouses during the arduous Long March in 1934 (Sun 2006). Their children certainly could not join the Long March column, and even Mao himself had to abandon two new-borns along the way (Pantsov and Levine 2012: 280). Thus, when the 20,000 or so survivors from the three Long March columns arrived in Yan'an in 1935 and 1936, they were mostly single men, including most in the top leadership. This was not remedied until the establishment of the Anti-Japan University drew women students and progressives from the cities to Yan'an, which led to a wave of marriages between veteran revolutionaries and leftist students and intellectuals in the late 1930s and early 1940s. Mao, for example, remarried to Shanghai film actress Jiang Qing, and others in the top leadership, including Lin Biao, Li Weihan, Chen Yi, Ye Jianying, Peng Dehuai, Kong Yuan, Dong Biwu, and many others, had all married much younger women from the cities. They began to have children in earnest in 1940, and this baby boom continued through much of the 1940s and 1950s (He and Gao 2000).

As Table 7.1 shows, just the ninety-seven 8th Party Congress Central Committee members produced 290 children, an average of nearly three children per CC member (Shih et al. 2015). Other revolutionaries of the Long March pedigree who had been alternate CC members or senior PLA officers produced additional hundreds of children in this period. This revolutionary baby boom thus engendered a large cohort of college students or students in senior high schools on the eve of the Cultural Revolution, who would have been in the prime age for senior offices in the 1990s and 2000s. Yet, among the children of CC members at the 8th Party Congress, only eleven ultimately made it to full ministerial level, or

TABLE 7.1 *Total number of children and ministerial-level children among 8th Party Congress (PC) Central Committee (CC) members and 8th PC CC members who also served as CC members at the 12th PC*

	Total Children	Children Who Achieved Full Ministerial Level by 2010	% Who Achieved Full Ministerial Level by 2010
8th PC CC Members	290	11	3.7 percent
8th PC CC Members Also 12th PC CC Members	64	5	7.8 percent

only a 3.7 percent probability. Although the various internal purges in the party since 1956 had removed many 8th Party Congress CC members from the elite by 1980, even among the sixty-four children of 12th Party Congress CC members, only five ultimately made it to full ministerial rank. To be sure, because of their parents' influence in the 1980s, the majority of these sixty-four princelings achieved director-general (司局级) level ranking, giving princelings much better odds of achieving these mid-level positions than an average person from their cohort. Still, as detailed in the next few pages, their Cultural Revolution activism, elite resistance, and the enticement of nascent capitalism prevented most of them from rising to full ministerial level, thus preventing them from being eligible for the top positions in the Chinese Communist Party.

The children of the revolutionary veterans, especially Long March veterans at or above the ministerial level in the 1950s, had led privileged childhoods despite frequent reminiscences of frugality and deprivation. Even before the CCP took over all of China, special schools for children of senior cadres were set up in Northeastern China with staff and provision from the Soviet Union (Yan 2017: 46). When the PLA took over Beijing, the regime immediately set up kindergarten, elementary schools, and high schools for children of senior CCP officials, as well as for orphans of deceased revolutionaries (Liu 2019). The military, for example, set up a boarding school at the elementary level for children of senior officers, as well as children of officers killed-in-action (Han 2019). By the mid-1950s, the major ministries and ministerial-level party organs in Beijing had set up their own elementary schools to accommodate the baby boom (Yan 2017: 55). At the high school level, an elite system of high school emerged in Beijing, which included established high schools founded in the late Qing or early Republic eras and newly established high schools attached to universities.

Princelings in Beijing, whose parents worked in government and military agencies in the city center, attended one of seventeen elite key-point high schools, including Bayi School, Beijing High School Four (BHSF), Beijing No. 6 High School, the high school attached to Tsinghua University, the high school attached to Beijing Normal University, and the high school attached to Beijing Aeronautical University (Sun 2012; Walder 2009: 124). While the Bayi School was set up by the party exclusively for the children of cadres and revolutionary martyrs, even princelings had to take entrance examinations to gain entry into the other elite high schools (Liu 2012). The most competitive entrance was arguably at the Beijing No. 4 High School (*Beijing Sizhong*), an all-boy school with an enrollment of 1,800 and located in the heart of the city (Chen 2012). There, the most competitive princelings matriculated alongside some of the most gifted children from ordinary or even capitalist background. Upon graduation, most gained entry into elite universities such as Tsinghua University, Peking University, and Harbin Institute of Technology, majoring in the sciences or in engineering, which were seen by the CCP elite as keys to future development in China.

Before the Cultural Revolution, the princelings enjoyed special treatment in these elite high schools and even at the university level because the authorities, that is, their parents and their friends, saw them as revolutionary successors who needed political cultivation. At BHSF, for example, children of senior officials were routinely asked to stay after class for special political study sessions, which excited much jealousy from the nonprinceling students (Chen 2012). At the elite Tsinghua University, the university president Jiang Nanxiang routinely met with children of the top leaders in order to convey to them the latest guidance from Mao and to tutor them in Marxist and Maoist texts (Xiao and Turner 1998: 33). Even during the summer, princelings congregated along with their parents at the Beidaihe resort, enjoying the beach and soaking up the political gossips (Kong and Mi 2013: 126). The special treatment bred a sense of superiority among most in the class of princelings. Chen Kaige, later a world-renowned film director and an alumnus of BHSF, observes that "(the revolutionary veterans) wanted their children to be fully satisfied in terms of honor and power, which produced a great sense of superiority among those children" (Chen 2012: 82). In other words, members of this revolutionary baby boom were groomed politically for their future leadership roles. Yet, as Table 7.1 shows, most of them did not achieve the most senior party and state positions.

Despite a promising start for this generation of princelings, many of their fortunes were undermined either by their parents falling from power before and during the Cultural Revolution or by their own actions during the Cultural Revolution. Even before the Cultural Revolution, the 1959 Lushan Conference, the purge against the Liu Zhidan splittist faction, and the Sino-Soviet split had led to the demotion and purges of scores of 8th Party Congress Central Committee members, including Peng Dehuai, Huang Kecheng, Xi Zhongxun, Wang Jiaxiang, and Bo Gu (MacFarquhar 1997a). With the beginning of the Cultural Revolution, the majority of 8th Party Congress CC members were purged or sidelined (Liu et al. 2018). Many children of purged parents, especially those who had passed away before the end of the Cultural Revolution, lost their political support as their careers were launched in the 1980s. However, for a sizable group of princelings, their sense of superiority also led to the formulation of a theory ultimately repudiated by both the conservatives and the Maoist radicals during the Cultural Revolution, the "bloodline theory" (血统论). This theory and the actions motivated by it casted a long shadow over the careers of many princelings for years to come.

In a way, the bloodline theory, which postulated a hereditary transmission of revolutionary loyalty from party veterans to their children, was a natural product of Marxist class theory and the special treatment of princelings in the 1950s and 1960s. Beyond the congregation of princelings in elite high schools, which consolidated their identities as members of the ruling class, the Chinese Communist Party also followed Soviet policies and officially designated every household in China into classes, which applied to parents as well as to children, even those who had been born after 1949 (White 1989). By 1960, all households had received their class designations, which placed them either in the "red" categories of soldiers, workers, poor peasants, and revolutionary cadres, or in the "black" categories of landlords, rich peasants, counterrevolutionaries, hooligans, and rightists (Wu 2014: 46). By the eve of the Cultural Revolution, class designation had played an important role in allocating scarce resources such as housing and university admissions (Wu 2014: 46).

For young people who grew up entirely in the new Communist regime, class designation had become second nature and a perfectly sensible way of organizing society. For the winners in this social system, children from "red" soldier and cadre families especially became enthusiastic enforcers of the system. In 1965, for example, the princeling students of several elite high schools in Beijing organized a petition and a walkout to protest against the perceived favoritism toward children from landlord and capitalist households by teachers and the perceived denigration of children from the "red" households (Sun 2012). Students from the "red" classes also advocated class-based education policies and the formation of class-based student associations, presumably only for those in the "red" classes (Kong and Mi 2013: 32). Although discrimination against the children of cadres almost certainly was not a systematic problem, it showed that princeling children were more than willing to break established procedures in order to enforce their status in the social order.

Thus, it was no surprise that the "bloodline" theory gained prominence soon after the Cultural Revolution had begun, popularized by the couplet "the son of a hero is a good lad; the son of a reactionary is a hoodlum" (老子英雄儿好汉； 老子反动儿混蛋) (Sun 2012). As the inventor of the "theory" and of the couplet Liu Huixuan explains decades later, "the couplet merely used coarse language to express unspoken rules (潜规则)" (Liu 2012). Even before the Cultural Revolution, official party policies in schools in Beijing already targeted children from "black" class background in ideological education. As Kong Dan, the son of China's security minister who attended BHSF in the mid-1960s, recalls "an important task for me then was to conduct ideological education for classmates from the exploiting classes, urge them to find the origin of their erroneous thinking and urge them to draw a clear line in the sand between themselves and their families" (Kong and Mi 2013: 35).

Guided by the ethos of the "bloodline theory," some of the most promising princelings committed atrocities and political acts that diminished their career prospects in the 1980s, even as their parents did their best to exonerate them. As Walder (2009: 126) points out, when Mao's call to rebel came in the middle of 1966, the first ones to heed the call were high school students from the "red" classes who took the lead to organize into Red Guards. Soon, Red Guards, dominated by those from the revolutionary "bloodlines," organized in all of Beijing's elite high schools and began to target school authorities and households with "black" class background in their neighborhoods (Walder 2009: 142). At the elite Beijing Normal Girls' High School, which had a student body dominated by princelings including the daughters of Mao, Deng Xiaoping, and Liu Shaoqi, Red Guards beat to death the party secretary of the school, Bian Zhongyuan (Walder 2009: 128).

Later accounts of that period suggest that the princeling Red Guards were among the more moderate ones. In fact, in August 1966, the early Red Guards at the high school level formed into the Western District Picket Group (西纠队), which was entrusted by Zhou Enlai to maintain order and to rescue some cadres from Red Guard struggles (Walder 2009: 142). However, that did not mean that princeling Red Guards did not engage in organized violence during the Cultural Revolution. As Liu Huixuan, the princeling author of the "bloodline" theory, recalls, "[A]ctually the Beijing Number Four High School was just like other schools and had large scale struggle meetings; we poured ink all over the heads and faces of the two principals Yang Bin and Liu Tieling...Yang Bin was beaten to a point that she could not stand up straight" (Liu 2012). Kong Dan, the son of the security minister, also recalls several rallies at BHSF that led to the beating of teachers and senior school administrators (Kong and Mi 2013: 54). Others at the BHSF also recall that princeling Red Guards had set up a "jail" to incarcerate school administrators and residents in the neighborhood who had belonged to the "black" categories (Mu 2012). After the Cultural Revolution, when the leadership called for the exclusion of Red Guard activists from fast-track promotions, these violent incidents implicated the princeling Red Guards.

For a few weeks in late August and early September 1966, the Western District Picket and other princeling Red Guard groups became Zhou Enlai's tool for maintaining some semblance of normality in key ministries and party organs (Walder 2009: 152). Chen Xiaolu (the son of Marshal Chen Yi), Dong Lianghui (the grandson of a CCP founder Dong Biwu), and Kong Dan, all princeling Red Guard leaders matriculating at the BHSF, received financial subsidies and logistical help directly from Zhou Enlai's State Council Administrative Office, where Kong Dan's mother Xu Ming had worked (Jie et al. 2010; Liu 2012). Their fortune soon turned, however, when Mao expressed his impatience with Zhou's pacification efforts at an October 1966 central work conference, which led to a slowdown in Western Picket activism (Walder 2009: 164). In a last ditch effort to retain influence, all the princeling Red Guards at the high school level banded together in December 1966 to form the United Action Committee (*liandong*), which, in contradiction with the prevailing ideology of the time, swore to protect pre-1960 Mao Zedong Thoughts (MacFarquhar and Schoenhals 2006: 197).

For a while, United Action gathered some momentum as they passed out leaflets criticizing the Central Cultural Revolution Group for "defrauding" Chairman Mao and even stormed the Ministry of Public Security in an ill-advised effort to free arrested members of their group (Liu 2012). Even in early January 1967, rebel Red Guards still expressed their fear of the Western Pickets and of their financial resources to Jiang Qing, to which Jiang replied, "[T]hey are only a small handful with behind-the-scenes backers, but we will help you, so do not be afraid" (Jiang 1967). On January 17, the CCRG finally moved to dismantle United Action and the remnants of the various pickets that had sprung up in central Beijing by arresting hundreds of leaders and activists in these organizations (Walder 2009: 193). According to one account, some sixty-five princelings accused of being ringleaders were incarcerated for up to five years in a secret jail in the south of Beijing, including nineteen children of national-level leaders such as He Long, Ye Jianying, Bo Yibo, Tan Zhenlin, Lu Dingyi, and Peng Zhen (Xiao and Turner 1998: 8). Other princelings like Kong Dan, Dong Liangfan, and Su Hansheng were incarcerated for four months before being released (Kong and Mi 2013: 94).

Many princelings also joined the military in 1967 in order to escape Red Guard persecution, which fundamentally altered their career trajectories.

Thus, while others in their cohorts toiled in work farms or factories or as junior cadres in Western China after the first two years of the Cultural Revolution, scores of activists in Western District Pickets and United Action were incarcerated for months to years, leaving a blank on their CVs, and many open questions about their activities at the beginning of the Cultural Revolution. Others spent the rest of their careers in the military, rising to mid-level positions but never having the opportunity to compete for national-level civilian positions. Meanwhile, the CCRG launched a propaganda campaign against leaders in United Action, highlighting their reactionary "bloodline" ideology and exaggerating their use of violence during the first few months of the Cultural Revolution (Walder 2009: 197). Although these princelings were fully exonerated of these charges by Hu Yaobang and Chen Yun later (Kong and Mi 2013: 170), whispers of their Red Guard activities continued to plague them for the rest of their careers.

With their parents and "uncles" back in power in 1978, members of the revolutionary baby boom were once again back in favor, and even those who had been active during the Cultural Revolution enjoyed rapid ascendance in their careers in the early 1980s. Even before veterans formally returned to powerful positions, mid-level cadres already saw which way the wind was blowing and began to give preferential treatment to some children of veteran revolutionaries. Deng Liqun, who had been appointed the vice head of the newly rehabilitated Chinese Academy of Social Sciences (CASS) in 1977, recruited as graduate students the children of several veterans who were still undergoing rehabilitation, including Bo Yibo and Peng Zhen (Deng 2005: 114). Kong Dan, a key leader of the Western District Pickets, even gained entrance into the graduate program in economics at CASS without ever having attended university as an undergraduate (Jie et al. 2010). After years of incarceration and manual labor in the countryside or in factories, admission to CASS was great relief for many princelings and put them back on a rapid track for career advancement.

Into the 1980s, as revolutionary veterans regained senior-level party, state, and military positions, they eagerly helped their children obtain sought-after positions after they had wasted the first ten years of their careers in jail or in work farms. A popular position for these young princelings in the early 1980s was to serve as the private secretary for high-level party or military officials, which afforded them connections with high-level politicians as well as knowledge of the inner workings of the center of power. Bo Xilai, the future Politburo member, obtained a position as secretary at the Central Secretariat, the nerve center of the entire party. Xi Jinping, the son of newly rehabilitated Xi Zhongxun, served as the private secretary of defense minister Geng Biao. Western District Picket activist Kong Dan served as State Economic Commissioner Zhang Jingfu's secretary after graduating from CASS with a degree in quantitative economics (Jie et al. 2010). After one or two years in these lowly *ke* (科) level positions, many of them were quickly promoted to *chu* (处) level positions, equivalent to a county chief.

Beijing Municipal Government (BMG), then under the tutelage of Long March veteran Duan Junyi, especially became a hotbed of princeling promotions. Within a couple of years of finishing schools and holding junior positions, several notable princelings, including Chen Yuan, Chen Haosu, Liu Yandong, and Bo Xicheng, obtained prefecture level (司局级) positions in BMG (Yan 2017: 224). Such rapid promotions departed from many standard procedures at the Central Organization Department, which itself was already staffed with many sympathetic princelings. For example, when the Central Organization Department recommended a vice-prefecture-level position for Bo Xicheng, his father and executive vice chairman of the powerful Central Advisory Committee, Bo Yibo, directly intervened and demanded a full prefecture-level position for his son, a request that was honored (Yan 2017: 199). Before he left Beijing in 1984, Duan Junyi even forcefully promoted Chen Yuan, the son of the powerful Chen Yun, into the standing committee of the Beijing Party Committee, but, as discussed later in this chapter, such rocket-like promotions in the early 1980s became a liability for many princelings in the late 1980s (Yan 2017: 224). After serving as Defense Minister Geng Biao's secretary for a few years, Xi Jinping likely could have landed a vice-prefecture-level position somewhere; instead, he opted for a county-level position outside of a major city, in Zhengding County in Hebei Province. Although still a rapid trajectory of promotion in a system where the vast majority of cadres spent a lifetime trying to achieve county-level positions, this was a humble step compared to those taken by many of his princeling peers. Xi's decision to leave Beijing likely saved him from concerted efforts to block princelings from high-profile central government positions and opened the way for a slower but much longer lasting career trajectory.

Despite making up for lost time with the help of their parents and their friends, princeling officials faced three major obstacles in the 1980s. First, their deeds during the Cultural Revolution continued to haunt them. Second, the emergence of the dual track economy provided an attractive alternative to life in the party-state for many princelings, especially those who saw that their Cultural Revolution activism had placed a ceiling on their careers. Finally, veterans not in the center of power or whose children had already fallen out of favor resisted the promotion of princeling officials.

During the elite conversation on promoting young cadres in the early 1980s, many revolutionary veterans, including Deng, Chen Yun, and Secretary General Hu Yaobang, also insisted that Red Guard activists during the Cultural Revolution should be eliminated from considerations for fast-track promotions due to their demonstrated tendency for opportunistic behavior (Li 2016b). In late 1982, the Central Committee officially issued a decree that sought to cleanse the influence of the Gang of Four and Lin Biao from the party. Importantly, this decree defined "three types of people" who needed to be expelled from the party, including close followers of the Gang of Four and Lin Biao, those who had engaged in serious factionalism, and those who had engaged in beating, destruction, and looting (打砸抢) during the Cultural Revolution (Central Committee 1982a). Because the "three types of people" represented "a factor for instability and a latent danger which cannot be overlooked," the party veterans decided that "they must be resolutely swept from leadership positions and be rotated out of sensitive or important positions" (Central Committee 1982a). A subsequent document on party rectification similarly called for "the expulsion from the party in principle" for the "three types of people" (Central Committee 1983). A factor working against the princeling Red Guards was that many veterans had little knowledge of the Red Guard movement and saw all Red Guards as guilty of overthrowing party institutions during the Cultural Revolution (Chen 2014).

This general revulsion against the Red Guards became a major problem for the former princeling Red Guards. Even though they argued that they had resisted the Gang of Four and Lin Biao, they had engaged in the "beating, destruction, and looting" of the third type of people, even by their own admission. According to Kong Dan, detractors of the princelings were linking them to "three types of people" in debates over promotions (Chen 2014). These arguments threatened to render them unqualified for leadership positions.

In response to these charges, influential veterans and their children tried to exonerate themselves. First, Kong Dan wrote a letter to Chen

Yun in 1984 defending the "Old Red Guards," primarily made up of princelings at the high school level who had been active until the dissolution of United Action in early 1967. In the letter, Kong admitted that the "Old Red Guards" "beat teachers...and even in extreme, isolated cases beat them to death" (Chen 2014). However, Kong delineated Red Guards in the Western District Pickets and United Action from rebel Red Guards because they "stood on the side of the older generation of proletariat revolutionaries in their struggle against the Gang of Four and Lin Biao" (Chen 2014: 7). As further evidence of their innocence, Kong pointed out that these Red Guard organizations "had been stunted or repressed by the Central Cultural Revolution Group around December of 1966 and were labeled either as 'conservative organizations' or 'reactionary organizations'" (Chen 2014: 7). Although this was largely correct, it still did not exonerate the "Old Red Guards" from the "beating, destruction, and looting" type that party documents had forbidden from leadership positions. However, Kong Dan argued that the beating, destruction, and looting engaged by the Old Red Guard "were not in service of the political ends of the Gang of Four and of Lin Biao" and, therefore, the Old Red Guards should not be considered as "three types of people" (Chen 2014: 7).

This letter was read by Chen Yun and immediately passed on to Hu Yaobang, Li Xiannian, and the rest of the Politburo with the comment "these Red Guards do not belong to 'three types of people,' and the better ones among them should still be considered for promotions in the third ladder reserve cadre group" (Yan 2017: 203). As someone with children engulfed by the Cultural Revolution, Chen Yun clearly was sympathetic to the plight of the princeling Red Guards. Soon after this discussion, the Central Organization Department issued a supplement to the document on "the three types of people," which specifically exonerated princeling Red Guards at the high school level: "Among student Red Guards below the age of 18, some people committed errors due to political ignorance, influence by 'left' thinking, or instructions from others, which included serious problems of beating people to death in a mob during the 'smash the four olds.' If they admit to their errors, are serious about their understanding, and are behaving well in reality, we do not need to raise it as a problem" (Central Committee 1984). Furthermore, as a part of the campaign to cleanse the "three types of people" from the party, universities were asked to compile a list of Red Guard activists on their campuses, but the Central Organization Department instructed universities that they had no need to record the activities of princeling Red Guards (Yan 2017: 200).

Despite these decrees, the stain on princeling Red Guards was difficult to remove, especially after the Central Organization Department circulated a document in 1983 that provided minute details of the Red Guard movement in Beijing (Chen 2014). After successfully exonerating princeling Red Guards like himself, Kong Dan heard through the grapevines that a senior party leader nonetheless commented that "even if those like Kong Dan are not 'three types of people,' surely they cannot be promoted into the ranks of reserve cadres" (Kong and Mi 2013: 171). At a time when party policy made the reserve cadre list a reservoir for the future leaders of China, exclusion from that list meant significantly lower chance of competing for top positions in the party ten to twenty years down the road. This became a disadvantage that most princeling officials who had participated in the Red Guard Movement could not overcome. The only Western District Picket participant to make it into the Politburo was Vice Premier Ma Kai.

Although the campaign against the "three types of people" erected a potentially insurmountable barrier for many princelings' career advancement in the government, they soon saw an attractive alternative in a new breed of state-owned enterprises, which promised both an alternative route for obtaining higher bureaucratic ranks and the accumulation of wealth – relatively new commodities in China's largely planned economy. In China's traditional planned economy, nearly every industrial sector was led by a central ministry, which coordinated much of the production and investment in that sector (Naughton 1996). At the apex of the planned economy were the State Planning Commission and the State Economic Commission, which coordinated investment and the relationships between different firms and sectors in the entire economy (Chen 1982a). Yet, in the late 1970s, after the post-Mao leadership conducted a series of research tours in Western and Asian capitalist countries, China's new leaders realized that the traditional planned economy had many problems and would be insufficient in making China into a globally competitive economy. At the heart of the problem was that many European and Japanese companies actually were interested in investing in China to take advantage of lower labor costs in China, but the line ministries and the State Planning Commission were too ossified to take advantage of these opportunities (Wang 2011: 11). At the same time, Deng and the other leaders saw that China needed to earn more foreign exchange to replace the rapidly dwindling supply of it. Again, the traditional planning bureaucracy was too cumbersome to launch tourism projects quickly, which would have immediately earned much-needed foreign exchange from willing tourists from Hong Kong and the rest of Asia (Wang 2011: 20).

In early 1979, Deng invited Rong Yiren, a recently rehabilitated "patriotic" capitalist with extensive ties to wealthy relatives in Hong Kong and the US, to a meeting and asked Rong to set up a new state-owned company that circumvented the traditional planned economy and directly answered to Vice Premier Gu Mu, China's tsar for external trade (Wang 2011: 30). Within weeks of the meeting, Rong handed Deng a business plan for an entity called China International Trust and Investment Company (CITIC), which aimed at absorbing foreign capital, acquiring foreign technologies through joint ventures or licensing, and "gaining an understanding of the economic situation around the world" (Wang 2011: 54).

Rong was given a free hand to hire his staff, which initially included mostly capitalists from Shanghai from the prerevolution period, including Wang Qianshi, Wu Zhichao, and Jing Shuping (Wang 2011: 60). However, two princelings in their late thirties, Wang Jun and Ye Xuanji, also joined the ranks of CITIC's founding management team. While Wang was the son of Politburo member and Deng ally Wang Zhen, Ye Xuanji was the trusted nephew of Marshal Ye Jianying, who had served as a confidential messenger for Marshal Ye in the run-up to the coup against the Gang of Four in 1976 (Xiong 2008). Although CITIC initially had very little real business due to bureaucratic hurdles, it soon became a major vehicle for China's external borrowing and for Chinese acquisitions of major Hong Kong assets in the run-up to the 1997 return of the city to China (Wang 2011: 140–200). As their footprints in the capitalist enclave of Hong Kong grew, other princelings soon saw CITIC as an attractive alternative to the grinds in a government agency or in a traditional SOE. Soon, Wang Jun's brother Wang Bing, as well as princelings like Qin Xiao, joined the ranks of CITIC (Qin 2019).

The success of CITIC soon led other princelings to lobby for the formation of lightly regulated state-owned conglomerates. Kong Dan soon joined Everbright Group, an entity similar to CITIC, while Deng's son, Deng Pufang, formed Kanghua, which had the stated purpose of generating profit for the China Association for the Disabled (Quan 1994). Because Deng was the most powerful leader in China in the 1980s, many princelings gravitated toward Kanghua after its formation. For example, future Politburo Standing Committee member Yu Zhengsheng, as well as his renegade brother Yu Minsheng, took up important positions in Kanghua (Quan 1994). As the head of a Kanghua subsidiary describes the makeup of personnel at the subsidiary, "[O]f the fewer than one hundred in the company, most personnel were '*guanxi* cases' with the majority being children of officials" (Yan 2017: 324).

Kanghua obtained special import licenses from government agencies and began to import much-desired consumer goods and to sell them at a high markup to Chinese consumers (Quan 1994). This earned Kanghua a high profit, but it also gave rise to accusations of corruption, which ultimately brought down the company after 1989 (Shih 2008a). Although many princelings doubtless earned fabulous wealth by working in these state-owned conglomerates or by starting their own businesses, few of them ever emerged from the business world as a high-level cadre. As the Chinese Communist Party began to standardize cadre evaluation and promotion procedures, even those with high-level connections found it increasingly difficult to continue a rapid pace of promotion after a stint in the new breed of state-owned conglomerates. The only exception was Yu Zhengsheng, who only worked at Kanghua for one year before resuming a rapid trajectory of promotions in the government, which ultimately made him a Politburo Standing Committee member.

Besides errors committed during the Cultural Revolution and the draw of the commercial world, princelings also were stymied by many cadres' resistance to their promotions. In the early 1980s, rehabilitated veteran cadres rebuilt their power bases in the various provinces and ministries. As the previous sections discussed, they promoted young, technical protégés without too many senior political connections. Meanwhile, these senior cadres also orchestrated a silent campaign to stymie the careers of princelings. This silent campaign ultimately trumped the efforts by some senior leaders and their allies to push their children toward the top echelon. In 1983, a cadre in the Youth Cadre Department of the Central Organization Department commissioned a report on the history of the Beijing Red Guard movement, which was drafted by former Tsinghua Red Guard Chen Chusan (Chen 2014). Chen's report argued that the princeling Red Guards were really no different than Red Guards formed by ordinary students or workers because they all heeded the call by Mao to rise up and rebel (Chen 2014). This was a damning indictment against the princeling Red Guards at a time when the party was preventing "three types of people" from holding leadership positions. Instead of squashing the letter, the head of the Youth Department, former Mao aide Li Rui, circulated the letter through the COD and even among the leadership (Chen 2014). Finally, Chen Yun, whose son was an ambitious princeling, harshly criticized the report and its author Chen Chusan, stating that "we must be vigilant against people like Chen Chusan" (Chen 2014). However, this criticism did not prevent this report from being widely read in the elite circle.

In 1983, Beijing Party Secretary Duan Junyi and Politburo member Wang Zhen also directly asked the Central Organization Department to consider Chen Yuan, the son of Chen Yun, as the vice secretary of Beijing, a promotion that would have catapulted the princeling from a lowly graduate student to a vice-ministerial-level official in the space of four years (Li 2016b). Chen Yeping, a longtime Deng protégé and Central Organization Department head, and Li Rui both balked at the request, thus stopping Chen Yuan's meteoric rise (Li 2016b). Chen Yuan did not obtain a vice-ministerial-level position until the late 1980s, and he ultimately did not achieve a ministerial-level position until the early 1990s. In 1984, Chen Yun, who was in charge of organizational work, found a pretext to remove Li Rui from the Central Organization Department, likely in retaliation against Li Rui's principled stand against his son's promotion (Yan 2017: 245).

Besides the contingent in the COD, however, even Party Secretary General Hu Yaobang seemed against the rapid rise of the princelings in the 1980s. After some princelings, including the child of a Politburo member, were caught as culprits of major crimes, Hu Yaobang called on the Central Organization Department to draft a decree that dictates "the management and education of the children of cadres" (Yan 2017: 204). In March 1984, Li Rui convened a group of senior princelings, including Chen Yun's son Chen Yuan, Kong Dan, Chen Yi's son Chen Haosu, and CCP founder Li Dazhao's granddaughter Li Hong (Li 2016b). During a heated exchange, the princelings argued that they should be regulated by the same rules that applied to any other cadres and party members instead of by a special set of decrees (Li 2016b). Chen Yuan used a subtle version of the "bloodline theory" to make his case "if a class cannot even handle its own children, it does not deserve to be a ruling class" (Yan 2017: 205). Similar to the "bloodline theory" of their youth, the princelings of the 1980s, now in their thirties and forties, still believed that they were members of a ruling class with noble qualities.

Given the stiff resistance by princelings and their parents, Hu Yaobang's suggestion of a decree regulating princeling behavior was dropped. Still, the intraparty resistance against princelings persisted. In 1987, the Beijing Party Committee (BPC) held its party congress, which augured a change in its top leadership. Although Chen Yuan, already a standing committee member of BPC, was nominated for the vice secretary position, Chen Xitong, Beijing mayor and vice secretary at the time, signaled to lower-level cadres that although Chen was an excellent cadre, it would have been better if "he can train for a longer period," which led to an embarrassing no-confidence vote result for Chen (Yan 2017: 253). A similar fate obstructed the careers of other princelings as they attempted to obtain full or vice-ministerial-level positions in the second half of the 1980s. Liu Yuan, the son of Liu Shaoqi, received very low votes for his appointment as the vice governor of Henan, while Youth League veterans rejected the appointment of Liu Yandong, the daughter of New Fourth Army General Liu Ruilong, as the head of the Communist Youth League (Yan 2017: 254).

For Chen Yuan, whose father was still a powerful "immortal" through the 1980s, obstructions to his career became both intractable and embarrassing. Even newly promoted ministerial or Politburo officials resisted the princelings, despite their general eagerness to please senior politicians such as Deng Xiaoping and Chen Yun. In the mid-1980s, as Chen Yuan searched for a way to obtain a vice-ministerial-level position, he contemplated a vice minister position in the Ministry of Electronics, then headed by future secretary general Jiang Zemin. Jiang indicated to a friend of Chen Yuan that he had no desire for Chen to be vice minister, since a princeling of that caliber would certainly meddle with top-level decision making and become a shadow minister (Yan 2017: 276). This recollection, if true, reflects the ambiguous attitude of many cadres toward princelings, whose connections brought additional resources to their work units but also had a much higher tendency for meddling. For many rehabilitated veterans, they would rather promote meek, obedient "always nice people" to ministerial positions, which guaranteed them some degree of postretirement influence (Manion 1993).

THE REIGN OF "ALWAYS NICE PEOPLE"

The year 1989 represented another critical juncture for the elite coalition that ruled China. The Tiananmen Square crisis again forced the surviving Long March veterans to reshuffle the leadership. In this crucial transition, instead of party veterans with extensive ties with the party and the military, they chose as successors a group of largely inexperienced and weakly networked technocrats whose main qualification had been their ability to pander to revolutionary veterans. Thus, the period between 1989 to the appointment of Xi Jinping as the secretary general in late 2012 can be characterized as the age of weak successors in China. Two "always nice people" favored by their veteran patrons took the helm in succession, which meant they governed via coalitions of similarly weak officials. In the meantime, because of Deng's decision to preappoint Jiang's successor, an entire generation of older princelings, whose careers were already frustrated by veteran opposition in the 1980s, had no chance of competing for top positions in the party. Except for one person, even the younger princelings who could qualify for the top position after Hu Jintao's term each had their own inadequacies by the norms of the party. This left the supreme position in the party to one qualified princeling, Xi Jinping. Although the selectorate at the 17th Party Congress, which decided on the successor to Hu Jintao, did not need to select a princeling, they did so because they thought the age of "always nice people" needed to come to an end. Indeed, the appointment of Xi Jinping as the secretary general of the party brought about the end of the reign of weak successors, as he eradicated or marginalized every faction that potentially challenged his power.

The reign of weak successors began with the appointment of Jiang Zemin as the secretary general of the CCP in 1989. His appointment was a surprising one forced on the leadership by the Tiananmen Square protests. However, Jiang's reign also was blessed by his ability to rule largely without intense competition from the princelings, whose careers were frustrated by their deeds during the Cultural Revolution and obstructions during the 1980s. Immediately after the decision was made to remove Zhao Ziyang from power in late May 1989, the jockeying for his successor began. Deng convened a series of intense meetings with various Long March stalwarts to discuss the question of succession, and at first almost everyone had their own favorites. Notably, none of the candidates discussed at that time were true princelings in that their parents were high-level officials in the party. Although Li Peng was the son of a revolutionary martyr and was raised by various veteran families, including by Zhou Enlai and Deng Yingchao, he had no blood relative who could help with his career.

Among the older princelings who had been inducted into the Central Committee at the 12th Party Congress, Li Tieying, the son of former Politburo member Li Weihan, and Ye Xuanping, the son of Marshal Ye Jianying, constituted the most likely competitors in the succession. The other princelings in the Central Committee in 1989, including Bu He, Liao Chengzhi, and Qiao Zonghuai, either were ethnic minorities or only oversaw minor departments. Li Tieying had been a career central technocrat like Li Peng but did not play a significant role in the 1989 crackdown and therefore lacked the political gravitas of Li. Ye Xuanping's career stalled after his promotion to the governorship of Guangdong Province in 1985, partly due to his father's passing in 1986 and partly due to the obstruction by Fourth Front Army (FFA) veterans, who still were a formidable presence in the 1980s. Having never served as the party secretary of a major province or ministry, Ye was naturally eliminated from serious consideration for the top job in 1989.

At a preliminary meeting on the issue on May 21, Chen Yun and Li Xiannian favored Jiang Zemin, a career factory boss, while Deng Xiaoping and Deng Yingchao proposed Li Ruihuan, a nationally well-known model construction worker. Wang Zhen voted for Li Peng, the son of a revolutionary martyr and a career technocrat, while Yang Shangkun supported Qiao Shi, the only candidate with extensive experience in the party center (Party Central Office Secretariat 2001a). Although multiple candidates emerged at that stage, Jiang Zemin might have been the front-runner even then due to backing from two major groups in the party, the central technocrats led by Chen Yun and the New Fourth Army faction represented by Wang Daohan (Gilley 1998: 35). Because Li Xiannian and most of the FFA voted with Chen Yun, Jiang also obtained the support of FFA veterans along with Chen Yun's support. The others were backed by smaller coalitions.

On the same evening in May, Jiang was hurriedly summoned to Beijing to meet with Wan Li, who had been the chairman of the National People's Congress and had just returned from Canada. Jiang's mission was to persuade the liberal Wan Li to support the martial law, which he finally did on May 27 (Wu 2004). Jiang's willingness to do the elders' dirty work might have been a final test of his loyalty before he was chosen. On May 27, Deng, Chen Yun, and Li Xiannian had a private meeting and decided on Jiang. They then convened a larger meeting with the other elders to announce their decision, who then also backed Jiang, but demanded the promotion of Li Ruihuan and Song Ping to the Politburo Standing Committee (Party Central Office Secretariat 2001b). Jiang was then ordered to fly to Beijing to join the elders in witness of the final suppression of the democracy movement (Wu 2004). On June 23, Jiang was formally voted into the position of Secretary General of the CCP by the fourth Plenum of the Central Committee (Li 2007: 321).

Tellingly, the veterans chose the new leadership never expecting Jiang or another member of the PSC to become particularly powerful. They wanted the new leadership to continue to rule collectively, which afforded surviving veterans considerable latitude to play one member of the leadership against another. As Deng put it to an audience of party veterans on May 31, 1989, "Without a doubt, in terms of administrative experience and experience in carrying out struggles, the (new) leadership has weaknesses. This is a fact…but we do not need to be satisfied with everyone in the leadership, just with the leadership as a whole" (Deng 1993: 298). At that point, Deng and the other veterans had a choice of appointing a younger Long March veteran or even an older princeling to be the secretary general of the party, who could have been a more powerful leader from the beginning. Yet they refrained from doing so in favor of an "always nice person" with obvious "weaknesses."

As multiple accounts have documented, the beginning of the age of weak successors was a rocky one with Jiang facing the prospect of removal for failing to pursue reform with sufficient vigor (Fewsmith 2001; Gilley 1998; Nathan and Gilley 2002). Veterans such as Yang Shangkun and his brother Yang Baibing also undermined Jiang's authority, especially in the military, forcing him to orchestrate an extremely risky purge of the Yang Brothers at the 1992 14th Party Congress (Gilley 1998: 95). To help him navigate the complex politics in Zhongnanhai, Jiang relied on the advice and machination of a princeling, Zeng Qinghong, whose father had joined the party in 1926. As Jiang increasingly relied on Zeng's help to fight off challenges from both the surviving veterans and from his contemporaries, Zeng, whose own career had stalled as the vice secretary of Shanghai at the age of fifty in 1989, saw a rocket-like series of promotions after Jiang's move to Beijing (Wu 2004). His new positions in Beijing allowed him to enter the Politburo as an alternate member in 1999 and a full member of the Standing Committee by 2002. He thus became the first "bloodline" princeling to enter the supreme body.

As shown in Figure 7.2, even if one were to consider princelings broadly as children and in-laws of 8th Party Congress CC members, of founding generals (开国将领), and of vice-ministerial or above officials by the 8th Party Congress, the share of princelings never exceeded 7 percent of the Central Committee or 4.5 percent of the combined full and alternate CC body. At the 16th Party Congress, when Zeng Qinghong entered the PSC and was at the height of his power, princeling representation in the CC also entered a high watermark of 6–7 percent, compared to below 4 percent in earlier congresses. Others have noticed this rise of the princeling or elitist coalition between the 16th and the 18th Party Congress (Li 2016a). However, considering a cohort of over 1,000 senior princelings (290 for 8th PC CC members alone), princeling full CC

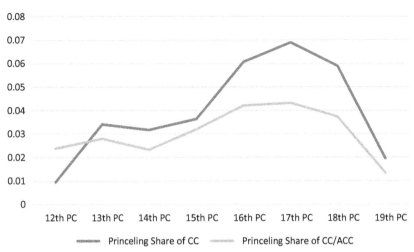

FIGURE 7.2 The share of full Central Committee members and the share of full and alternate Central Committee members who were children of the 8th Party Congress Central Committee members, founding generals, and vice-ministerial-level officials

members reached a high of fourteen, or less than 2 percent of the full cohort. If the Cultural Revolution and obstruction in the 1980s had not stymied the careers of so many princelings, many more of them, such as Chen Yuan, Kong Dan, Chen Xiaolu, Chen Haosu, Liu Yuan, Fu Yang, Dong Lianghui and so forth, would have vied for Politburo seats in the 2000s. This would have produced a markedly different political dynamic during the crucial transitional congresses of the 16th through the 18th Party Congress, which also represented the height of the princeling baby boom in high politics (Figure 7.2).

For the small number of princeling officials who had survived the race to the top by the early 2000s, Figure 7.3 shows that they, even during their first term in the Politburo, had significantly more ties with the Central Committee elite than their nonprinceling counterparts. Through most of the post-reform congresses, princeling Politburo members had ten to twenty more ties with full or alternate CC members than nonprinceling counterparts. Some princeling first-term Politburo members, such as Li Tieying and Zou Jiahua, had thirty to forty more ties with the CC elite than their nonprinceling counterparts. Meanwhile, if one were to take out nonprinceling Politburo members with close ties to powerful princelings, such as Zhou Yongkang and Luo Gan, the average ties of nonprinceling Politburo members would be even lower. Although not a perfect measure,

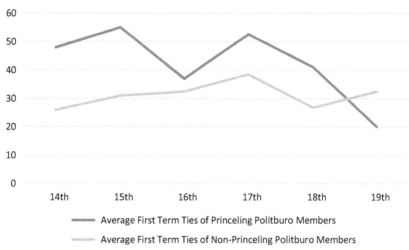

FIGURE 7.3 Average number of ties of first-term Politburo members, princelings and nonprincelings: 14th PC to 19th PC

Figure 7.3 shows that in head-to-head competitions against nonprincelings, princeling Politburo members, even in their first term, likely had an advantage because of the larger size of their networks. The significantly higher number of ties likely stemmed from greater ability by princeling Politburo members to influence the promotion trajectories of former colleagues than nonprinceling Politburo members (Shih and Lee 2018). This metric of network size also does not take into account ties with non-CC senior military officers and the commercial elite. If they were included, the princeling advantage likely was even bigger (Gilley 2004; He and Gao 2000). The weakness of the princelings as a group, instead, stemmed from their small numbers in the highest level due to events in the 1980s, but this likely worked to the advantage of princeling officials who had made it into the upper echelon by the 17th Party Congress.

The absence of princeling rivals led to a singularly advantageous position for Xi as he entered the Politburo at the 2007 17th Party Congress. The 16th and the 17th Party Congress were presided by another "always nice person" who had climbed to the top of the party, Hu Jintao. Identified early as a promising foot soldier for the party, Tsinghua University president Jiang Nanxiang, who had mentored Hu at the university, recommended him to Song Ping, who had been the party secretary of the remote Gansu Province in the early 1960s (Li 2000: 33). After proving himself as a consistent executor of orders from higher levels, Song Ping recommended him for higher-level offices as China emerged from the Cultural Revolution in the 1980s. With Song's patronage and with additional boosts from Hu Yaobang, Hu Jintao served successively as the secretary of the Communist Youth League, the party secretary of Guizhou, and party secretary of Tibet, all while Hu was in his forties in the 1980s (Nathan and Gilley 2002: 33). Given these rapid rotations, Hu was groomed for the highest offices, which became reality when his patron Song Ping, who presided over personnel decisions at the 14th Party Congress, ensured Hu's induction into the Politburo Standing Committee, thus indicating his role as the designated successor even in 1992 (Li 2000).

After a ten-year apprenticeship at the top of the party hierarchy, at the 2002 16th Party Congress, Hu was smoothly voted into office as the new party secretary general of the party, as Deng and the other veterans had planned in 1992. Several "always nice people" officials who had been on the reserve cadre list in the 1980s also were inducted into the Politburo Standing Committee at the congress, including He Guoqiang, Jia Qinglin, Li Changchun, and Wen Jiabao. Hu knew that his position was far from secure with Jiang's influence still looming large in the party, especially in the PLA, and undertook to staff many central party and provincial positions with former officials in the Communist Youth League, where Hu himself had served as the secretary in the 1980s (Li 2005a). Instead of staffing high-level positions with the savviest politicians with dense elite networks, however, Hu likewise staffed them with "always nice people" who had shown a track record of obeying his commands, such as Li Keqiang, Hu Chunhua, and Sun Zhengcai.

Meanwhile, between the 16th and the 17th Party Congress, princelings finally began to enter high politics at the Politburo level and above, fulfilling the promise of their "bloodlines." As shown in Figure 7.4, however, instead of a heated competition for the next secretary general position between connected princelings and other highly networked officials at the 17th PC, the most connected Politburo members then either were due to retire at the 18th PC (textured bars) or had significantly fewer ties than Xi Jinping. Even among the princelings (dark bars) in the Politburo then, two were unqualified for the party secretary general position in the run-up to the 2012 transition because of established internal party rules or norms. Liu Yandong was a woman and faced an unspoken glass ceiling at the Politburo level. The only princelings who were male, not too old, not in the military, and had extensive administrative experience were Bo Xilai, Xi Jinping, Li Yuanchao, Wang Qishan, and Yu Zhengsheng, but Yu was disqualified because his brother had

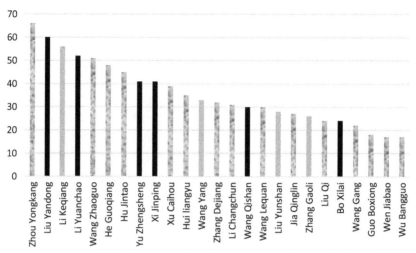

FIGURE 7.4 17th PC Politburo members by the number of ties with CC and ACC members (princelings in dark bars; 18th PC retirees in textured bars)

defected to the US in the 1980s. This left four princelings in the running in the run-up to the 18th Party Congress. Both Bo and Wang actually had significantly fewer ties than Xi. This left Li Yuanchao, whose father had a much more junior revolutionary pedigree than Xi's father, as the only viable competitor against Xi among the princeling group. Li Yuanchao also had the advantage of being a core member of Hu Jintao's Youth League faction and thus had a large network among CYL veterans. Among the nonprinceling group, future Premier Li Keqiang clearly was a contender, as he had a larger network than Xi at the 17th PC (Figure 7.4).

As events turned out, intense political drama unfolded in the run-up to the 18th Party Congress surrounding Bo Xilai, the son of revolutionary stalwart Bo Yibo. As Figure 7.4 shows, however, Bo had fifteen fewer connections than Xi Jinping, then already the anointed successor to Hu Jintao. Available evidence suggests that although Bo Xilai grumbled about Xi, he did not have any immediate design to be the secretary general but merely tried to obtain a promotion into the Politburo Standing Committee (Ho and Huang 2013: 54–74). His panic reaction in the aftermath of his protégé Wang Lijun's escape to the US Consulate in Chengdu had to do with his strong desire to preserve his planned promotion to the PSC rather than with any plot to usurp the power of the incumbent or the future leader of China (Ho and Huang 2013: 74). Even the rumored coup attempt in mid-2012 was allegedly launched by

PSC member Zhou Yongkang, who had the most extensive network among the CC elite before the 18th PC (Figure 7.4) (Anderlini 2012). The only true princeling competitor to Xi was Li Yuanchao, who was the one person that Xi had insisted could not join the Politburo Standing Committee at the 18th Party Congress, according to Beijing sources (SCMP Reporters 2012). Li's exclusion from the PSC meant that no other princeling could or would challenge his authority at the Politburo Standing Committee level. After Li Yuanchao was excluded from the PSC, none of the other nonprinceling PSC members demonstrated any appetite to resist Xi's consolidation of power. After he took power, Xi also made use of his princeling network to consolidate power in the regime, especially in the military. Because they were military officers, princelings such as Liu Yuan, Zhang Youxia, and Zhang Haiyang could not compete for the top party position, yet they were indispensable to Xi, as he removed the powerful Xu Caihou faction from the military (Buckley 2014).

In a hypothetical world where princelings never engaged in Red Guard activities and the veterans in the 1980s never resisted their promotions, princelings would have taken up a much higher share of Politburo seats from the 15th PC through the 18th PC, perhaps as high as 20–30 percent. At the crucial 17th and 18th PC, a whole slate of qualified princelings, such as Liu Yuan, Liu Yazhou, Kong Dan, and Chen Yuan, would have either qualified for the top job or would have been powerful kingmakers for the future leadership of China. To be sure, the inheritors of the "red bloodline" would have dominated elite politics in China in any event, but none of them likely would have had the capacity to dominate politics in a manner that Xi had done.

CONCLUSION

The coalitions of the weak pursued by Mao in his last years produced a collective leadership of FFA veterans and rehabilitated veterans with Deng as the uniquely capable balancer in the middle. As the leadership set about to repair damages to the party-state inflicted by the Cultural Revolution, their thoughts soon turned to rejuvenation of the aging leadership. Instead of cultivating successors from among veteran officials with decades of experience, however, the rehabilitated leaders opted to promote a cohort of young and relatively inexperienced technocrats with college degrees in the sciences. Instead of choosing those with proven records of upholding the rule of the party, the veteran leadership favored "always nice people" who could guarantee their postretirement influence.

In the 1980s, many children of the first-generation revolutionaries also came of age and began to serve in mid-level government positions. However, most of them soon faced a ceiling to their advancement due to their own checkered history during the Cultural Revolution, their exit from the government in favor of lucrative careers in the commercial world, and resistance to their rise from mid- and high-level veterans. These forces combined to create a situation where a few densely networked princelings entered high politics along with a large group of technocratic but thinly networked officials in the 2010s. This created the preconditions for a daring official with the right political network to upend decades of collective leadership and become the dictator of China. As events after the 18th Party Congress revealed, Xi Jinping took advantage of the elite alignment born of decades of weak coalition strategies pursued by his predecessors to become the most powerful leader of China since Mao.

8

Conclusion and the Future of the Chinese
Communist Party

Authoritarian regimes must grapple with a fundamental source of
instability that a significant redistribution of power, often unseen or only
partially observed, can radically alter the incentives of regime insiders and
overturn initially stable equilibria (Acemoglu et al. 2008). Although institutional features such as authoritarian legislatures and a ruling party can
alleviate the incentives to usurp the incumbent leader to some extent,
especially among lower-level officials (Gandhi 2008; Svolik 2012), they
cannot fundamentally remove the incentives to grab power forcefully in
the top echelon of these regimes. For one, one-party states by design
entrust enormous power in the hands of the top few officials or even in
the hands of one person. For ambitious officials just one layer below the
very top facing a low probability of ordinary promotion, the reward for
achieving an extra step upward can be enormous and can justify a risky
gamble, especially if an external shock leads to a significant redistribution
of power. Even for those who are already in the top echelon of the ruling
party, a gamble to break the existing power-sharing equilibrium can reap
enormous rewards as the power and resources of authoritarian colleagues
are consolidated into one's hands. Knowing the dangers of these
possibilities, authoritarian leaders also have the incentives to preempt
potentially threatening colleagues by removing them from power with
coercive measures. In the absence of credible constitutional frameworks
or electoral pressure to stop the actions of the top leadership, the stable
façade of authoritarian politics can quickly descend into coups, purges,
and assassinations.

   For dictators in authoritarian regimes, they face the dilemma of surrounding themselves with densely networked and experienced officials

who can mobilize resources across these regimes to fend off external shocks and to institutionalize these regimes' power but who also can use their connections and experience in elite intrigues to usurp the power of the dictators. Their presence becomes especially dangerous to dictators in the aftermath of shocks that redistribute power away from the dictators to other members of the ruling elite. When faced with this dilemma, some dictators responded by purging potentially threatening colleagues whole-sale (Getty and Naumov 1999; MacFarquhar 1997a).

The theoretical framework provided in this book further specifies that in addition to purging well-connected and resourceful colleagues, dicta-tors also gain by replacing them with *coalitions of the weak*. Potential members of these weak coalitions include those who are either shunned by the other elite for historical or cultural reasons or inexperienced and sparsely networked officials who can scarcely navigate the complexity of elite politics. By replacing experienced, well-networked officials with the coalitions of the weak, dictators and other experienced officials obtain higher probability of surviving the choppy water of authoritarian politics through two channels. First, weaker officials filling more positions in an elite that is relatively fixed in size means fewer challengers to the dictator's power or fewer contenders to become a part of the real ruling coalition. Second, the appointments of officials with obvious flaws provide infor-mation to the dictator about the relative balance of power, not just today but also for some time into the future. For the dictator, while the gains of appointing progressively weaker officials are limited, the gains from replacing a large proportion of experienced veterans with the coalition of the weak can be significant from a balance of power perspective and from an information standpoint. These gains, however, may be shared between the dictator and any other surviving veteran officials with dense networks, which can lead to further rounds of instability. A complete replacement of the elite with the coalition of the weak affords the dictator a high degree of protection against usurpation of power and ease in making major policy changes, although the agency problem never com-pletely disappears. However, governing with the coalition of the weak also leads to volatile policy making, a period of instability after the passing of the dictator, as well as institutional devolution toward neopa-trimonialism. For some dictators, these were a small price to pay for secure rule.

In the comparative context, the case of late-Mao politics calls for greater research on the role of elite agency and exogenous shocks in determining authoritarian stability, in addition to institutional factors that have been the focus of the extant literature. The installation of the coalition of the weak may well explain the ability of some bloodthirsty dictators to remain in power for life, whereas a different coalition strategy might have led to greater instability or even successful coups. The case of Maoist China also calls for more empirical research on the interaction between external shocks and elite political equilibria, as the theoretical work by Acemoglu, Egorov, and Sonin (2008) also suggests. For Mao, a major policy failure attributable to him opened the way for power redistribution, which forced the dictator to change his strategy from one of divide and rule to a riskier path of mass purge, followed by the coalition of the weak. The institutions in the CCP did not change much before and after the Great Leap Forward, but Mao's preferred strategy changed tremendously due to this exogenous shock, ultimately leading to an entirely new coalition alignment, which then brought about enormous institutional changes during the Cultural Revolution. Without the Great Leap shock and without Mao's preference for a high-risk strategy, the power-sharing arrangement of the mid-1950s likely would have persisted for quite some time.

The theory of the coalition of the weak also creates new space for future research on the incentives and strategy of lieutenants of the dictator as the dictator's own strategy changes. Under a collective leadership equilibrium, which implies competition between factions, dictators may prefer lieutenants with a history of loyalty to their patrons and perhaps even some capacity to build up their own networks. This is consistent with the empirical pattern of faction-based promotions in reform-era China, but the data used to derive these findings have largely come from an era of collective leadership (Jia et al. 2014; Meyer et al. 2016; Shih and Lee 2018). However, if the dictator begins to pursue a coalition of the weak strategy, previously favored lieutenants may suddenly find themselves out of favor. Faced with this changing environment, officials can respond by rendering themselves "weak" by engaging in high-profile corruption or by purging their own followers in order to shrink their networks. Less ominously, technocrats with opportunities to enlarge their networks by serving as senior provincial administrators may forgo such opportunities in order to limit the size of their networks. This reaction would intensify the formation of siloed interests in the regime. Uncovering the linkage between elite dynamics and mid-level incentives provides fruitful avenues of research for China and for other large authoritarian regimes.

Finally, the case of late-Mao politics suggests a potentially generalizable lag effect between coalition strategy in one period and likely equilibrium coalition in a subsequent period. In an institutionalized dictatorship, installation of the coalition of the weak by the dictator in one period likely elevated the chance of power sharing among several elite in a subsequent period. Because a key objective of the coalition of the weak is to provide the dictator with more certain signals about the weaknesses of his lieutenants, these weak lieutenants also would have better information on each other's weaknesses, thus encouraging them toward power sharing upon the dictator's death. Thus, power sharing might be a more likely outcome among a group of known weaklings, compared to a group of well-networked officials unsure of each other's power. To be sure, post-Mao politics saw a few rounds of reshuffling before surviving officials arrived at a stable power-sharing arrangement, but that mainly was caused by the mass rehabilitation of densely networked elite, which is unlikely to be replicated elsewhere. In post-Stalin Soviet Union, for example, the top leadership quickly arrived at a power-sharing arrangement after Beria's execution (Taubman 2003: 258). The reverse, the higher likelihood of dictatorship after a period of power sharing, also might be true, although that likely is more contingent on the personality and information set of the elite actors. In any event, the causal relationship between different configurations of elite coalitions presents another potentially fruitful avenue of future research.

COALITIONS OF THE WEAK AND POLITICS IN THE MAO AND DENG ERAS

Although numerous works have examined the life and deeds of Mao Zedong, the chairman of the Chinese Communist Party from the 1940s to his death in 1976, few works have abstracted away from his globally influential ideology or his symbolic importance for the Chinese revolution and considered him as purely a politician in an authoritarian regime. This book takes this approach and finds new interpretations of his actions after the disastrous Great Leap Forward. Agreeing with existing accounts of the period (MacFarquhar 1997a; Tsou and Nathan 1976), this work sees the Great Leap Forward as a major shock to the CCP elite, which depleted Mao's erstwhile reputation for being nearly invincible and infallible. This led other leaders, such as Liu Shaoqi, to intensify their own effort to build up their own image with the potential aim of replacing Mao one day (Perry 2012). Although Mao was still nominally in charge, subtle moves by the other elite to circumvent his decision-making and his direct control over policies greatly alarmed him. Into the mid-1960s, Mao became increasingly determined to remove several high-ranking colleagues who were seen as subtly usurping his power (Dittmer 1977; MacFarquhar 1997a; Pantsov and Levine 2012).

While the preparation for and the eventual removal of highly networked and experienced rivals and the ascendency of his loyal lieutenant Lin Biao is a well-known story, Mao also cultivated two groups of unlikely leaders to take up some of the highest offices in the party-state. On the one hand, a sizable group of military officers with the label "counterrevolutionary splittists" in their dossiers were rotated into increasingly powerful positions in the military even as officers with long records of loyalty to Mao were being purged. The conventional account of factionalism benefiting followers of powerful factions cannot explain why Mao favored officers of the Fourth Front Army (FFA) who had betrayed the party and him personally.

On the other hand, a group of junior propagandists, the scribblers (笔杆子), also gained prominence during the Cultural Revolution. Existing accounts focus on their ideological zeal and prodigious ability to author polemics in support of Mao's latest ideological campaign to explain their ascendance (Gao 2003; MacFarquhar 1997b; Perry and Li 1997). However, if they were meant as successors of Mao's continuous revolution (MacFarquhar 1997b), why were the vast majority of them purged by Mao with scarcely a second thought in 1967 and 1968? Beyond the polemics they authored, what other roles did they play in Mao's power strategy during the Cultural Revolution? If they were not meant to be revolutionary successors, how did they help Mao stay in power in the twilight of his life?

The coalition of the weak framework explains both the removal of Mao's powerful colleagues and the appointment of traitors and inexperienced writers into senior party and military positions. For members of the traitorous FFA, if they had dared to plot against Mao in any manner, Mao easily could have mobilized the rest of the party to purge them by pointing out their glaring historical errors. Their tainted status also made them unlikely allies of potential challengers of Mao because of the limited payoffs to them of joining a rival coalition and the additional costs to the challengers of including them in a rival coalition. Their vulnerability was made clear in the aftermath of the Wuhan incident in 1967, when Lin Biao nearly managed to remove them wholesale. Their vulnerability made them perfect material for the "sand" that Mao mixed into the military to dilute the rising power of Lin Biao. As Lin Biao's power rose in the military in the run-up to the 9th Party Congress in 1969, Mao elevated more FFA veterans to counterbalance Lin Biao, knowing that the veterans of the tainted faction would side with Mao in any ensuing power struggle not out of loyalty but out of fear of their own vulnerability and Mao's wrath. Mao's insurance policy against Lin Biao paid off handsomely because Lin Biao indeed began to deviate from Mao's wishes, especially during and after the 1970 Lushan Conference. This deviation ultimately necessitated the mobilization of FFA veterans in the military to arrest Lin Biao followers wholesale.

As for junior propagandists, some of them saw an opportunity in the mid-1960s to serve the highest power in the country. Most of them likely did not know the full extent of the rewards and risks their participation in Mao's plot to launch the Cultural Revolution entailed. For Mao, however, the political ignorance of these junior officials made them the perfect weapons against his established enemies. First, they wrote polemics against a junior member of Liu Shaoqi's Northern Bureau faction, which ultimately lured Politburo member Peng Zhen into supporting an erroneous ideological line, giving Mao sufficient justification for his removal. Also important for Mao, in case their attack had led to a collective backlash, Mao could have sacrificed these scribblers at little cost to himself because he had not been the author, merely the silent backer, of these polemics. As the Red Guard movement emerged, these junior writers were then entrusted with the power to communicate with and convey Mao's wishes to the emerging movement. Again, in case the other elite staged a strong backlash, the scribblers would have been blamed for the entire Red Guard movement and purged.

After the removal of scores of veteran revolutionaries from party positions, a few of the scribblers were rapidly elevated into key positions in the party, especially in the propaganda bureaucracy. However, they remained easily dispensable pawns in Mao's complex political game and also in the political strategy of Mao's emerging rival, Lin Biao. In 1967, Lin Biao manipulated a group of scribblers into believing that Mao had intended to attack and purge all FFA veterans from the military. The circumstances of the Wuhan incident certainly lent themselves to that interpretation, but Lin Biao, who had witnessed the FFA's treachery firsthand and had noticed Mao's intentional elevation and protection of these officers, almost certainly knew of Mao's true intention. Still, in order to eradicate the last obstacle to his complete dominance of the military, Lin Biao used the scribblers to write polemics against FFA veterans in Wuhan and beyond. In this case, this campaign against FFA veterans drew Mao's wrath, but Lin Biao escaped without a scratch by blaming the entire campaign on a handful of junior scribblers. Suddenly, scribblers like Wang Li, Guan Feng, and Qi Benyu, who had enjoyed the limelight as "central leaders," were thrown into prison, condemned to decades of isolated confinement without a clear explanation as to why their lives were laid to waste. When Mao finally purged Lin Biao's faction in 1971, the surviving scribblers were elevated to some of the highest offices in the CCP, although they continued to have little influence beyond the propaganda bureaucracy.

With the doomed flight of Lin Biao to the Soviet Union, Mao's coalition of tainted military officers and junior propagandists occupied the most powerful positions in the party. None of them dared to usurp Mao's power in any overt way or to disagree with Mao's decisions. In the absence of any rival leaders with their own agendas, Mao ruled for a time as a true dictator of China. Ever watchful of potential threats, Mao was weary of the FFA's dominance in the military and rehabilitated Deng Xiaoping as a counterweight to senior leaders in the FFA bloc. However, when Deng clearly deviated from the Maoist line by rapidly rehabilitating the economic bureaucracy and veteran cadres, a sickly Mao easily mobilized the coalition of the weak to first criticize, then purge him. As long as Mao was alive, members of the coalition of the weak dared not move against Mao or even against each other without Mao's blessing. Politics in the late-Mao period, however, degenerated to competing whispering campaigns by weak officials to gain Mao's favor. This style of neopatrimonial politics, however, was well suited for an increasingly ill dictator with declining cognitive capacity to rule until his dying day.

After Mao's passing in 1976, however, junior officials promoted by Mao were soon purged or sidelined by the surviving veterans. The tainted veterans of the FFA chose to ally themselves with the few surviving veterans who were not sullied by historical errors and facilitated the rehabilitation of Deng Xiaoping. Deng, never having a large faction of his own in the PLA, had to corule with FFA veterans and other rehabilitated veterans, thus setting the stage for a long period of collective rule in the Chinese Communist Party.

COALITIONS OF THE WEAK AND THE DAWN OF THE XI JINPING ERA

Scholars of elite politics in China have long debated whether the elite political equilibrium in China was domination by one-man or collective rule (Nathan and Tsai 1995; Tsou 1976). Empirically, both types of equilibria have persisted for long periods in the CCP (Shih et al. 2010a). An analysis of the politics of the 1980s and 1990s in China suggests that collective rule, especially by weakly networked elite, left a power vacuum of which daring and ambitious politicians could well take advantage. This logic might have laid the groundwork for the complete domination of the CCP by Xi Jinping. Having achieved domination of the CCP, Xi will be incentivized to pursue a coalition of the weak strategy to maintain his dominance in the party after the 20th Party Congress in 2022. This logic will present payoffs and challenges to the CCP and to Xi himself.

The surviving revolutionary veterans of the 1980s cultivated "always nice people" successors who relied on the political connections of their patrons, thus prolonging the postretirement influence of these veterans in their respective policy domains. In other words, although power was decentralized in the 1980s, each of the senior patrons in each policy domain pursued their own coalition of the weak strategy. Although a sizable group of princelings, the children of the revolutionary veterans, came of age in the 1980s, they ran into a glass ceiling in the government because of their activism during the Cultural Revolution, their own enthusiasm for capitalist wealth, and because of elite resistance to these connected princelings. Thus, some of the most networked officials of a younger generation were prevented from competing for top positions in the regime in the 1990s and 2000s. Instead, the Tiananmen Crisis saw the elevation of two generations of thinly networked technocrats to the helm of the party even though veteran revolutionaries like Deng had known that individually they lacked the connections across the regime to be effective leaders.

During the reign of the weak successors, a small handful of princelings left the capital and its intense jockeying for power and settled down as mid-level officials in several of the hundreds of nameless cities in China. Out of the limelight, they proved themselves valuable to local leaders by using their connections in Beijing to lobby for greater resources for the localities. They also cultivated ties with members of the military stationed in their jurisdictions and also with SOE bosses in those localities. Seeing them as potential national leaders in the future, some officials in these nameless cities wisely gravitated toward princeling officials and stood with them as they fought at times fierce factional battles with rival local leaders. Thus, over time, these princeling officials also built up sizable followings in localities where they served. Some of these princelings made use of local resources to curry favors with the technocrat successors in charge in Beijing. Others kept their heads low and relied on the princeling networks of influential officials, generals, and businessmen to lobby for their steady promotions up the bureaucratic ladder.

As the succession issue loomed for Hu Jintao in the early 2000s, a small handful of princelings became probable candidates for the next secretary general of the CCP. Most of them, however, were flawed in their own way. As experienced and capable as Liu Yandong was, she could not overcome the entrenched sexism in the party that had barred women from its highest offices since communism had touched down in China. Yu Zhengsheng, who was closed to the Deng family, could not take the highest office because his brother had defected to the US. The charismatic and learned Wang Qishan had married into a revolutionary family but was a few years too old to become the successor to Hu. This left three princelings and one nonprinceling – Xi Jinping, Bo Xilai, Li Yuanchao, and Li Keqiang – as potential candidates for the top position.

The story of the elite jockeying for the top position in 2012 remains vague, but Bo Xilai likely was eliminated from the race early on because of his nakedly ambitious and confrontational personality, as well as his smaller network among the elite compared to the other candidates. Meanwhile, princeling officials and military officers, led by Zeng Qinghong, gravitated around Xi Jinping, whose father had belonged to the weakest of the revolutionary era faction to emerge out of the Cultural Revolution. Despite receiving the fewest number of votes in the election for alternate members of the Central Committee at the 1997 15th Party Congress, or perhaps because of it, Xi's career continued to prosper as he moved to ever more prestigious positions (Wong and Ansfield 2011). Meanwhile, although Li Yuanchao came from a mid-level revolutionary family, he had long ago thrown his lot in with nonprinceling officials in the Chinese Communist Youth League. Thus, as the succession decision came to a head, princeling officials singularly supported Xi Jinping and not Li Yuanchao, who found himself excluded from the Politburo Standing Committee at the 18th Party Congress (Brown 2014; SCMP Reporters 2012). The Youth League faction also concentrated their political resources on ensuring Li Keqiang's promotion to the premier position instead of backing Li Yuanchao (SCMP Reporters 2012).

Had several more princeling officials been in the running in the crucial 2007–2012 period, though, Xi might not have been the chosen successor, and even if he had succeeded Hu, he would have been balanced in the PSC by several more "bloodline" princes without the apparent vulnerabilities of Liu Yandong or Yu Zhengsheng. Xi likely would not have been able to launch a wide-ranging anticorruption campaign because it hurt many princeling interests, and, almost certainly, his ability to reshuffle the military would have been curtailed by other senior-level princelings, who also had strong ties in the military. The resulting balance of power politics would have produced different policy outcomes, including foreign policy outcomes.

Instead, Xi established almost complete domination of the Politburo after the 19th Party Congress by promoting his followers into nearly all the available Politburo slots. He also revealed his probable intention to serve as China's leader for life at the 2018 National People's Congress, when the state constitution was revised to remove the term limit for state presidency, in which he served. Into his third term after the 20th Party Congress in 2022, will we see a replay of the coalition of the weak logic that dominated late-Mao politics?

EVOLVING POLITICS IN XI'S CHINA AFTER THE FIRST TEN YEARS

Several factors suggest near-term elite stability in China. First, unlike the mid-Mao period of the 1960s, when Mao's peers undermined his power in the aftermath of the Great Leap, Xi already has eliminated or sidelined most potential challengers from his age group. Li Yuanchao did not obtain a PSC promotion and was entirely forced out of the Politburo at the 19th Party Congress. Even Wang Qishan, who was instrumental in Xi's consolidation of power and had built his own faction in the financial sector and in the anticorruption bureaucracy, had been forced out of the Politburo Standing Committee into the symbolic vice president position. Moreover, unlike Mao, Xi has avoided any major policy mistake that caused a sharp decline in the welfare of millions of Chinese up through his first two terms. Although the Chinese government's reaction to Covid-19 likely was delayed by two weeks or so due to political considerations, China has largely controlled the spread of Covid-19, and Xi has claimed credit for this outcome (Shih 2021). Short of a major disaster attributable to him, latent opponents of Xi will find it difficult to coalesce against him.

At the same time, we are beginning to see an emerging coalition of the weak in the Xi Jinping Era, which portends stable rule in the latter years of his administration but also institutional and political challenges. Figure 8.1 shows that the number of ties that Hu Jintao and Xi Jinping had with Central Committee members were roughly the same at the 17th Party Congress and the 19th Party Congress, respectively. These two congresses were roughly comparable because they were both the second

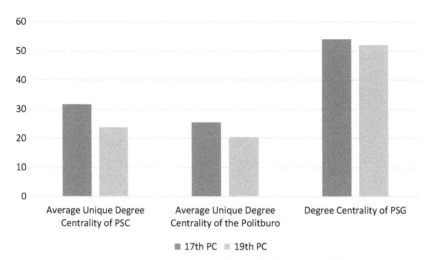

FIGURE 8.1 Average unique degree centrality of Politburo and PSC members and the degree centrality of the party secretary general: 17th PC versus 19th PC

congress presided by the two secretary generals. However, the average PSC and Politburo member at the 19th PC had fewer unique ties than their 17th PC counterparts. At the 17th Party Congress, PSC members like Xi Jinping, Li Keqiang, Zhou Yongkang, and He Guoqiang on average had over thirty unique ties with members of the Central Committee elite, which they did not share with Hu Jintao. By the 19th Party Congress, no PSC member (besides Xi) could claim over thirty ties that were not a part of Xi's network. PSC member Wang Hunning, who had worked in academia and think tanks for most of his career, only had ties with one other Central Committee elite. At the Politburo level, the network density of its members was more comparable between the 17th PC and the 19th PC. However, unlike the 17th PC, the 19th PC saw the elevation of several Politburo members, including Ding Xuexiang, Liu He, and Cai Qi, with sparse networks of ten or fewer unique elite ties each. To the extent that these Politburo members had elite networks, they shared the bulk of them with Xi Jinping and therefore could not claim independent power bases. If one sees densely networked elite replaced by more sparsely networked ones at the 20th Party Congress, one can be even more certain that Xi is pursuing a coalition of the weak strategy in the latter years of his rule. This book has argued that coalitions of the weak helped aging dictators consolidate tranquil rule in the twilight years of their lives.

As time passes, however, two factors likely will erode the current state of stability at the top level, even if China faces a perfectly stable external environment. These factors may further drive Xi toward an increasingly comprehensive coalition of the weak strategy even if it meant large-scale purges and institutional devolution. First, as his own health and cognition deteriorate, his worries about a potential usurpation of power will intensify, thus escalating the possibility of a preemptive strike against potential rivals. Second, some of his lieutenants, especially younger ones who will join the Politburo at the 20th Party Congress, will begin to accumulate power and knowledge of the complexities of elite politics, making them potential rivals of Xi. The case of Maoist China and the theory of the coalition of the weak suggest that Xi will intensify his strategy by speeding up the pace of high-level reshuffling, especially for sensitive positions where power can be used to usurp Xi's own power. This need not take place through purges, although the chance of them will increase after the 20th Party Congress in 2022.

Even at the height of his power, Xi has begun to replace highly networked and charismatic officials with less networked ones, especially for holders of sensitive offices. For example, his close friend and comrade Wang Qishan stepped down from the secretary of the Central Discipline and Inspection Commission position presumably for age reason, but if Xi had wanted him to stay in that position, no one, certainly not Wang himself, would have objected. He already has bent the rule for others close to him such as Xia Baolong. Similarly, for fellow princeling Liu Yuan, instead of promoting him to the Central Military Commission after he lent Xi a hand in cleansing the military of the Xu Caihou faction, he retired from active duty in 2015, which a CMC promotion would have negated. Finally, former Beijing police chief Fu Zhenghua helped Xi consolidate control over the public security ministry and carry out a crackdown on online dissent. However, Fu was first moved out of the public security ministry and then gently eased into a powerless National People's Congress position, ultimately ending up in jail after his arrest in 2021. For most officials in the defense and security establishments, they may well face frustrating career outcomes even if they have done a lot for the top leadership. Even promising Politburo members in Xi's own faction such as Li Xi and Chen Xi may find their relatively large unique networks greater liabilities than assets after the 20th Party Congress. They may find themselves on an accelerated schedule for retirement much as that faced by Li Yuanchao, or even implicated in anticorruption investigations. Of course, Politburo member Hu Chunhua, who is not in Xi's faction and has a relatively large network of thirty-seven unique ties among the CC elite, faces the greatest danger after the 20th Party

Congress, unless he too is forced into an early retirement in 2022. In general, Figure 8.1 suggests that Xi still has ample room to weaken the average network of the elite selectorate, thus consolidating his power even more.

In terms of party institutions, Xi already reshaped them to concentrate policy-making power to his own hands through the leading groups, which channeled authorities away from the collectively governed Politburo Standing Committee (Johnson and Kennedy 2015). However, as the leading groups gain more power and policy influence by transforming into commissions, Xi will need to rotate away or purge senior officials in these commissions to prevent them from accumulating too much power. If this is the case, the upper echelon of the party will be populated by technocrats and party administrators who have a record of seeking Xi's patronage but have relatively thin networks in the party-state because of their fear of Xi's suspicion. Thinly networked officials in these commissions will jockey with each other to convey the latest "instructions" from Xi to the ministries and provinces below, even though they themselves will not have much informal influence over these units through their own networks.

This policy-making structure will have important implications on policy formation and implementation in the second and perhaps even third decade of Xi's rule. In brief, politics may be characterized by neo-patrimonialism at the top and bureaucratic turf war and fragmented authoritarianism in the middle. First, for Politburo and PSC members running the day-to-day business of the leading groups and commissions, they know they cannot accumulate power by having independent policy agendas or their own networks of officials in these commissions. Thus, they will focus on gauging Xi's policy preferences by seeking audiences with him and rendering his wishes into decrees for lower-level officials, perhaps obtaining rent in the process. This patrimonial policy process at the top will produce a cascade of decrees reflecting Xi's policy preferences at a given moment. Actual policy outcomes, short of major disasters, will not matter for senior officials, since they cannot accumulate power or obtain further promotions in any event. For mid-level officials at the director-general or ministerial level, they will spend enormous energy on apparently implementing Xi's policies and ideologies and on currying favors with Xi and his family members. As recent promotions have shown, having a past history with Xi has been a much more important precondition for promotion than other attributes (Shih and Lee 2018). They will not spend energy on policy innovation or in cultivating their own networks across the regime beyond their own narrow bureaucratic hierarchy, or *xitong*, because Xi's growing suspicion will limit the expected payoffs of such actions. For the vast majority of officials who never had dealings with Xi and therefore have no hope of ever rising to the Politburo or to one of the central leading groups, they will spend much of their energy on protecting their own bureaucratic turfs while appearing to comply with Xi's policies issued by the leading groups.

These incentives will generate powerful interest groups surrounding the most powerful agencies in the government, including the military-industrial complex, the security apparatus, and the technology bureaucracy, much as the late-Brezhnev Era in the USSR (Bunce 1983). This especially will be the case if Xi allowed his close followers to occupy Politburo seats for long periods along with himself, which would stop promotions for officials below the top level. Like the late-Brezhnev period, officials heading these silos may see the protection of these special interests superseding overall objectives of continual growth or maintaining a peaceful environment with China's neighbors. As Xi's health declines, members of the top elite will be increasingly unable to dictate the behavior of entrenched sectoral interests, again similar to the late-Brezhnev years.

Similar to the late-Mao years, although Xi will have overall security in his power, the agency problem will not go away completely. Richly endowed interests and their patrons in the Politburo will feed false or exaggerated information to the dictator in order to better position themselves for the coming power transition. This may lead to elite instability in the twilight years of Xi's life. For one, one can already foresee potential power struggles between the internal security apparatus and the internet security apparatus. While one bureaucracy oversees a vast network of police forces and surveillance capabilities, the other bureaucracy commands vast troves of personal and commercial data on all of China's population and companies. Both bureaucracies have close working relationships with some of China's leading technology companies, which have cutting-edge capabilities and enormous databases. Even if Xi places weak figures at the top of these bureaucracies, longtime insiders and commercial stakeholders in them will have incentives to misrepresent information to the dictator in order to obtain greater resources and power (Milgrom 1988), and ambitious younger officials will be tempted to exert greater control over these powerful agencies in the run-up to the succession. These dynamics may form the foundation of political tension in the twilight years of Xi's rule.

In the late-Mao period, at least some surviving officials, such as Li Xiannian, had followers across wide swaths of the regime, who were mobilized during crises such as the Tangshan Earthquake. In the late-Xi period, besides the dictator's own command and the formal bureaucracy, most of the officials will only have relatively narrow networks and may not have the capacity to mobilize all the resources at the regime's disposal effectively. Mid-level officials also will be highly motivated to suppress information on insipient crises for fear of being accused of policy failure. This may exacerbate the impact of a shock on China in the late-Xi years. To be sure, China responded to Covid-19 rapidly and effectively after an initial delay, but the effectiveness of China's response may have been contingent on a common understanding in the entire government that Xi had total control over the party and would remain the dictator of China in the foreseeable future. As such, a cover-up of a major disaster likely will lead to harsh punishment by Xi. These incentives will erode over time if mid-level bureaucrats expect higher payoffs from misrepresenting information due to greater ability to lie convincingly or lower probability of being discovered and punished as the transition looms. Also, as the dictator becomes more vulnerable to information manipulation due to cognitive decline, competing special interests will have stronger incentives to present favorable information to sway the dictator's decisions, leading to greater volatility in policy making. This is a serious concern even in a system with relatively decentralized power, such as the United States (Ainsworth 1993; Austen-Smith 1993). Lobbying, counter-lobbying, and policy volatility are expected to be increasingly common features of policy making in the latter Xi years, potentially delaying the resolution of crises, especially chronic ones like China's collapsing birthrates.

Finally, both Stalin and Mao were able to pursue the coalition of the weak strategy to a large extent due to relatively benign international environment in their last years. Likewise, the political equilibrium in the late-Xi period also will depend on external or internal pressure confronting the regime. In the absence of external pressure, which was the case in China after the Sino–US rapprochement in 1972, Xi can fully pursue the coalition of the weak strategy. However, if the regime becomes besieged by external and internal challenges, Xi will need to entrust senior officials with the authority to deal with these challenges, especially the authority to mobilize disparate resources across the regime. Although some of these officials will show an aptitude for resolving challenges, they also will accumulate power, networks of trusted officials across the regime, and

prestige in the process. The bigger the challenges resolved by these subordinates, the more power they will accumulate, even to a point of usurping
Xi's own role in the party. Major domestic and foreign policy challenges,
in brief, will force Xi into a choice between policy successes and a halcyon
reign in his twilight years.

References

Acemoglu, Daron, Georgy Egorov, and Konstantin Sonin. 2008. "Coalition formation in non-democracies." *Review of Economic Studies* 75 (4):987–1009.

Ainsworth, Scott. 1993. "Regulating lobbyists and interest group influence." *Journal of Politics* 55 (1):41–56.

Anderlini, Jamil. 2012. "Beijing on edge amid coup rumors." *Financial Times*, March 21.

Austen-Smith, David. 1993. "Information and influence: lobbying for agendas and votes." *American Journal of Political Science* 37 (3):799–833.

Bachman, David M. 1991. *Bureaucracy, Economy, and Leadership in China: the Institutional Origins of the Great Leap Forward.* Cambridge and New York: Cambridge University Press.

Baidu. 2014a. "Liu Jingsong." In *Baidu Baike.* Beijing: Baidu. Retrieved 8/2/2014 from http://baike.baidu.com/view/178764.htm

———. 2014b. "Zhou Yibing." In *Baidu Baike.* Beijing: Baidu. Retrieved 8/2/2014 from http://baike.baidu.com/view/305860.htm

Baum, Richard. 1994. *Burying Mao: Chinese Politics in the Age of Deng Xiaoping.* Princeton, NJ: Princeton University Press.

Bell, Daniel. 2016. *The China Model: political Meritocracy and the Limits of Democracy.* Princeton, NJ: Princeton University Press.

Berger, Peter L., and Thomas Luckmann. 1990. *The Social Construction of Reality: A Treatise in the Sociology of Knowledge.* New York: Anchor Books.

Bo, Yibo. 1993. *Ruogan Zhongda Juece yu Shijian de Huigu Xia (Recollections on Certain Important Decisions and Events, Volume 2).* Beijing: Central Party School Publisher.

Bosworth, Barry, and Susan L. Collin. 2008. "Accounting for growth: comparing China and India." *Journal of Economic Perspectives* 22 (1):45–66.

Brandt, Loren, Debin Ma, and T. G. Rawski. 2014. "From divergence to convergence: reevaluating the history behind China's economic boom." *Journal of Economic Literature* 52 (1):45–123.

Braun, Otto. 1982. *A Comintern Agent in China 1932–1939*. Stanford, CA: Stanford University Press.

Brown, Kerry. 2014. *The New Emperors: power and the Princelings in China.* London and New York: I. B. Tauris.

Brownlee, Jason. 2007. *Authoritarianism in an Age of Democratization.* Cambridge and New York: Cambridge University Press.

Brzezinski, Zbigniew K., and Carl J. Friedrich. 1956. *Totalitarian Dictatorship and Autocracy.* Cambridge, MA: Harvard University Press.

Buckley, Chris. 2014. "China's antigraft push snares an ex-general." *New York Times*, June 30.

Bueno de Mesquita, Bruce, Alastair Smith, Randolph M. Silverson, and James D. Morrow. 2003. *The Logic of Political Survival.* Cambridge, MA: MIT Press.

Bunce, Valerie. 1983. "The political economy of the Brezhnev era: the rise and fall of corporatism." *British Journal of Political Science* 13 (2):129–158.

Calhoun, Craig. 1994. *Neither Gods nor Emperors: students and the Struggle for Democracy in China.* Berkeley: University of California Press.

Central Committee. 1966. "Zhongguo gongchandang zhongyang weiyuanhui tongzhi ji yuanjianfujian (Notice of the CCP Central Committee and the original and appendix)." In *China Contemporary Political Movement Archive.* Los Angeles, CA: Song Yongyi.

1979. "Guanyu Zhang Guotao Tongzhi chengli dier 'zhongyang' de jueding (Decision concerning Comrade Zhang Guotao forming the second 'center')." In *Zhonggong Dangshi Cankao Ziliao Diqice (Reference Material on Party History, Volume 7)*, ed. Party History Research Center of the PLA Political Academy. Beijing: PLA Publisher, 191–192.

1982a. "Guanyu qingli lingdao banzizhong 'sanzhongren' wenti de tongzhi (Notice concerning the issue of cleansing the leadership ranks of 'three types of people')." In *China Contemporary Political Movements Database.* Los Angeles, CA: Song Yongyi.

1982b. "Zhonggong zhongyang guanyu jianli laoganbu tuixiu zhidu de jueding (Decision concerning constructing a system for cadre retirement)." In *San Zhong Quanhui Yilai Zhongyao Wenxian Huibian (Compilation of Important Documents since the Third Plenum (of the 11th Central Committee))*, ed. Document Research Center of CCP Central Committee. Beijing: People's Publisher, 1158–1168.

1982c. "Zhonggong zhongyang pizhuan zhongyang jilu jiancha weiyuanhui guanyu Kang Sheng, Xie Fuzhi wenti de liangge shencha baogao (The Central Committee forwards two evaluation reports authored by the Central Discipline and Inspection Committee on Kang Sheng and Xie Fuzhi)." In *San Zhong Quanhui Yilai Zhongyao Wenxian Huibian (Compilation of Important Documents since the Third Plenum (of the 11th Central Committee))*, ed. Document Research Center of CCP Central Committee. Beijing: Renmin, 684–713.

1982d. "Zhonggong zhongyang zhuanfa zhongyang zuzhibu 'guanyu 'liushiyi ren anjian' de diaocha baogao' de tongzhi (Notice on the Central Committee Forwarding the Central Organization Department's 'Investigation Report on the '61 Persons' Case')." In *San Zhong Quanhui Yilai Zhongyao Wenxian*

Huibian (Compilation of Important Documents since the Third Plenum (of the 11th Central Committee)), ed. Document Research Center of CCP Central Committee. Beijing: People's Publisher, 12–13.

1983. "Zhonggong zhongyang guanyu zhengdang de jueding (Decision on rectification of the party)." In *China Contemporary Political Movements Database*. Los Angeles, CA: Song Yongyi.

1984. "Guanyi qingli 'sanzhongren' de buchong tongzhi (Supplemental notice concerning cleansing 'three types of people')." In *China Contemporary Political Movements Database*. Los Angeles, CA: Song Yongyi.

1990. "Guanyu ruogan lishi wenti de jueyi (Decision concerning certain historical issues)." In *Zhonggong Zhongyang Wenjian Xuanji 15 (A Selection of CCP Central Committee Documents, Volume 15)*, ed. Central Archive. Beijing: Central Party School Publisher, 87.

2010. "Guanyu tongyi yibufen laotongzhi buzai danren zhongyang sange weiyuanhui chengyuan de qingqiu (Concerning agreeing with the requests by some old comrades to no longer serve on the three committees in the Central Committee)." *People's Daily*, October 15. Available at http://cpc.people.com.cn/GB/64162/64168/64565/65379/4429520.html.

Central Organization Department, and Party History Research Center of CCP CC. 2004. *Zhongguo Gongchandang Lijie Zhongyang Weiyuan Da Cidian, 1921–2003 (The Dictionary of Past and Present CCP Central Committee Members)*. Beijing: Party History Publisher.

Central Organization Department, Central Party History Research Center, and Central Archive. 1997a. *Zhongguo Gongchan Dang Zuzhishi Ziliao (Material on the Organization History of the Chinese Communist Party)*. 6 vols. Beijing: Party History Publisher.

1997b. *Zhongguo Gongchan Dang Zuzhishi Ziliao (Material on the Organization History of the Chinese Communist Party)*. 7 vols. Beijing: Party History Publisher.

Chang, Jung, and Jon Halliday. 2005. *Mao: the Unknown Story*. 1st American ed. New York: Knopf.

Chen, Boda. 2000. *Chen Boda Yigao: Yuzhong Zihu ji Qita (The Writing of Chen Boda: His Self Portrait in Jail and Others*. Hong Kong: Tiandi Tushu.

Chen, Chusan. 2014. "Guanyu hongweibing de yizhuang lishi gongan (A public case concerning red guards)." *Yanhuang Chunqiu* 2014 (7):2–8.

Chen, Guohua. 2018. "Nu'er zhuiyi haijun silingyuan Ye Fei rongma yisheng (Daughter remembers a life of service for naval commander Ye Fei)." *Beijing Youth Daily*, March 26.

Chen, Kaige. 2012. "Qingchun jian (The knives of youth)." In *Fengbao de huiyi: 1965-1970 de Beijing Sizhong (Memory in the midst of a storm, Beijing number four high school between 1965 and 1970)*, ed. D. Bei, Y. Cao and Y. Wei. Shanghai: Sanlian Publisher.

Chen, Xilian. 2007. *Chen Xilian Huiyilu (The Memoir of Chen Xilian)*. Beijing: People's Liberation Army Publisher.

Chen, Yingci. 2008. *Chen Yonggui Benshi (The Talent of Chen Yonggui)*. Hong Kong: Shidai Guoji Publisher.

Chen, Yun. 1982a. "Jiaqiang jihua jingji (Strengthening the planned economy)."
    In *San Zhong Quanhui Yilai Zhongyao Wenxian Huibian (Compilation of
    Important Documents since the Third Plenum (of the 11th Central
    Committee))*, ed. Document Research Center of the CCP Central
    Committee. Beijing: People's Publisher.
    1982b. "Zai sheng, shi, zizhiqu dangwei shuji zuotanhui shang de tanhua
    (Remarks during the province, city, autonomous region party secretary dis-
    cussion meeting)." In *San Zhong Quanhui Yilai Zhongyao Wenxian Huibian
    (Compilation of Important Documents since the Third Plenum (of the 11th
    Central Committee))*, ed. Document Research Center of the CCP Central
    Committee. Beijing: People's Publisher.
Chen, Zaidao. 1988. "Wuhan '7.20' shijian de shimo (The story of the Wuhan
    '7.20' Incident)." In *Wenhua Dageming Yanjiu Ziliao (Research Material for
    the Cultural Revolution)*, ed. research Center for Party History and Party
    Construction at the National Defense University. Beijing: PLA Publisher.
Chen, Zutao. 2006. "Huiyi Fuqin Chen Changhao (Remembering my father Chen
    Changhao)." *Zhonggong Dangshi Ziliao (Material for CCP History)* 2006
    (1):66–79.
Cui, Wunian. 2003. *Wode 83 ge yue (My 83 Months)*. Hong Kong: Ko Man
    Publishing Co.
Debs, Alexandre. 2007. *The Wheel of Fortune: agency Problems in Dictatorships*.
    Rochester, NY: University of Rochester. Available from https://www
    .researchgate.net/publication/248065710_The_Wheel_of_Fortune_Agency_
    Problems_in_Dictatorships.
Deng, Liqun. 2005. *Shi'erge Chunqiu: 1975-1987 (Twelve Springs and Autumns:
    1975-1987)*. Hong Kong: Boszhi Publisher.
    2015. *Deng Liqun Zishu 1915-1974 (The Self Portrait of Deng Liqun: 1915-
    1974)*. Beijing: Renmin Publisher.
    2016. *Wowei Shaoqi Tongzhi Shuoxiehua (I Will Speak on Behalf of Comrade
    Shaoqi)*. Beijing: Contemporary China Publisher.
Deng, Maomao. 1995. *Deng Xiaoping : my Father*. New York: BasicBooks.
Deng, Xiaoping. 1994. "Lao ganbu diyiwei de renwu shi xuanba zhongqing nian
    ganbu (The first task of elderly cadres is to promote young and middle age
    cadres)." In *Deng Xiaoping Wenxuan Di'er Juan (The Collected Works of
    Deng Xiaoping: Second Volume)*, ed. Document Research Center of CCP
    Central Committee. Beijing: Renmin Publisher, 384–388.
    1993. "Zucheng yige shixing gaige de you xiwang de lingdao jiti (Form a
    leadership collective that is hopeful and will realize reform)." In *Deng
    Xiaoping Wenxuan Disan Juan (The Collected Works of Deng Xiaoping:
    Third Volume)*, ed. D. R. C. o. t. C. C. Committee. Beijing: Renmin Publisher,
    296–301.
    1993a. "Zai zhongguo gongchandang quanguo daibiaohuiyishang de jianghua
    (Remarks at the CCP National Representative Conference)." In *Deng
    Xiaoping Wenxuan Di'san Juan (The Collected Works of Deng Xiaoping:
    Third Volume)*, ed. D. R. C. o. C. C. Committee. Beijing: Renmin Publisher,
    141–147.

Deng, Xiaoping, Shangkun Yang, and Ziyang Zhao. 2001. "Memoranda of conversations supplied by a friend of Yang Shangkun who cannot be further identified (May 13, 1989)." In *The Tiananmen Papers*, ed. A. Nathan and P. Link. London: Little, Brown & Company.

Dikötter, Frank. 2016. *The Cultural Revolution: a People's History, 1962-1976.* First U.S. edition. ed. London: Bloomsbury Press.

Ding, Sheng. 2008. *Luolan yingxiong: Ding Sheng jiangjun huiyi lu (A hero in trouble: the memoirs of General Ding Sheng).* Hong Kong: Xingke'er Publisher.

Dittmer, Lowell. 1977. "'Line struggle' in theory and practice: the origins of the Cultural Revolution reconsidered." *The China Quarterly* (72):675–712.

1998. *Liu Shaoqi and the Chinese Cultural Revolution.* revised edition ed. Armonk, NY: ME Sharpe.

Document Research Center of CCP Central Committee. 1983. *Guanyu Jianguo Yilai Dangde Ruogan Lishi Wenti de Jueyi-Zhuxi Ben (Commentaries on 'Decisions on Certain Historical Problems in the Party Since the Founding of the Republic').* Beijing: CCP CC Document Research Center.

Document Research Center of the CCP CC. 2000. *Chen Yun Nianpu (The Chen Yun Chronicle).* Vol. 3. Beijing: Central Documentation Publisher.

2004. *Deng Xiaoping Nianpu: 1975-1997 (The Deng Xiaoping Chronicle: 1979-1997).* Beijing: Central Document Publisher.

Easter, Gerald M. 1996. "Personal networks and postrevolutionary state building: Soviet Russia reexamined." *World Politics* 48 (4):551–578.

Editorial Committee. 2009a. *Chi Haotian Zhuan (The Biography of Chi Haotian).* Beijing: PLA Publisher.

2009b. *Li Xiannian Zhuan- xia (The Biography of Li Xiannian: Volume 2).* 2 vols. Beijing: Central Literature Publisher.

Editorial Staff of One Spark Lighting the Plains. 2006. *Zhongguo Renmin Jiefangjun Jiangshuai Minglu (Biographical List of Generals in the People's Liberation Army).* Beijing: PLA Publisher.

Egorov, Georgy, and Konstantin Sonin. 2011. "Dictators and their viziers: endogenizing the loyalty-competence trade-off." *Journal of the European Economic Association* 9 (5):903–930.

Evans, Peter B. 1995. *Embedded Autonomy: states and Industrial Transformation.* Princeton, NJ: Princeton University Press.

Fang, Weizhong, Renzhi Wang, Shipu Gui, and Suinien Liu. 1984. *Zhonghua Renmin Gongheguo Fang Jingji Dashiji: 1949-1980 (An Account of Major Economic Events in the PRC).* Beijing: Chinese Social Science Publisher.

Fearon, James. 1995. "Rationalist explanations for war." *International Organization* 49:379–414.

Fewsmith, Joseph. 1994. *Dilemmas of Reform in China: political Conflict and Economic Debate.* Armonk, NY: M E Sharpe.

2001. *China Since Tiananmen: the Politics of Transition.* Cambridge; New York: Cambridge University Press.

Gandhi, Jennifer. 2008. *Political Institutions Under Dictatorship.* New York: Cambridge University Press.

Gandhi, Jennifer, and Adam Przeworski. 2006. "Cooperation, cooptation, and rebellion under dictatorships." *Economics & Politics* 18 (1):1–26.

Gao, Hua. 2000. *Hong taiyang shi zeme shengqide: Yan'an zhengfeng yundong de lailong qumai (How did the red sun rise: the origin and consequences of the Yan'an Rectification Movement)*. Hong Kong: Chinese University of Hong Kong Press.

Gao, Wenqian. 2003. *Wan nian Zhou Enlai (The Last Years of Zhou Enlai)*. 21st ed. Carle Place, NY: Ming jing chu ban she.

Gao, Xin. 1999. *Taming of the Guangdong Gang*. Hong Kong: Mirror Press.

Geddes, Barbara. 1999. "What do we know about democratization after twenty years?" *Annual Review of Political Science* 2:115–144.

Getty, J. Arch, and Oleg V. Naumov. 1999. *The Road to Terror: Stalin and the Self-Destruction of the Bolsheviks, 1932-1939*. New Haven, CT; London: Yale University Press.

Gilley, Bruce. 1998. *Tiger on the Brink: Jiang Zemin and China's New Elite*. Berkeley: University of California Press.

2004. "China's princelings." *Wall Street Journal*, August 27.

Goldstein, Avery. 1991. *From Bandwagon to Balance-of-Power Politics: structuralConstraints and Politics in China, 1949-1978*. Stanford, CA: Stanford University Press.

Goodman, David S. G. 1994. *Deng Xiaoping and the Chinese Revolution: a Political Biography*. London; New York: Routledge.

Gregory, Paul R. 2009. *Terror by Quota: state Security from Lenin to Stalin: an Archival Study*. New Haven: Yale University Press.

Guan, Feng. 1966. "Guan Feng deng zai zhongyang wenge jiedaishi dui tongxue de guangbo jianghua (Broadcasted remarks by Guan Feng and others at the reception room of the Central Cultural Revolution Group)." In *China Contemporary Political Movement Archive*. Los Angeles: Song Yongyi.

Han, Guang. 2019. "Beijing Shiyi Xuexiao de hongse ji'yin (The red gene of the October One School in Beijing)." *Yanhuang Chunqiu* 2019 (5):4–7.

Harding, Harry. 1997. "The Chinese state in crisis: 1966-1969." In *The Politics of China*, ed. R. MacFarquhar. New York: Cambridge University Press, pp. 148–247.

He, Husheng, Yaodong Li, and Changfu Xiang. 1993. *Zhonghua Renmin Gonghe Guo Zhiguan Zhi (A Gazette of Officials in the People's Republic of China)*. Beijing: China Society Publisher.

He, Libo, and Fengying Song. 2004. "Xie Fuzhi Zhegeren (A man called Xie Fuzhi)." *Wenshi Jinghua (Digest of Literature and History)* 2004 (6):29–40.

He, Yi, and Xin Gao. 2000. *The 'Princeling Faction' in the Chinese Communist Party (Zhonggong 'Taizidang')*. Taipei: Shibao Wenhua Publisher.

Ho, Pin, and Wenguang Huang. 2013. "A Death in the Lucky Holiday Hotel: murder, Money, and an Epic Power Struggle in China." New York: Public Affairs.

Hongqi Editorial Committee. 1967. "Wuchan jieji bixu yuyu zhangwo qiangganzi —jinian zhongguo renmin jiefangjun jianjun sishi zhounian (The proletariat must tightly control the guns– commemorating the 40th anniversary for the founding of the PLA)." *Hongqi (Red Flag)* 1967 (12):1.

Hu, Jiwei. 1998. *Cong Huaguofeng Xiatai dao Hu Yaobang Xiatai (From the Fall of Hua Guofeng to the Fall of Hu Yaobang)*. Hong Kong: Mirror Books.

Huang, Chunguang, and Hedu Mi. 2013. "Huang Yongsheng ren zongcanmouzhang de yixie shi (Some events during the period when Huang Yongsheng was the chief of the general staff)" *Yanhuang Chunqiu* 2013 (9).

Huang, Da, Yu Zhu, and Jingzeng Gao. 2010. "Shuobujin de Li Xiannian (Much can be said about Li Xiannian)." *Bainian Chao (Century Tide)* 2010 (1):38–46.

Huang, Jing. 2000. *Factionalism in Chinese Communist Politics*. New York: Cambridge University Press.

Huang, Shukang. 2007. "Fangzhi nugong dangshang fuzongli, Wu Guixian daqi daluo rensheng zhilu (From a textile worker to vice premier, the big rise and fall in the life of Wu Guixian)." In *Xinhua*. Beijing: Xinhua.

Huang, Yasheng. 1996. *Inflation and Investment Controls in China: the Political Economy of Central-Local Relations During the Reform Era*. New York: Cambridge University.

Inside Mainland China. 1998. "Military and police exchange fire in the Yellow Sea for an hour." *Inside Mainland China* 1998 (11):1.

Iqbal, Zaryab, and Christopher Zorn. 2006. "Sic semper tyrannis? Power, repression, and assassination since the second world war." *Journal of Politics* 68 (3).

Jia, Ruixue, Masayuki Kudamatsu, and David Seim. 2014. "Complementary roles of connections and performance in the political selection in China." *Journal of European Economic Association* 13 (4):631–668.

Jiang, Guanzhuang, and Jingzeng Gao. 2006. "Li Xiannian chuxi zhonggong bada de qingkuang (Li Xiannian at the Eighth Party Congress)." *Dang de Wenxian (Party Literature)* 2006 (5):37–38.

Jiang, Jian. 2004. "'caodi midian' zhenxiang tanjiu (Examining the truth of the 'secret telegram on the grassland'." *Wenshi Jinghua (Digest of Literature and History)* 2004 (10):17–25.

Jiang, Qing. 1967. "Zhongyang shouzhang yu 'Mao Zedong sixiang hongweibing shoudu bingtuan' zuotan jiyao (Summary of discussion between central leaders and 'Capital Brigade on Mao Zedong Thoughts')." In *China Contemporary Political Movements Database*. Los Angeles: Song, Yongyi.

Jiang, Qing, Enlai Zhou, and Boda Chen. 1967. "Zhongyang shouzhang yu Beijing Hongdaihui daibiao zuotan jiyao (Summary of discussion between central leaders and representatives from the Beijing Red Representatives)." In *China Contemporary Political Movements Database*. Los Angeles: Song, Yongyi.

Jiangsu Party History Work Office. 2012. *Su Yu Nianpu (Su Yu Chronicle)*. Beijing: Contemporary China Publishing House.

Jie, Suwei, Xiaping Kang, and Bin Zheng. 2010. "Buzou xunchanglu: fang Zhongxin jituan dongshizhang Kong Dan (Never trod the usual path: an interview with the chairman of CITIC Group Kong Dan)." *Lao You* 2010 (12):4–8.

Johnson, Chalmers. 1982. *MITI and the Japanese Miracle: the Growth of Industrial Policy, 1925-1975*. Stanford, CA: Stanford University Press.

Johnson, Chris, and Scott Kennedy. 2015. "China's un-separation of power." *Foreign Affairs*, July 24.

Kai, Feng. 1979. "Dang zhongyang yu Guotao luxian fengqi zai nali (The discrepencies between the party center and the Guotao line)." In *Zhonggong Dangshi Cankao Ziliao Diqice (Reference Material on Party History, Volume 7)*, ed. party history research center of the PLA Political Academy. Beijing: PLA Publisher.

King, Gary, Robert O. Keohane, and Sidney Verba. 1994. *Designing Social Inquiry: scientific Inference in Qualitative Research.* Princeton, NJ: Princeton University Press.

Kong, Dan, and Hedu Mi. 2013. *Nande Bense Ren Tianran- Kong Dan Koushu Shi (A Trial of One's Nature: an Oral History of Kong Dan)*. Hong Kong: CNHK Publications.

Kung, James Kai-sing, and Justin Lin. 2003. "The causes of China's Great Leap famine, 1959–1961." *Economic Development and Cultural Change* 52 (1):51–73.

Lam, Willy Wo-Lap. 1995. *China after Deng Xiaoping*. New York: John Wiley & Sons.

1999. *The Era of Jiang Zemin.* New York: Simon and Schuster.

Landry, Pierre F. 2008. *Decentralized Authoritarianism in China: the Communist Party's Control of Local Elites in the Post-Mao Era*. New York: Cambridge University Press.

Lee, Hong Yung. 1991. *From Revolutionary Cadres to Party Technocrats in Socialist China*. Berkeley: University of California Press.

Leng, Meng. 2009. "wenge zhong the Xu Shiyou yu Xiao Yongyin (Xu Shiyou and Xiao Yongyin in the Cultural Revolution)." *Laonian Kanglebao (Elderly Health News)* 2009 (598).

Levitsky, Steven R., and Lucan A. Way. 2012. "Beyond patronage: violent struggle, ruling party cohesion, and authoritarian durability." *Perspectives on Politics* 10 (04):869–889.

Li, Cheng. 2000. "Jiang Zemin's successors: the rise of the fourth generation of leaders in the PRC." *The China Quarterly* 2000 (161):1–40.

2005a. "New provincial chiefs: Hu's groundwork for the 17th Party Congress." *China Leadership Monitor* 2005 (13).

2016a. *Chinese Politics in the Xi Jinping Era Reassessing Collective Leadership.* Washington, DC: Brookings Institution Press.

Li, De, and Yun Shu. 2009. *Lin Biao Riji (The Diary of Lin Biao)*. Hong Kong: Mirror Publisher.

2015a. *Lin Biao Yuanshuai Nianpu, Shangce (The Chronicle of Marshal Lin Biao: Volume 1)*. Hong Kong: Phoenix Books.

2015b. *Lin Biao Yuanshuai Nianpu, Xiace (The Chronicle of Marshal Lin Biao, Second Volume)*. Hong Kong: Pheonix Books.

Li, Jiantong. 2005b. *Fangdan Xiaoshuo 'Liu Zhidan' An Shilu (A True Record of the Counterrevolutionary Novel 'Liu Zhidan')*. Hong Kong: Xingke'er Publisher.

Li, Junru. 2007. *Zhongguo gongchandang lici quanguo daibiao dahui yanjiu (Studies of the Past Party Congresses of the Chinese Communist Party)*. Beijing: Dongfang Publisher.

Li, Qing. 2009a. "Sanchao yuanlao Li Xiannian zai 'zhengzhi zhibian' shi (Three dynasty veteran Li Xiannian in the midst of 'political transition'." Laonian Wenhuibao (Elderly Digest Daily), May 7.

Li, Rui. 2016b. "Xuanba disan tidui de youguan huiyi (Memories about selecting the third tier)." *Yanhuang Chunqiu* 2016 (1):39–45.

Li, Wei, and Tao Yang. 2005. "The great leap forward: anatomy of a central planning disaster." *Journal of Political Economy* 113 (4):840–878.

Li, Wenqing. 2002. *Jinkan Xu Shiyou (A Close Look at Xu Shiyou)*. Beijing: PLA Arts Publisher.

Li, Yigen. 2009b. "Hong Sifangmianjun ganbu 'gaozhuang shijian' shimo (The story of cadres in the Fourth Front Army 'submitting a petition')." *Wenshi Jinghua (Digest of Literature and History)* 2009 (4):42–52.

Liang, Jinying. 2010. "Li Xiannian: 'sanchao yuanlao' gongxunzhuozhe (The accomplishments of Li Xiannian "an elder who survived three dynasties *Fujian Dangshi Yuekan (Fujian Party History Monthly)* 2010 (19):10–13.

Lieberthal, Kenneth, James Tong, and Sai-cheung Yeung. 1978. *Central Documents and Politburo Politics in China*. Ann Arbor: Center for Chinese Studies University of Michigan.

Lin, Justin Yifu. 1992. "Rural reforms and agricultural growth in China." *The American Economic Review* 82 (1):34–51.

Linz, Juan J. 2000. *Totalitarian and Authoritarian Regimes*. New York: Lynne Rienner.

Liu, Chongwen, and Shaochou Chen. 1996. *Liu Shaoqi Nianpu Xiace (The Liu Shaoqi Chronicle, Volume 3)*. Beijing: Central Document Publisher.

Liu, Huixuan. 2012. "Zuoye xingchen zuoyefeng (The stars and wind of yester years)." In *Fengbao de huiyi: 1965-1970 de Beijing Sizhong (Memory in the Midst of a Storm, Beijing Number Four High School between 1965 and 1970)*, ed. D. Bei, Y. Cao and Y. Wei. Shanghai: Sanlian Publisher.

Liu, Mingxing, Dong Zhang, and Victor Shih. 2018. "Fall of the old guards: explaining decentralization in China." *Studies in Comparative International Development* 2018 (May):1–26.

Liu, Shaocai. 2008. "Xilujun bingbai hou Chen Changhao weishenme xiaosheng yeji (After the defeat of the Western route Army, why did Chen Changhao disappear)." *Dangshi Congheng (Aspects of Party History)* 2008 (3):51–56.

Liu, Shihong. 1999. "xilujun canmouzhang Li Te bei cuosha de shuizhong (Investigating the wrongful killing of Western march chief of staffs Li Te)." *Yanhuang Chunqiu* 1999 (1):14–21.

Liu, Wei. 2019. "Jianzhuan sanqianli de 'mabeiyaolan'- Yan'an di'er baoyuyuan de zhanlue zhuanyi (Transferring the 'cradle on horseback' by 3000 li–the strategic transfer of Yan'an Second Child Care Center)." *Yanhuang Chunqiu* 2019 (6):14–18.

Lohmann, Susanne. 2003. "Why do institutions matter? An audience-cost theory of institutional commitment." *Governance* 16 (1):95–110.

MacFarquhar, Roderick. 1983. *The Great Leap Forward, 1958-1960*. New York: Columbia University Press.

1997a. *The Coming of the Cataclysm, 1961-1966.* Edited by R. MacFarquhar. Oxford; New York: Published for the Royal Institute of International Affairs Studies of the East Asian Institute by Oxford University Press and Columbia University Press.

1997b. "The succession to Mao and the end of Maoism, 1969-1982." In *The Politics of China: the Eras of Mao and Deng*, ed. R. MacFarquhar. New York: Cambridge University Press.

MacFarquhar, Roderick, and Michael Schoenhals. 2006. *Mao's Last Revolution.* Cambridge, Mass: Belknap Press of Harvard University Press.

Magaloni, Beatriz. 2006. *Voting for Autocracy: hegemonic Party Survival and its Demise in Mexico.* Cambridge; New York: Cambridge University Press.

Mahoney, James. 2012. "The logic of process tracing tests in the social sciences." *Sociological Methods & Research* 41:570–597).

Man, Mei. 2005. *Huiyi Fuqin Hu Yaobang (Remembering Father Hu Yaobang).* Beijing: Beijing Publisher.

Manion, Melanie. 1993. *Retirement of Revolutionaries in China: public Policies, Social Norms, Private Interests.* Princeton, NJ: Princeton University Press.

Mao, Zedong. 1967a. "Zai Bada erci huiyi shang de jianghua (remarks at the second plenum of the 8th CC)." In *Mao Zedong Sixiang Wansui 1958-1960 (Long Live the Thoughts of Mao 1958-1960)*, ed. Cultural Revolution Group of the Xi'an Metal Construction Academy. Beijing.

1967b. "Jiguanqiang pojipao de laiji ji qita (The origin of machine guns and mortars and other)." In *Mao Zedong Sixiang Wansui 1958-1960 (Long Live the Thoughts of Mao 1958-1960)*, ed. Cultural Revolution Group of the Xi'an Metal Construction Academy. Xi'an.

1975. "Tong zaijing zhongyang zhengzhiju weiyuan de tanhua (Discussions with Politburo members in Beijing)." In *China Contemporary Political Movements Database.* Los Angeles: Song, Yongyi.

1986. "Zai kuodade zhongyang gongzuo huiyishang de jianghua (Remarks at the enlarged central work conference)." In *Zhonggong dangshi jiaoxue cankao ziliao 24 ce (Reference material for party history curriculum, Volume 24)*, ed. Research Center for Party History and Party Construction at the National Defense University. Beijing: National Defense University.

1987a. "Guanyu 'Fengqing' lun wenti de piyu (Instructions on the issue of the ship 'Fengqing')." In *Jianguo Yilai Mao Zedong Wengao (Mao Zedong's Writings since the Founding of the People's Republic)*, ed. Document Research Center of CCP Central Committee. Beijing: Central Document Publisher.

1987b. "Zai waidi xunshi qijian tong yuantu gedi fuzeren tanhua jiyao (Summary of his remarks to local leaders during his inspection trip)." In *Jianguo Yilai Mao Zedong Wengao (Mao Zedong's Writings since the Founding of the People's Republic)*, ed. Document Research Center of CCP Central Committee. Beijing: Central Document Publisher.

1987c. "Dui Zhongyang gei Xinjiang binggao Xibeiju de liangfen dianbao de piyu (Instruction on two telegrams that the central committee is sending to Xinjiang and the Nothwestern bureau)." In *Jianguo Yilai Mao Zedong Wengao (Mao Zedong's Writings since the Founding of the People's*

Republic), ed. Document Research Center of CCP Central Committee. Beijing: Central Document Publisher.

1987d. "Dui Wu Faxian jiantaoxin de piyu he pizhu (Instructions on Wu Faxian's self critcism letters)." In *Jianguo Yilai Mao Zedong Wengao (Mao Zedong's Writings since the Founding of the People's Republic)*, ed. Document Research Center of CCP Central Committee. Beijing: Central Document Publisher.

1987e. "Dui Mao Yuanxin guanyu chuanda Hua Guofeng, Chen Xilian gong-zuo anpai wenti qingshi baogao de piyu (Instructions on report submitted by Mao Yuanxin on the work arrangement of Hua Guofeng and Chen Xilian)." In *Jianguo Yilai Mao Zedong Wengao (Mao Zedong's Writings since the Founding of the People's Republic)*, ed. Document Research Center of CCP Central Committee. Beijing: Central Document Publisher.

1987f. "Gei Jiang Qing de xin (A letter to Jiang Qing)." In *Jianguo Yilai Mao Zedong Wengao (Mao Zedong's Writings since the Founding of the People's Republic)*, ed. Document Research Center of CCP Central Committee. Beijing: Central Document Publisher.

1991. "Zhongguo geming zhanzheng de zhanlue wenti (Strategic issues in the Chinese revolutionary war)." In *Mao Zedong Xuanji (Selected Works of Mao Zedong)*, ed. Editorial Committee. Beijing: Remin Publisher.

Meng, Xin, Nancy Qian, and Pierre Yared. 2015. "The institutional causes of China's Great Famine: 1959-1961." *Review of Economic Studies* 82:1568–1611.

Meyer, David, Victor C. Shih, and Jonghyuk Lee. 2016. "Factions of different stripes: gauging the recruitment logics of factions in the reform period." *Journal of East Asian Studies* 16 (Special Issue 01):43–60.

Miao, Jinsheng. 2011. "Wo gei Chen Boda zuo mishu (I was Chen Boda's secretary)." *Zhongguo Gaige (China Reform)*.

Milgrom, Paul. 1988. "Employment contracts, influence activities, and efficient organization design." *Journal of Political Economy* 96 (1).

Mill, John Stuart. 1846. *A System of Logic, Ratiocinative and Inductive Being a Connected View of the Principles of Evidence and the Methods of Scientific Investigation*. New York: Harper.

Miller, Alice L. 2008. "Institutionalization and the changing dynamics of Chinese Leadership politics." In *China's Changing Political Landscape: prospects for Democracy*, ed. C. Li. Washington DC: Brookings.

Mitter, Rana. 2004. *A Bitter Revolution: China's Struggle with the Modern World*. Oxford; New York: Oxford University Press.

Moe, Terry M. 2005. "Power and political institutions." *Perspectives on Politics* 3 (2):215–233.

Montefiore, Sebag. 2003. *Stalin: the Court of the Red Tsar*. London: Weidenfeld & Nicolson.

Mu, An. 2006. "Xu Shiyou Yan'an yujin shoushen shimo (The story of Xu Shiyou's detainment and trial in Yan'an)." *Wenshi Yuekan (Literature and History Monthly)* 2006 (2):27–30.

Mu, Zhijing. 2012. "Sishui Liunian (Years pass away like water)." In *Fengbao de huiyi: 1965-1970 de Beijing Sizhong (Memory in the Midst of a Storm,*

Beijing Number Four High School between 1965 and 1970), ed. D. Bei, Y. Cao and Y. Wei. Shanghai: Sanlian Publisher.

Nathan, Andrew. 2003. "Authoritarian resilience." *Journal of Democracy* 14 (1):6–19.

Nathan, Andrew, and Bruce Gilley. 2002. *China's New Rulers: the Secret Files.* New York: The New York Review of Books.

Nathan, Andrew J., and Kellee S. Tsai. 1995. "Factionalism: a new institutionalist restatement." *The China Journal* 34:157–192.

National Defense University Editorial Committee for 'Xu Xiangqian Chronicle'. 2016. *Xu Xiangqian Nianpu, Xiajuan (Xu Xiangqian Chronicle, Volume 2).* 2 vols. Beijing: PLA Publisher.

Naughton, Barry. 1996. *Growing Out of the Plan: Chinese Economic Reform 1978-1993.* New York: Cambridge University Press.

New fourth Army research society, Huang Gang city archive, Museum of Li Xiannian, and Association for China social work. 2009. *Li Xiannian Zhuanqi zhilu (The Amazing Journey of Li Xiannian).* Beijing: Red Flag Publisher.

Oksenberg, Michel, and James Tong. 1991. "The evolution of central-provincial fiscal relations in China, 1971-1984: the formal system." *The China Quarterly* 125:1–32.

Pantsov, Alexander, and Steven I. Levine. 2012. *Mao: the Real Story.* 1st Simon & Schuster hardcover ed. New York: Simon & Schuster.

2015. *Deng Xiaoping: a Revolutionary Life.* New York: Oxford University Press.

Party Central Office Secretariat. 2001a. "Minutes of important meeting, May21, 1989." In *The Tiananmen Papers*, ed. A. Nathan and P. Link. London: Little, Brown & Company.

2001b. "Minutes of important meeting, May 27, 1989." In *The Tiananmen Papers*, ed. A. Nathan and P. Link. London: Little, Brown & Company.

Pepinsky, Thomas B. 2014. "Institutional turn in comparative authoritarianism." *British Journal of Political Science* 44:631–653.

Perry, Elizabeth J. 2012. *Anyuan: mining China's Revolutionary Tradition.* Berkeley: University of California Press.

Perry, Elizabeth J., and Xun Li. 1997. *Proletarian Power: Shanghai in the Cultural Revolution.* Boulder, Colo: Westview Press.

Pierson, Paul. 2000. "Increasing returns, pathdependence, and the study of politics." *American Political Science Review* 94 (2):251–267.

Politburo. 1979. "Guanyu Zhang Guotao Tongzhi de cuowu de jueding (Decision concerning the mistake of Comrade Zhang Guotao)." In *Zhonggong Dangshi Cankao Ziliao Diqice (Reference Material on Party History, Volume 7)*, ed. party history research center of the PLA Political Academy. Beijing: PLA Publisher.

1996. "Politburo decision concerning Zhang Guotao's mistakes." In *The Rise to Power of the Chinese Communist Party: documents and Analysis*, ed. A. Saich and B. Yang. Armonk, NY: ME Sharpe.

Pomfret, John. 2000. "Chinese Tie Leaders to Smuggling; Party, Military Chiefs among the suspects." *Washington Post*, January 22.

Powell, Robert. 2006. "War as a commitment problem." *International Organization* 60 (1):169–203.

Pye, Lucian W. 1995. "Factions and the politics of guanxi: paradoxes in Chinese administrative and political behaviour." *The China Journal* 34:35–53.

Qi, Benyu. 2016. *Qi Benyu Huiyilu (The Memoire of Qi Benyu)*. Hong Kong: China Cultural Revolution History Publisher.

Qin, Jiwei. 2007. *Qin Jiwei Huiyilu (The Autobiography of Qin Jiwei)*. Beijing: PLA Publisher.

Qin, Xiao. 2019. "Wo yanzhong de Wang Jun (Wang Jun in my eyes)." *Caixin*, June 22.

Quan, Yanchi. 1994. *Deng Pufang he Kanghua Gongsi (Deng Pufang and Kanghua Company)*. Hong Kong: Cosmos Books.

Research Center for Party Material in the Central Archive. 1986. "Jieshao1962nian wuyue zhongyang gongzuo huiyi (Introducing the central work conference in May 1962)." In *Zhonggong dangshi jiaoxue cankao ziliao 24 ce (Reference Material for Party History Curriculum, Volume 24)*, ed. Research Center for Party History and Party Construction at the National Defense University. Beijing: National Defense University Press.

Revolutionary Masses of the Central Organization Department. 1967. "Fan Geming xiuzheng zhuyi fenzi An Ziwen shida zuizhuang (The ten crimes of counter-revolutionary revisionist An Ziwen)." In *China Contemporary Political Movements Database*. Los Angeles: Song, Yongyi.

Ross, Robert S. 1989. "From Lin Biao to Deng Xiaoping: elite instability and China's US Policy." *The China Quarterly* 118:265–299.

Ruan, Ming, Nancy Liu, Peter Rand, and Lawrence R. Sullivan. 1994. *Deng Xiaoping: chronicle of An Empire*. Boulder, Colo: Westview Press.

Rudolph, Lloyd I., and Susanne Hoeber Rudolph. 1979. "Authority and power in bureaucratic and patrimonial administration: a revisionist interpretation of Weber on Bureaucracy." *World Politics* 31 (2):195–227.

Saich, Tony, and Bingzhang Yang. 1996. *The Rise to Power of the Chinese Communist Party: documents and Analysis*. Armonk, NY: M.E. Sharpe.

Saunders, Phillip C., Arthur S. Ding, Andrew Scobell, Andrew N. D. Yang, Joel Wuthnow, and National Defense University. "Chairman Xi remakes the PLA: assessing Chinese military reforms."

Schoenhals, Michael. 1996. "The Central Case Examination Group, 1966-1979." *The China Quarterly* (145):87–111.

SCMP Reporters. 2012. "Li Yuanchao tipped to oversee Hong Kong and Macau affairs." *South China Morning Post*, November 10, 1.

Shambaugh, David. 1993. "Deng Xiaoping: the politician." *The China Quarterly* (135):457–490.

Shih, Victor. 2008a. *Factions and Finance in China: elite Conflicts and Inflation*. New York: Cambridge University Press.

2008b. "'Nauseating' displays of loyalty: monitoring the factional bargain through ideological campaigns in China." *Journal of Politics* 70 (4):1177–1192.

2017. "How the party-state runs the economy: a model of elite decision making in the financial market." In *Routledge Handbook of the Chinese Communist Party (Routledge Handbooks)*, ed. W. W.-L. Lam. London: Routledge.

2021. "China's Leninist response to COVID-19: from information repression to total mobilization." In *Coronavirus Politics: the Comparative Politics and Policy of COVID-19*, ed. S. Greer, E. King, A. Peralta-Santos and E. Massard da Fonseca. Ann Arbor MI: University of Michigan Press.

Shih, Victor, and Jonghyuk Lee. 2018. "Locking in fair weather friends: assessing the fate of Chinese communist elite when their patrons fall from power." *Party Politics* 26 (5).

Shih, Victor, Jonghyuk Lee, and David Meyer. 2015. *The Database of CCP Elite*. San Diego: Institute of Global Conflict and Cooperation.

Shih, Victor, Wei Shan, and Mingxing Liu. 2008. "Biographical data of Central Committee members: first to sixteenth Party Congress."

2010a. "Gauging the elite political equilibrium in the CCP: a quantitative approach using biographical data." *China Quarterly* 201:79–102.

2010b. "The Central Committee past and present: a method of quantifying elite biographies." In *Sources and Methods in Chinese Politics*, ed. M. E. Gallagher, A. Carlson and M. Manion. New York: Cambridge University Press.

Shirk, Susan. 1993. *The Political Logic of Economic Reform in China*. Berkeley, CA: The University of California Press.

Slantchev, Branislav, and R. Blake McMahon. 2015. "The guardianship dilemma: regime security through and from the armed forces." *American Political Science Review* 109 (2):297–313.

Slater, Dan. 2003. "Iron cage in an iron fist: authoritarian institutions and the personalization of power in Malaysia." *Comparative Politics* 35 (1):81–101.

Snyder, Richard. 1992. "Explaining transitions from neopatrimonial dictatorships." *Comparative Politics* 24 (4):379–399.

Sun, Dannian. 2013. "Chuanbei de hongjun 'yuanlie' ("Falsely accused martyres" of the Northern Sichuan Red Army)." *Yanhuang Chunqiu* 2013 (11).

Sun, Shuyun. 2006. *The Long March: the True History of Communist China's Founding Myth*. New York: Doubleday.

Sun, Yancheng. 2012. "Xuetonglun yu Daxing 'basanyi' shijian (The blood line theory and the '831' incident at Daxing)." *Yanhuang Chunqiu* 2012 (2):24–27.

Supreme People's Court. 1982. "Tebie fating panjueshu (Sentencing of the Special Court)." In *San Zhong Quanhui Yilai Zhongyao Wenxian Huibian (Compilation of Important Documents since the Third Plenum (of the 11th Central Committee))*, ed. Document Research Center of the CCP Central Committee. Beijing: People's Publisher.

Svolik. 2009. "Power sharing and leadership dynamics in authoritarian regimes." *American Journal of Political Science* 53 (2):477–494.

Svolik, Milan. 2012. *The Politics of Authoritarian Rule*. New York: Cambridge University Press.

Svolik, Milan, and Carles Boix. 2013. "The foundations of limited authoritarian government: institutions, commitment, and power-sharing in dictatorships." *Journal of Politics* 75 (2).

Taubman, William. 2003. *Khrushchev: the Man and his Era*. New York: Norton.

Teiwes, Frederick. 1993. *Politics and Purges in China: Rectification and the Decline of Party Norms, 1950-1965*. Armonk, NY: M E Sharpe.

Teiwes, Frederick C., and Warren Sun. 1996. *The Tragedy of Lin Biao: Riding the Tiger During the Cultural Revolution, 1966-1971*. Honolulu: University of Hawaii Press.

2007. *The End of the Maoist Era: Chinese Politics During the Twilight of the Cultural Revolution, 1972-1976*. Armonk, NY: M.E. Sharpe.

Teiwes, Frederick, and Warren Sun. 1997. "The politics of an 'un-Maoist' interlude: the case of opposing rash advance, 1956-1957." In *New Perspectives on State Socialism in China*, ed. T. Cheek and A. Saich. Armonk, NY: M.E. Sharpe.

1999. *China's Road to Disaster: Mao, Central Politicians, and Provincial Leaders in the Unfolding of the Great Leap Forward, 1955-1959*. Armonk, NY: ME Sharpe.

Thelen, Kathleen. 1999. "Historical institutionalism in comparative politics." *Annual Review of Political Science* 2 (1):369–405.

2004. *How Institutions Evolve: the Political Economy of Skills in Germany, Britain, the United States, and Japan*. New York: Cambridge University Press.

Thornton, Patricia M. 2007. *Disciplining the State: virtue, Violence, and State-Making in Modern China*. Cambridge, Mass: Harvard University Asia Center; Distributed by Harvard University Press.

Tsou, Tang. 1976. "Prolegomenon to the study of informal groups in CCP politics." *The China Quarterly* 65:98–114.

Tsou, Tang, and Andrew J. Nathan. 1976. "Prolegomenon to the study of informal groups in CCP politics." *The China Quarterly* (65):98–117.

Tullock, Gordon. 1987. *Autocracy*. Boston: Kluwer Academic Publishers.

Vogel, Ezra F. 2011. *Deng Xiaoping and the Transformation of China*. Cambridge, Mass: Belknap Press of Harvard University Press.

Wade, Robert. 1990. *Governing the Market: Economic Theory and the Role Government in East Asian Industrialization*. Princeton, NJ: Princeton University Press.

Walder, Andrew G. 2009. *Fractured Rebellion: the Beijing Red Guard Movement*. Cambridge, Mass: Harvard University Press.

2015. *China under Mao : a Revolution Derailed*. Cambridge, MA: Harvard University Press.

Walder, Andrew G., and Guoqiang Dong. 2011. "Local politics in the Chinese cultural revolution: Nanjing under military control." *Journal of Asian Studies* 70 (2):425–447.

Wang, Fang. 2006. *Wang Fang Huiyilu (Wang Fang's Autobiography)*. Hangzhou: Zhejiang People's Publisher.

Wang, Li. 1967. *Wang Li zai Zhonggong zhongyang zuzhibu de jianghua (Remarks by Wang Li at the Central Organization Department)*. Los Angeles: Song, Yongyi.

2001. *Wang Li Fansilu (The Reflections of Wang Li)*. Hong Kong: Beixing Publisher.

Wang, Li, and Benyu Qi. 1966. "Wang Li deng jiejian Beijing Yixueyuan 'bayiba' bufen zhanshi zuotan jiyao (Summary of discussion when Wang Li and others received some fighters from the '8-18' brigade from the Bejing School of Medicine)." In *China Contemporary Political Movements Database*. Los Angeles: Song, Yongyi.

Wang, Nianyi, and Yu Zhu. 2004. "Yetan Hongjun Changzheng zhong de 'midian' wenti (Discussion on the 'secret telegram' issue during the Long March)." *Xibei Shida Xuebao-shehuikexueban (Journal of the Northwestern Normal University-Social Sciences Edition)* 41 (6):43–49.

Wang, Shaoguang. 1995. *Failure of Charisma: the Cultural Revolution in Wuhan*. Hong Kong; New York: Oxford University Press.

Wang, Weiqun. 2011. *Zhongxin 30nian: 1979-2009 (30 Years of CITIC: 1979-2009)*. Hong Kong: Strong Wind Press.

Way, Lucan, and Steven Levitsky. 2002. "Elections without democracy: the rise of competitive authoritarianism." *Journal of Democracy* 13 (2):51–67.

Wedeman, Andrew. 2003. *From Mao to Market*. New York: Cambridge University Press.

Wen, Zichun, and Yongchun Li. 1998. "Xu Shiyou in 1966-1976 (Part 2)." *Dangshi Wenhui (Party History Literature Collection)* 1998 (6):33–37.

White, Lynn T. 1989. *Policies of Chaos: the Organizational Causes of Violence in China's Cultural Revolution*. Princeton, NJ: Princeton University Press.

Whitson, William W., and Chen-hsia Huang. 1973. *The Chinese High Command; A History of Communist Military Politics, 1927-1971*. New York: Praeger.

Williamson, Oliver E. 2000. "The new institutional economics: taking stock, looking ahead." *Journal of Economic Literature* 38:595–613.

Wintrobe, Ronald. 1990. "The tinpot and the totalitarian: an economic theory of dictatorship." *American Political Science Review* 84:142–157.

1998. *The Political Economy of Dictatorship*. Cambridge, UK; New York, NY: Cambridge University Press.

Wong, Edward, and Jonathan Ansfield. 2011. "China grooming deft politician as next leader." *New York Times*, January 23.

Wu, Faxian. 2006. *Suiyue Jiannan: Wu Faxian Huiyilu (Difficult Time: the Memoire of Wu Faxian)*. 2 vols. Hong Kong: Beixing Publisher.

Wu, Guoguang. 1995. "'Documentary politics': hypotheses, process, and case studies." In *Decision Making in Deng's China: persepctives from Insiders*, ed. C. L. Hamrin and S. Zhao. Armonk, NY: M.E. Sharpe.

1997. *Political Reform Under Zhao Ziyang (Zhao Ziyang yu Zhengzhi Gaige)*. Hong Kong: Pacific Century Institute.

Wu, Kegang. 2004. *Zeng Qinghong–Zhonggong Gang'ao Daguanjia (Zeng Qinghong–the Head Manager for Hong Kong and Macau)*. 2nd ed. Hong Kong: Xinhua Caiyin Publisher.

Wu, Renhua. 2007. *1989 nian Tian An Men guang chang xue xing qing chang nei mu (The Bloody Inisde Story of Tiananmen Square in 1989)*. Chu ban. ed. Alhambra: Zhen xiang chu ban she.

Wu, Yiching. 2014. *The Cultural Revolution at the Margins Chinese Socialism in Crisis*. Cambridge, MA: Harvard University Press.

Xia, Fei. 2005a. "Li Xiannian zai 'wenhua dageming zhong' (Li Xiannian in the midst of the Cultural Revolution)." *Dangshi Congheng (Aspects of Party History)* 2005 (11):5–11.

2005b. "Qiekai Xie Fuzhi de shenmi miansha (Unveil the mysterious mask of Xie Fuzhi)." *Dangshi Bocai (An Overall View of Party History)* 2005 (10):13–18.

2008. "Zhang Chunqiao yu Yao Wenyuan (Zhang Chunqiao and Yao Wenyuan)." *Dangshi Tiandi (Party History World)* 2008 (6):45–51.

Xia, Mingxing, and Zhenlan Su. 2010. "Deng Xiaoping moxia de zhanjiang Chen Xilian (The military commander under Deng Xiaoping, Chen Xilian)." *Dangshi Zonglan (Wide View of Party History)* 2010 (3):27–32.

Xiang, Shouzhi. 2006. *Xiang Shouzhi Huiyilu (The Memoir of Xiang Shouzhi)*. Beijing: People's Liberation Army Publisher.

Xiao, Han, and Mia Turner. 1998. *789 Jizhongying (789 Concentration Camp)*. Edited by P. Ho. Hong Kong: Mirror Books.

Xiong, Lei. 2008. "1976nian, Hua Guofeng he Ye Jianying zeme liangshou de (In 1976, how did Hua Guofeng make an alliance with Ye Jianying)." *Yanhuang Chunqiu* 2008 (10):3–21.

Xu, Jingxian. 2003. *Shinian Yimeng, Xu Jingxian Huiyilu (The Dream that Lasted 10 Years, the Memoire of Xu Jingxian)*. Hong Kong: Shidai Publisher.

Xu, Xiangqiang. 1987. *Lishi de Huigu (Revisiting History)*. Beijing: PLA Publisher.

Yan, Huai. 2017. *Jinchu Zhongzubu: Yige Hongerdai Lixiang Zhuyizhe de Linglei Rensheng (Into and out of the Central Organization Department: the Separate Lives of an Idealistic Red Second Generation)*. Hong Kong: Mirror Books.

Yang, Jisheng, Edward Friedman, Jian Guo, and Stacy Mosher. 2012. *Tombstone: the Great Chinese Famine, 1958-1962*. 1st American ed. New York: Farrar, Straus and Giroux.

Yang, Shangkun. 1980. "Yang Shangkun tan Liu Shaoqi (Yang Shangkun's remarks on Liu Shaoqi)." In *China Contemporary Political Movements Database*. Los Angeles: Song, Yongyi.

2001a. "Yang Shangkun's talk to a small group meeting at the enlarged meeting of the central military commission." In *Tiananmen Papers*, ed. A. Nathan and P. Link. London: Little, Brown & Company.

2001b. *Yang Shangkun Riji (The Diary of Yang Shangkun)*. 2 vols. Beijing: Central Document Publisher.

Yang, Shengqun, and Pu Chen. 2006. *Wushinian de Huiwang- Zhonggong Bada Jishi (Reviewing after 50 years- a True Record of the 8th Party Congress)*. Beijing: Sanlian Publisher.

Yang, Yinlu. 2014. *Ting yuan shen shen Diaoyutai: wo gei Jiang Qing dang mi shu (The Deep Gardens of Diaoyutai: I Served as Jiang Qing's Secretary)...* Beijing: Contemporary China Publisher.

Yao, Yang. 2016. *The Anatomy of Chinese Selectocracy*. ed. The National School of Development. Beijing: Peking University.

Ye, Yonglie. 2009. *Si Renbang Xingwang (The Rise and Fall of the Gang of Four)*. Vol. 1. Beijing: People's Daily Publisher.

Yu, Shiping. 2009. *Xin Taizijun (New Princeling Army)*. Hong Kong: Mirror Press.

Zakharov, Alexei. 2016. "The loyalty-competence tradeoff in dictatorships and outside options for subordinates." *Journal of Politics* 78 (2).

Zhang, Gensheng. 2004. "Hua Guofeng tan fensui 'Sirenbang' (Hua Guofeng on crushing 'the Gang of Four')." *Yanhuang Chunqiu* 2004 (7).

Zhang, Guotao. 1971. *Wode Huiyi Diyice (My Rememberance–Volume 1)*. Hong Kong: Ming Pao Publisher.

    1996. "Telegram from Zhang Guotao to the Party Center." In *The Rise to Power of the Chinese Communist Party: documents and Analysis*, ed. A. Saich and B. Yang. Armonk, NY: M.E. Sharpe.

    1998. *Wo de Huiyi Disan Ce(My Rememberance-Volume 3)*. Beijing: Dongfang Publisher.

Zhang, Tingdong. 2008a. *Ye Jianying Weida de Yisheng (The Great Life of Ye Jianying)*. Beijing: Central Document Publisher.

Zhang, Yaoci. 2008b. *Zhang Yaoci Huiyilu (The Memoire of Zhang Yaoci)*. Beijing: Party History Publisher.

Zhang, Zhaojin, and Huanyu Hu. 2010. "Li Xiannian yu Chen Yun de zhanyouqing (The friendship through warfare between Li Xiannian and Chen Yun)." *Dangshi Bocai (An Overall View of Party History)* 2010 (12):26–30.

Zhang, Zhen. 2007. *Zhang Zhen Huiyilu (The Memoir of Zhang Zhen)*. 3 ed. Vol. 2. Beijing: Liberation Army Publisher.

Zhang, Zhenglong. 2002. *Xuebai Xuehong (White Snow, Red Blood)*. Hong Kong: Cosmos Books.

Zhao, Fugui. 1997. "Xu Shiyou yu Mao Zedong (Xu Shiyou and Mao Zedong)." *Guizhou Wenshi Tiandi (Guizhou Literature and History)* 1997 (2):21–26.

Zhao, Guang. 2006. "1971, cuiwei Lin Biao sidang de mohouzhan (1971, the secret war to destroy Lin Biao's proteges)." *Wenshi Chunqiu (Literature and History Times)* 2006 (9):8–10.

Zhao, Yuansan. 2011. "Wosuo jiesudao de 'Jiefang Ribao' wenyibu zhuren Yao Wenyuan (The head of arts and literature section of the Liberation Daily Yao Wenyuan that I knew)." *Dangshi Bolan (Grand View of Party History)* 2011 (1):51–52.

Zhao, Ziyang. 2009. *Prisoner of the State: the Secret Journal of Premier Zhao Ziyang*. New York: Simon and Schuster.

Zheng, Zhong. 2017. *Zhang Chunqiao: 1949 Ji Qihou (Zhang Chunqiao: 1949 and After)*. Hong Kong: Chinese University of Hong Kong Press.

Zhu, Tingxun. 2007. *Li Desheng zai dongluan suiyue (Li Desheng During Chaotic Times)*. Beijing: Central Document Publisher.

Zhu, Yongjia, and Xunzhong Gu. 2011. "Shanghai 'wenge' shiqi de junzheng guanxi-'jiuyisan' shijian 40 zhounian qianji fangtan Zhu Yongjia (Civil military relations in Shanghai during the 'Cultural Revolution' an interview with Zhu Yongjia in the event of the 40th anniversary of the '913' incident." *Yanhuang Chunqiu* 2011 (3).

Zhu, Yu. 2008. "Li Xiannian dui xilujun he zhengque renshi xilujun wenti de gongxian (the contribution of Li Xiannian to the Western route Army and the issues surrounding the Western route Army)." *Gansu Shehui Kexue (Gansu Social Sciences)* 2008 (1):48–55.

Index

Acemoglu, Daron, 187
"always nice people" (*laohaoren*), 5, 151, 154, 158, 175; as successors, 175–183, 192
An Ziwen, 39, 40, 48
anti-AB League purge, 38
Anti-Japan University, 63, 69, 111, 117, 126, 161
Anti-Lin Biao, Anti-Confucius Campaign, 22, 113
Anting incident (1966), 83–84, 87, 95–96
Anti-Rightist Movement (1957), 86
Anyuan strike, 40, 46
Army Cultural Revolution Group, 68
authoritarian regimes: challenges to, 7, 8, 9, 11, 20, 32; and coalitions of the weak, 2–6; exogenous shocks to, 186–187; information asymmetry in, 7, 8, 9–10; oligarchical, 15, 18, 20, 33; one-party, 7–10; selectorates in, 7–10, 11, 14–18; stability of, 4, 8–10, 186–187, 195–196; transfers of power in, 20–21

Beidaihe Conference (1962), 47
Beijing: Capital Garrison of, 112, 118, 119, 138; Municipal Government (BMG) of, 168; Party Committee (BPC) of, 174–175; princelings in, 162–163, 168, 174–175; Red Guards in, 92–93, 171, 173–174
Beijing Military Region, 111, 112, 115, 119, 138, 148

Beijing No. 4 High School (*Beijing Sizhong*), 162–163, 165–166
Beijing Ribao (newspaper), 90
Beria, Lavrentiy, 188
Bian Zhongyuan, 165
bloodline theory, 164–165, 167, 174, 181, 183
Bo Gu, 60, 163
Bo Xicheng, 168
Bo Xilai, 160, 168, 181, 182–183, 193
Bo Yibo, 42, 48, 67, 147, 151, 160; children of, 166, 167, 168, 182; purge of, 50; rehabilitation of, 141; and white area group, 40, 56
British Embassy, attack on (1967), 99, 100
Bu He, 176
Bukharin, Nikolai, 57, 64

Cai Chang, 27
Cai Qi, 195
Cao Diqiu, 50, 91, 95, 129
Central Case Examination Group, 69, 79
Central Committee (CC): and 8th Party Congress, 39–40, 163; degeneration of, 110, 121; and Deng Xiaoping, 130–131; enlargement of, 19, 22; and factions, 26, 37, 39–40, 151; and FFA, 58–62, 145; and FFA veterans, 64–68, 75, 76, 78, 79; and Great Leap, 42; and Jiang Zemin, 177; and 9th Party Congress, 103; plenums of, 47, 50, 94, 135, 149; and Politburo, 52–53; and

For EU product safety concerns, contact us at Calle de José Abascal, 56–1°, 28003 Madrid, Spain or eugpsr@cambridge.org.

www.ingramcontent.com/pod-product-compliance
Ingram Content Group UK Ltd.
Pitfield, Milton Keynes, MK11 3LW, UK
UKHW010250140625
459647UK00013BA/1774